Anabaptism in Outline

CLASSICS OF THE RADICAL REFORMATION is an English language series of Anabaptist and Free Church documents translated and annotated under the direction of the Institute of Mennonite Studies, which is the research agency of the Associated Mennonite Biblical Seminaries, 3003 Benham Avenue, Elkhart, Indiana 46514, and published by the Mennonite Publishing House, (Herald Press), Scottdale, Pennsylvania 15683.

1. *The Legacy of Michael Sattler.* Translated and edited by John H. Yoder, 1973.

2. *The Writings of Pilgram Marpeck.* Translated and edited by William Klassen and Walter Klaassen, 1978.

3. *Anabaptism in Outline: A Collection of Primary Sources.* Edited by Walter Klaassen, 1981.

Anabaptism in Outline

Selected Primary Sources

Edited by
Walter Klaassen, Conrad Grebel College, Waterloo, Ontario

In Cooperation with
John S. Oyer, Goshen College, Goshen, Indiana
John H. Yoder, Notre Dame University, Notre Dame, Indiana
Jarold K. Zeman, Acadia Divinity College, Wolfville, Nova Scotia
Cornelius J. Dyck, Institute of Mennonite Studies,
Elkhart, Indiana

1981

herald press kitchener, ont.
scottdale, pa.

Canadian Cataloguing in Publication Data

Main entry under title:
Anabaptism in outline

(Classics of the radical Reformation ; 3)
Bibliography: p.
Includes index.
ISBN 0-8361-1240-7 (bound). - ISBN 0-8361-1241-5 (pbk.)

1. Theology – Collected works – 16th century.
2. Anabaptists – Collected works. I. Klaassen,
Walter, 1926–   II. Series.

BX4930.A52   230'.43   C81-094169-4

ANABAPTISM IN OUTLINE
Copyright © 1981 by Herald Press, Kitchener, Ont. N2G 4M5
   Published simultaneously in the United States by
   Herald Press, Scottdale, Pa. 15683
Library of Congress Catalog Card Number: 81-80185
International Standard Book Numbers:
   0-8361-1240-7 (hardcover)
   0-8361-1241-5 (paper)
Printed in the United States of America
Book designed by Jan Gleysteen

81 82 83 84 85 86 10 9 8 7 6 5 4 3 2 1

2189227

To Ruth

Contents

General Editors' Preface

For many years a committee of German and North American historians known as the *Täuferaktenkommission* (TAK) has published source materials of the sixteenth-century Anabaptist movement under the title *Quellen zur Geschichte der Täufer* (QGT). More recently a similar organization has begun work in the Netherlands with Dutch source materials. It is known as the *Commissie tot de uitgave van Documenta Anabaptistica Neerlandica* (CUDAN). These developments have, obviously, been deeply rewarding to scholars and others as the multitude of articles and books using these documents amply verifies.

There are, however, still relatively few sixteenth-century Anabaptist materials available in the English language, though their number is increasing. It is to meet this need that the *Classics of the Radical Reformation* (CRR) series was begun some years ago with the aim of making available in the English language a scholarly and critical edition of the primary works of major Anabaptist and Free Church writers of the late fifteenth, sixteenth, and early seventeenth centuries. The first volume in this series, *The Legacy of Michael Sattler* by John H. Yoder, appeared in 1973, and *The Writings of Pilgram Marpeck* by William Klassen and Walter Klaassen, appeared in 1978. Other volumes are in preparation.

In preparing these translations it has not been considered essential to the purposes of the series to include every known document of the writers under translation and, unless some contribution can be made to a fuller understanding of the text, it has not been considered essential to pursue at length critical textual issues. Those scholars interested in the details will, in any case, turn to the original language text. Where a choice had to be made between clarity and awkward literalism, the translators were encouraged to favor readability but without compromising the text.

Most of the volumes being included in CRR include the writings of one author only. The present volume, however, is an exception, bringing together the key comments of many Anabaptists under seventeen theological categories. It is hoped and believed that this will facilitate specific theological study of issues which it might be impossible for the uninitiated reader to find in the wealth of materials available in Anabaptist writings. The limitations and dangers of compiling short selections which may, by the necessity of brevity, lose their full contextual meaning are recognized. However, every effort has been made by the translator-editor to prevent this, both in the translations he himself has made and in the adaptation of the translations of others.

It is appropriate to express appreciation to the translator-editor for his "labor of love," as well as to those translators whose works have been used and acknowledged for permission granted. The North American Committee for the Documentation of Free Church Origins (NACDFCO), of which Professor George H. Williams, Harvard Divinity School, serves as chairman and Walter Klaassen as secretary, was helpful with its encouragement and counsel during the initial stages of the launching of the CRR series. Finally, without the commitment to the work of the church on the part of Mennonite Publishing House and its willingness to include the series in its responsibility to society and the church, this venture could not have been undertaken.

Cornelius J. Dyck, Editor, CRR
Institute of Mennonite Studies
Elkhart, Indiana

Introduction

I have felt for a long time the need for a compendium of Anabaptist source materials which would give an overview of their positions on basic Christian affirmations. This volume is an attempt to provide such a tool. It grew out of my experience of teaching undergraduates. Frequently I had to translate sections from sources unavailable to students because they did not have the language skills to use even sources already published.

This collection will illustrate the variety and colour of the Anabaptist movement. There are expressions from academics, artisans, and peasants, from leaders and followers. They will show that even on what are normally considered basic issues in Anabaptism, such as nonresistance, there was no unanimity.

I have tried faithfully to represent all major points of view on the various subjects. The categories used will have excluded one point or another. That is the problem with artificial categories. Moreover there is a limit to the size of the volume. The sources represent the views of the bulk of the Anabaptist movement. Only the Italian and the English Anabaptists are not represented.

Some parts of the movement are not as extensively represented as some others. This is especially true of Swiss Anabaptism. The reason for this is that there was simply not as much written material available. Apart from Hubmaier, who is extensively represented, the Swiss Brethren had no Peter Riedeman, no Pilgram Marpeck, no Bernhard Rothmann, no Menno Simons, and no Dirk Philips. With the exception of the small group of Sattler writings, and a few other documents, the Swiss Brethren produced virtually no written monuments to their faith. Even the Swiss Täuferakten have remarkably lit-

11

tle of direct theological interest. All the material available was mined for relevant statements.

The sources are arranged in chronological order in each section. This is partly an arbitrarily chosen sequence, but it may also, here and there, suggest lines of influence and dependence. Each selection is identified by author, title, date, and source. If one of these is missing the reader may conclude that it was not available. This is true especially with regard to dates. There are, for example, no precise dates available for a number of the works of Dirk Philips.

Wherever possible I have used existing translations. In the cases of Balthasar Hubmaier and Dirk Philips I revised, sometimes extensively, the existing translations of Davidson and Kolb respectively. Where no modern author is given it may be assumed that I have done the translation myself. In the translation of Peter Riedeman's *Account of Our Religion,* I have, with permission, modernized the archaic English, but have otherwise left the translation intact.

The time span represented in these sources is 1524-1560, that is, the formative period of Anabaptism ending with the death of Menno Simons.

The list of secondary literature in English on the various subjects is designed to aid the reader and researcher to interpret the primary documents. The lists are, of course, not exhaustive, and important contributions will have been omitted inadvertently.

I am pleased to acknowledge the many helpful suggestions made by the many persons who read the first draft of the manuscript. I mention especially John H. Yoder, John S. Oyer, John C. Wenger, and Cornelius J. Dyck. They alerted me to weaknesses and omissions. For any that remain I am responsible.

I am grateful to the Institute of Mennonite Studies for taking this volume into the series, Classics of the Radical Reformation.

I hope that readers in college, university, church, and home will enjoy the use of this volume as much as I enjoyed assembling it. Special thanks to Mrs. Pauline Bauman for carefully and painstakingly typing this manuscript more than once and to Michael Klaassen for preparing the index.

Walter Klaassen
Conrad Grebel College
Waterloo, Ontario

Sources
and Abbreviations

Armour, Rollin. *Anabaptist Baptism*,
Scottdale: Herald Press, 1966.

Armour

*Ausbund, Das ist: Etliche schöne
Christliche Lieder...*, Germantown:
Christoph Saur, 1742.

Ausbund

Beck, Joseph. *Die Geschichtsbücher der
Wiedertäufer in Oesterreich-Ungarn
1526-1785*, Nieuwkoop: B. de Graaf,
1967.

Beck, *Geschichtsbücher*

Davidson, George Duiguid. *The Works of
Balthasar Hubmaier*, English
translation revised by Walter
Klaassen. Microfilm in the Conrad
Grebel College Library, 1930.

Davidson/Klaassen,
Hubmaier

Fast, Heinold. *Der Linke Flügel der
Reformation*. Bremen: Carl
Schünemann Verlag, 1962.

Fast, *Der Linke Flügel*

Fast, Heinold. *Quellen zur Geschichte der
Täufer in der Schweiz. II Band.
Ostschweiz*, Zürich: Theologischer
Verlag, 1973.

Fast, *Quellen*

Fellmann, Walter. *Hans Denck. Schriften
2. Teil Religiöse Schriften*.
Gütersloh: C. Bertelsmann Verlag,
1956.

Fellmann, *Denck I*

Fellmann, Walter. *Hans Denck. Schriften 3. Teil Exegetische Schriften.* Gütersloh: C. Bertelsmann Verlag, 1960.

Fellmann, *Denck II*

Fischer, Hans. *Jakob Huter: Leben, Froemmigkeit, Briefe*, Newton, Kansas: Mennonite Publication Office, 1956.

Fischer, *Huter*

Franz, Günther. *Urkundliche Quellen zur hessischen Reformationsgeschichte. IV. Band Wiedertäuferakten 1527-1626.* Marburg: N. G. Elwert'sche Verlagsbuchhandlung, G. Braun, 1951.

Quellen: Hesse

Geiser, Samuel. "An Ancient Anabaptist Witness for Nonresistance," *Mennonite Quarterly Review* XXV (Jan. 1951), 66-69, 72

Geiser, *Witness*

Haas, Martin. *Quellen zur Geschichte der Täufer in der Schweiz: IV. Band: Drei Täufergespräche.* Zürich: Theologischer Verlag, 1974.

Haas, *Quellen*

Hoffman, Melchior. *Das xii Capitel des prophete Danielis ausz gelegt . . .* M.d.xxvj.

Melchior Hoffman, *Daniel XII*

Horsch, John. *Mennonites in Europe*, 2 ed., Scottdale: Mennonite Publishing House, 1950.

Horsch, *Mennonites*

Hulshof, Abraham. *Geschiedenis van de Doopsgezinden te Straatsburg van 1525-1557.* Amsterdam: J. Clausen, 1905.

Hulshof

Klassen, William and Walter Klaassen. *The Writings of Pilgram Marpeck.* Kitchener, Ont., and Scottdale, Pa.: Herald Press, 1978.

The Writings

14

Kolb, A. B. Dietrich Philips. *Enchiridion*,
Aylmer, Ont.: Pathway Publishing
Corp., 1966. English translation
revised by Walter Klaassen, based on
*De Geschriften van Dirk Philipsz,
Bibliotheca Reformatoria
Neerlandica*, vol. X ed. S. Cramer
and F. Pijper, Nijhoff, 1914.

Kolb/Klaassen, *Philips*

Krebs, Manfred. *Quellen zur Geschichte
der Täufer IV. Band. Baden und
Pfalz*, Gütersloh: C. Bertelsmann
Verlag, 1951.

Quellen: Baden und Pfalz

Krebs, Manfred and H. G. Rott. *Quellen
zur Geschichte der Täufer VIII.
Band: Elsass II. Teil*. Gütersloh:
Verlagshaus Gerd Mohn, 1960.

Quellen: Elsass II

Loserth, Johann. *Pilgram Marbecks
Antwort auf Kaspar Schwenckfelds
Beurteilung des Buches der
Bunddesbezeugung von 1542*, Wien
und Leipzig: Carl Fromme, 1929.

Loserth, *Marbeck*

Manschreck, Clyde L. *A History of
Christianity*, Englewood Cliffs, N.J.:
Prentice-Hall, Inc., 1964.

Manschreck, *History*

Meyer, Christian. "Die Anfänge des
Wiedertäuferthums in Augsburg,"
*Zeitschrift des historischen Vereins
für Schwaben und Neuburg*, I, 1874,
207-253.

Meyer

Müller, Lydia. *Glaubenszeugnisse
oberdeutscher Taufgesinnter* I,
Leipzig: M. Heinsius Nachfolger,
1938.

Müller, *Glaubenszeugnisse*

Muralt, Leonhard von and Walter
Schmid. *Quellen zur Geschichte der
Täufer in der Schweiz: I. Bd. Zürich*,
Zürich: S. Hirzel Verlag, 1952.

Muralt and Schmid,
Quellen

15

Peachey, Shem and Paul Peachey.   Peachey, *Answer*
"Answer of Some Who Are Called
Anabaptists—Why They Do Not
Attend the Churches: A Swiss
Brethren Tract," *Mennonite
Quarterly Review* XLV (Jan. 1971),
5-32.

Riedeman, Peter. *Account of Our*   Riedeman, *Account*
Religion, Doctrine and Faith,
London: Hodder and Stoughton in
conjunction with the Plough
Publishing House, 1950.

Rupp, Gordon. *Patterns of Reformation,*   Rupp, *Patterns*
London: Epworth Press, 1969.

Schornbaum, Karl. *Quellen zur*   Schornbaum, *Quellen*
*Geschichte der Täufer II. Bd.
Markgraftum Brandenburg,* Leipzig:
M. Heinsius Nachfolger, 1934.

Schornbaum, Karl. *Quellen zur*   *Quellen: Bayern II*
*Geschichte der Täufer. V. Band.
Bayern II. Abteilung.* Gütersloh: C.
Bertelsmann Verlag, 1951.

Stupperich, Robert. *Die Schriften*   *SBR*
Bernhard Rothmanns, Münster i.
Westfalen: Aschendorffsche
Verlagsbuchhandlung, 1970.

van Braght, Thieleman J. *The Bloody*   *Martyrs Mirror*
*Theater or Martyrs Mirror of the
Defenseless Christians,* Scottdale,
Pa.: Herald Press, 1950.

Wenger, J. C. *The Complete Writings of*   *CWMS*
Menno Simons, Scottdale, Pa.:
Herald Press, 1956.

Wenger, John C. "Martin Weninger's Vindication of Anabaptism," *Mennonite Quarterly Review* XXII, (July 1948), 180-187.

Wenger

Westin, Gunnar and Torsten Bergsten. *Quellen zur Geschichte der Täufer IX. Bd. Balthasar Hubmaier: Schriften*, Gütersloher Verlagshaus Gerd Mohn, 1962.

Westin, *Quellen*

Williams, George H. and A. M. Mergal. *Spiritual and Anabaptist Writers*, Philadelphia: Westminster Press, 1957.

Williams, *Spiritual*

Yoder, John H. *The Legacy of Michael Sattler*, Scottdale, Pa.: Herald Press, 1973.

Legacy

Zuck, Lowell. *Christianity and Revolution*, Philadelphia: Temple University Press, 1975.

Zuck

zur Linden, Friedrich Otto. *Melchior Hoffman: Ein Prophet der Wiedertäufer*, Haarlem: De Erven F. Bohn, 1885.

Zur Linden

Abbreviations for Secondary Literature

Rollin Armour, *Anabaptist Baptism*,
Scottdale, Pa.: Herald Press, 1966.

Armour, *Baptism*

Alvin J. Beachy, *The Concept of Grace in
the Radical Reformation*,
Nieuwkoop: de Graaf, 1977.

Beachy, *Grace*

Peter Brock, *Pacifism in Europe to 1914*,
Princeton: Princeton University
Press, 1972.

Brock, *Pacifism*

Claus-Peter Clasen, *Anabaptism: A Social
History*, Ithaca: Cornell University
Press, 1972.

Clasen, *Anabaptism*

Cornelius J. Dyck ed., *A Legacy of Faith*,
Newton, Kansas: Faith and Life
Press, 1962.

Dyck, *Legacy*

William R. Estep, *The Anabaptist Story*,
Revised Edition, Grand Rapids:
Eerdmans, 1975.

Estep, *Anabaptist Story*

Robert Friedmann, *The Theology of
Anabaptism*, Scottdale, Pa.: Herald
Press, 1973.

Friedmann, *Theology*

John Horsch, *The Hutterian Brethren*,
Goshen College, Goshen, Ind.:
Mennonite Historical Society, 1931.

Horsch, *Hutterian Brethren*

18

Irvin B. Horst, A. F. de Jong, D. Visser
eds., *De Geest in het Geding*, Alphen
aan den Rijn: Tjeenk Willink, 1978.

Horst, *Geest*

William E. Keeney, *Dutch Anabaptist
Thought and Practice*, Nieuwkoop:
de Graaf, 1968.

Keeney, *Dutch Anabaptist*

Walter Klaassen, *Anabaptism: Neither
Catholic Nor Protestant*, Waterloo,
Ont.: Conrad Press, 1973.

Klaassen, *Anabaptism*

Peter J. Klassen, *The Economics of
Anabaptism*, London: Mouton,
1964.

Klassen, *Economics*

William Klassen, *Covenant and
Community*, Grand Rapids:
Eerdmans, 1968.

Klassen, *Covenant and
Community*

Cornelius Krahn, *Dutch Anabaptism*, The
Hague: Nijhoff, 1968; Scottdale, Pa.:
Herald Press, 1981.

Krahn, *Dutch Anabaptism*

Franklin H. Littell, *The Anabaptist View
of the Church*, Boston: Starr King
Press, 1958.

Littell, *Church*

Mennonite Quarterly Review

MQR

John S. Oyer, *Lutheran Reformers
Against Anabaptists*, The Hague:
Nijhoff, 1964.

Oyer, *Lutheran Reformers*

Steven E. Ozment, *Mysticism and
Dissent*, New Haven and London:
Yale University Press, 1973.

Ozment, *Mysticism*

James S. Stayer, *Anabaptists and the
Sword*, Manhattan, Kansas:
Coronado Press, 1976.

Stayer, *Anabaptists*

John C. Wenger, *Even Unto Death*,
Richmond: John Knox Press, 1961.

Wenger, *Even Unto Death*

19

A Collection of
Primary Sources

1

Jesus Christ: God's Revelation

For Anabaptists, as for other Christians, Jesus constituted the heart of Christian faith. Most statements about Jesus made by Anabaptists are orthodox in nature, that is, they accept the traditional creedal statements. Beyond that, however, the unanimity ends.

A major feature of Anabaptist Christology was the weight placed on the function of Jesus as model and example. That involved an emphasis on his human life with his actions and words as described in the Gospels. But it did not lead to a denial or even an underemphasis on the divine nature of Jesus. With a few exceptions (Italian Anabaptism, for example, which, after 1550 was unitarian) it was strongly asserted that, in order to be the Saviour, Jesus had to be divine, a member of the Trinity (see Hubmaier, Riedeman, Marpeck).

Pilgram Marpeck's view of the humanity of Jesus is unique in Anabaptism. Jesus had to be a human, material being, since God makes his spiritual reality known to man only through physical media. The humanity of Jesus is therefore not simply the basis for ethics but is also an important philosophical principle. For Marpeck, as indeed for all Anabaptists, Jesus is the revelation of God as loving and gracious.

The Dutch Anabaptist writers would have agreed totally with emphasizing both the humanity and divinity of Jesus. Nevertheless, beginning with Hoffman, and continuing with Rothmann, Menno Simons, and Dirk Philips, we encounter a docetic[1] Christology, which, while it used traditionally orthodox words, moved in a monophysite[2] direction. All these writers emphasized that Jesus did

23

not receive his flesh from Mary but rather came with heavenly flesh, since a body made impure by sin could not be a perfect sacrifice for sins. The balance then is that with these writers Jesus was more divine than human, the human characteristics being gradually swallowed up in the divine. This doctrine of the heavenly flesh, which they shared with Caspar Schwenckfeld, had important implications for their doctrine of the church as the body of Christ. It led to an almost impulsive concern for the purity of the church and directly into the harsh church discipline of early Dutch Anabaptism. See selections on the ban by Menno and Dirk 10.13-10.15.

There was also a third view represented by Hans Denck and Hans Hut, and his followers. Denck especially worked with a Logos-Christology. He could say, for example, that the Lamb that had suffered from the beginning of the world had now suffered in Jesus. While the humanity of Jesus remains unquestionably important in this part of the movement, the historical particular is universalized so that the danger exists that the historical basis will be abandoned. It is the road of the mystics.

All Anabaptists are united in emphasizing that the confession of Jesus as Lord must be combined with obedience to his words. If obedience is not there, the faith is, by definition, counterfeit.

1.1 Hans Schlaffer, "A Comforting Letter," 1527, Müller, *Glaubenszeugnisse*, 108

I do not quite know what to say to the [charge made against us] that Christ is not true God and man but only a prophet. I am afraid that in some it is more impertinence than love. However, I wish to judge no one; it is difficult and dangerous to speak about it. It should be more thought about with fear than talked about. It is true that there is only one God as Moses says: Hear, O Israel, the Lord your God is one Lord, etc. This scandalizes both Jews and Christians. The Jews are ready to suffer anything, but to accept Christ as God is their greatest stumbling block. Man's reason simply cannot grasp that a thing could be at the same time one and three.

· ·

Concerning this I choose to remain with the Scriptures. The Word

24

which was with God from the beginning, has become flesh. That is Christ, who says himself: the Father is in me and I am in the Father. I and the Father are one. Christ, who was born from the Jews according to the flesh is God. There is one God and one mediator, God and man, Jesus Christ. Summa summarum briefly: I confess with Thomas the holy apostle and say to my Lord and Saviour Christ: my Lord and my God.

1.2 Balthasar Hubmaier, "The Twelve Articles," 1526-7, Davidson/Klaassen, *Hubmaier*, 212-214

I believe also in Jesus Christ, your only Son, our Lord. I believe that he has made atonement to you, my Father, for the fall; that he has made peace between you and me, who am a poor sinner, and has won, through his obedience, an inheritance for me. He has now given me strength through the Holy Word which he has sent, so that I may become your child through faith. I hope and trust in him entirely. He will not allow the healing and comforting name of Jesus to be lost to me, a miserable sinner, but rather will save me from all my sins. For I believe that he is Christ, true God and true man.

Also I believe and confess, my Lord Jesus Christ, that you were conceived through the Holy Spirit without human seed, and born of Mary, a pure and eternally chaste virgin. This was to redeem me and all believing men and to obtain from your heavenly Father the grace of the Holy Spirit, which had been withdrawn from me on account of my sins. I believe and trust that the Holy Spirit has come to dwell in me, and that the power of almighty God has overshadowed my soul like Mary's, and that I was conceived a new man, and born again of your living immortal Word, and in the Spirit. I believe that I shall behold the kingdom of God. You are the Son of the living God, and have become man, that we poor mortals might through you become the children of God.

I believe and confess that you suffered under the judge Pontius Pilate, that you were crucified, dead, and buried. All this you did on account of my sins in order that you might save me from eternal suffering, torment and death, by your cross, anguish, torment, and bit-

25

ter death. Through your rose-coloured blood shed for me you purchased my redemption.

Your great love for us poor men can be seen in this: that you have given us, instead of a heavy cross, a light yoke; instead of your bitter sorrow, indestructible joy; instead of your awful death, eternal life. Therefore, I praise and thank my kind Lord Jesus Christ for ever and ever.

1.3 Hans Denck, "The Order of God," 1527, Fellmann, *Denck I*, 94-95

Thus God tolerated the sin of the evil world in man at the time of Noah until the Flood (Gen. 6), but began to produce righteousness in those in whom he had before tolerated sin until the time of the death of Jesus Christ. Through his suffering he became one with God and his Word (Lk. 24, Acts 17, Ps. 18), descended into hell in the spirit to preach to those unbelieving spirits (1 Pet. 3), to complete the work of faith begun in those who believed (1 Pet. 4). Yes, the same Lamb that suffered in Christ has suffered from the beginning of the world (Rev. 13) and suffers until the end of the world (Mt. 25). And the lion from the tribe of Judah (Gen. 49) who was victorious in Christ (Rev. 5) has been victorious in all the elect from the beginning (Num. 23, 24) and will be victorious until the last enemy is overcome (Is. 30, 1 Cor. 15). The lion and the lamb are the one Word of God which fills the whole world (Jer. 23, Wis. 1), and which is even in our hearts (Deut. 30, Rom. 10), not idle but doing the will of the Father (Jn. 4). As long as we seek only ourselves and do not esteem him it suffers in us as it is said, but to our condemnation (Jn. 3) which this Word works in us although we do not know it (Jn. 9).

1.4 Leonhard Schiemer, "Letter to the Church at Rattenberg," 1527, Müller, *Glaubenszeugnisse*, 50

If one asks a heathen how a Christian ought to live his answer is: our lords have forbidden it. But when I ask: who are your lords that forbid you to believe they answer: this or that sovereign. Christians obey the sovereigns of this world with body and goods.[3] But they are obedient to the Sovereign of heaven, our Lord Jesus Christ with the soul and everything that pertains and belongs to faith. For in him dwells the fullness of deity. He alone is the Lord of all lords and the King of all kings, a Healer and Saviour of the human race. To him is given all authority in heaven, on earth, and under the earth. Therefore we are properly subject to him, give him our obedience, and honour, fear, and love him above all creatures.

1.5 Melchior Hoffman, "Truthful Witness," 1533, *Zur Linden*, 441-443

No flesh can become good through any work except through an innocent death, that is through a pure flesh without spot that was not from the cursed seed. For through the cursed seed nothing could be accomplished as it is written.

And I saw a strong angel preaching with a clear voice: who is worthy to open the book and to break its seals? And no one in heaven or on earth or under the earth could open the book nor look at it.

Here we see that no angel above in heaven in the height could accomplish the opening, nor anyone in hell or in the depth of the earth, nor any man on earth, but only the eternal Word and paschal Lamb.

We have now heard enough that the whole seed of Adam, be it of man, woman, or virgin, is cursed and delivered to eternal death. Now if the body of Jesus Christ was also such flesh and of this seed, that is of Adam's flesh and blood as is openly affirmed, it follows that the redemption has not yet happened. For the seed of Adam belongs to Satan and is the property of the devil. Satan cannot be paid in his own coin. . . .

Since Christ is of this seed after the flesh he cannot introduce grace since Adam's seed was cursed and has died (Rom. 5, 1 Cor. 13). It is certain that death cannot produce life, nor the curse a blessing. Since this seed is caught in lies and is the lie itself it cannot erect the truth. This is shown by the prophet Ecclesiasticus 34 when he says: who can be cleansed by one who is unclean or get truth from a liar? And if it should be established that Christ's flesh was Mary's

27

natural flesh and blood, we would all have to wait for another redeemer, for in such a one we could get no righteousness.

And it is certain that all who put their trust in Adam's flesh will never by such faith be able to inherit eternal blessedness. Rather the wrath of God remains on such. For those who seek their sanctification in Adam's seed as well as their blessing, cleansing, justification, redemption and coming to life, they cast away the true foundation stone, the eternal Word, and thrust the Lamb of God away. They make God, Christ, the Holy Spirit and all the witnesses of God into liars. Through this accursed seed nothing can be made better. If salvation was to be established it would have to be a different seed through which the whole seed of Adam could again be liberated and set free, namely the seed of the heavenly Father Abraham (Gal. 3), which Mary received from the Holy Spirit. It is the eternal Word and the Son of the most High himself who was not of this world (Jn. 8), and did not come out of this world (Jn. 16). Rather he came into the world. He is the one through whom everything was made in heaven and on earth, visible and invisible (Col. 1, Heb. 1, Eph. 2, 3, Jn. 1). He also had the power to give his life, surrender it, and take it again (Jn. 10). For if he had been the seed of the first Adam he would have had to die for himself as all other men, that is certain. Yes, he would have had to die for his own inherited guilt and be cursed as all other men.

1.6   Peter Riedeman, *Account*, 1542, 22-26
WE ACKNOWLEDGE ALSO JESUS CHRIST,
THE ONLY BEGOTTEN
SON OF GOD

We have said and acknowledge that God is one, and apart from him there is none that remains of himself unchanging in his clarity and who lives for ever; for he is truth, and that is his name in all eternity. Therefore we acknowledge also his Son, who was in the Father before the world was made, and in whom it was prepared; who modelled all things together with the Father—that is the Word that in the beginning was with God, through whom all things were created, are maintained, and shall be completed. Thus, we have the Father and the Son—not, however, two, but one God, for the Son is not without the Father nor is the Father without the Son, for they are not two but one, the Son in the Father and the Father in the Son.

JESUS

This Word proceeded from the Father that the harm brought by the transgression of Adam might be healed, and the fall restored; he took upon himself human nature and character, became man, became flesh, that even as through a man death came, even so resurrection from the dead and salvation might come through a man.

Now since in him and in none other is salvation, he brought his true name with him: the name given him by the angel before he was conceived in his mother's womb—"Jesus," that is Saviour. He is the Saviour who has robbed death of its power, torn its bond and snare asunder and set us, his people, free.

CHRIST

Now, since death, which could be crushed and overpowered by the strength of no hero or giant, nor by any human strength, held such sway over us that we were not able to be free, a power other than human strength was necessary. Therefore the Word, that is God himself, although he took upon himself human nature, lost nothing of his strength, through which all things were created, that death might thereby be overwhelmed and overcome.

For although the Word put on human nature and became flesh, yet the divine nature remains completely in the same, as Paul testifies, "In him dwells all the fullness of the Godhead bodily and in essence." Hence is he also named "Christ" or the anointed of God, as is written of him, "The Spirit of the Lord is upon me; therefore he has anointed me and sent me to preach the gospel." Thus he alone has the power to overcome death, and to quicken whom he will and to give of his fullness to whomsoever and in what abundance he will. And those who take from and receive of him become through him likewise "God's anointed" or Christians—failing this, they have the name in vain.

ONLY BEGOTTEN

That is the only begotten Son of the Father, come as a light into the world that he might lighten and make bright the darkness in which we were bound and by which we were encompassed, as it is written, "The people which sat in darkness saw great light; and to them which sat in the region and shadow of death a great light is sprung up." And he also himself testifies, "I am the light of the world; he that believes in me shall not walk in darkness, but shall have the light of life."

He is the only begotten in that he proceeded in a unique way from the Father, being quite different from all other created things, in that he has inherited a better name than the angels. For he is the unique power of God by means of which all his holy angels and all other created things were formed, moulded and given shape, therefore he has from the Father the birthright of the first-born, that every knee should bow and confess that he is Lord, to the glory of God, the Father.

SON

Now, since the Word proceeded forth from Truth and was spoken by Truth it is named the Son, but the Truth which spoke is named the Father, as that from which the Word came. Now it came from God, yet it remained in him, for he is everywhere and in all places, filling the earth with his breadth and with his height reaching unto heaven. A word which proceeds from a man breaks away from him because he is weak, but the word that proceeds from God because of his strength, greatness, and power remains for ever and ever in him, and can in no way break away from him. Thus are the Word and Truth, or the Son and Father, one; yea, one strength and one nature (although there are two names) which upholds all things, in which also we live and move and are, and without his strength can no one have being; and it is the Son, the brightness of the glory of the Father and the likeness of his nature, who has now taken us captive into his obedience and leads us in his way, teaches us his character, ways, and goodness that he may thereby become more and more known to the children of men.

WE CONFESS CHRIST TO BE LORD

As we know right well that no one can call Jesus Lord except in the Holy Spirit, and that all those who confess him in truth to be Lord must be children of his Spirit or have the same, and since we are not unaware of his grace which has been given us by God through him and experienced by us, we likewise confess him to be Lord; as, indeed, he truly is, for all power is given him by the Father, not only in heaven but also on earth and in the abyss. For this reason also all unclean spirits fear and tremble before him, for he has overcome and bound them, and taken from them their power and delivered and set free the prey, namely us, whom they had held captive in death.

But none may in truth give or ascribe to him such glory and honour except he experience such a victory in himself, namely that Christ has overcome the devil in him also, and rent and removed his snare, that is sin; delivered him, set him free, and reconciled him with God. For whosoever else may do so, speaks not from truth but out of delusion and from an improvised faith, or because others say so, therefore is Christ not confessed to be Lord as is said above by Paul, no man can say that Christ is Lord but by the Holy Spirit. For he in whom Christ is thus to overcome must surrender himself wholeheartedly to him, and endure and suffer his work. Since, however, this is not so, Christ works not in the same; therefore he remains forever in his sins.

1.7   **Pilgram Marpeck, "Concerning the Love of God in Christ,"** *The Writings.* **529-530; 534-536**

Love is all power, authority, strength, might, wisdom, reason, skill, understanding, truth, righteousness, mercy, forbearance, patience, meekness in all humility and lowliness. She is fully God in all, in, with, and through her summation Jesus Christ our Healer. He is the complete, whole, eternally coming true love of the Father, and the Father himself is the true love of the Son, one Spirit, God, and Lord forever, not mixed but One from eternity to eternity, not separated into two or three but three in One eternally.

Only what God himself is from eternity in and of himself is everlasting (understand: not "in" but "from" eternity), and remains eternally, God the Word and Spirit. The incarnate Word is taken into the unity, and, according to the measure of time, one in and with God. He is two natures, one Man, two natures, one God, divine and human in one.

. . . .

No creature has been found to express, teach, and to witness and state with power what love is, along with its virtues and powers except the Man Jesus, Jesus, Jesus Christ, the Son of God. The same was brought forth, glorified, and revealed by the Father with that glory which he as the incarnate Word had before the Father from eternity, as he also with love declares himself to be the true Son of God commissioned even to the death of condemnation, and has achieved the fullest, greatest, exalted love in that he gives his life for his friends. For no one has greater love than he who gives his life for his friends.

To this Christ has witnessed and in love declared himself, with the incarnate Word, deed, and power. This is the Lamb that was found worthy to open the sealed and closed book, that is the hidden-ness of all the virtue, power, and effulgence of love and himself to reveal before the Father the glory of love in himself, according to his Holy Manhood. He declares that the Father himself has glorified him with that glory which he had with the Father before the foundation of the world was laid. And as he was glorified in love in and before the Father, before the beginning of the world, so he also glorified himself before men and angels, and so the Father will glorify him again. In him virtue, such as the power of love, is completed and revealed before time, in the time of his flesh, as well as after this time to eternity. As this [power of love] is declared and witnessed to in that manner before the Father, so the Father will fully glorify the Son in the fulfillment of time in all of Christ's elect, and they will be as he is and he as his own in God and God in them eternally. It is not as though he had just become love, but this shows that he is from eternity. Thus, the incarnate Word is God and Man, Man and God, two natures, one God, and also two natures, one Man, the beginning of time, the center, and end of all things, A and O. For his sake are

32

all things. He is the breaking in of time out of eternity and into eternity.

Thus for the sake of love the lamb of God, which has taken away the sin of the world, was slain in love from the foundation of the world (Rev. 13:[8]). He, without guilt and sin, was sacrificed in history for the guilt and sin of man in order to restore the fall of man from the original love and raise him up into the blissful, joyful, eternally enduring love out of grace and more grace and be made worthy to be to the glory, praise, and honor of God as an eternal thanksgiving.

1.8 Pilgram Marpeck, "Judgment and Decision," 1543
The Writings, 314-315

Conceived by the Holy Spirit in Mary, Jesus Christ is the Son of God according to Spirit, Word, and power. The Father has certified God in him, through the power of his divine essence, with all powers, works, and miracles. He has also shown and certified his true humanity. As the Lord says in John 14 [10]: "Philip, do you not believe that I am in the Father and the Father is in me? If not, why do you not believe for the sake of the works that I do?" Thus, the Father is certified in the Son as true God and the Son in the Father, one God, manner, nature, and divine essence, all in the Son of Man. Brought forth from the seed and line of David, he was shown to be, in his weakness, a natural, earthly, true man. He was born of the race of man, but without the seed of man or sin. He was born of Mary, the spotless virgin in flesh and blood, in the manner of the human race; he grew and was brought up by earthly creatures as a truly earthly man. His physical life was sustained by eating and drinking and he died a natural death. Like those who also died a natural death, or who will yet die, he rose again from among the dead through the nature of God, Spirit, and Word, which is the resurrection and the life (as he said to Martha). He was taken up into heaven and seated himself at the right hand of his heavenly Father. We wait for his return and for our resurrection from the dead according to the flesh, to be received through him. Forgiveness and remission of sins come alone through the Lord Jesus Christ. That, briefly, is the testimony concerning the true divinity and true humanity of Christ. The divinity is testified to and known through power, and the humanity through weakness in death, for death does not come from heaven. I write on this matter because many Antichrists have now appeared who deny both the divinity and humanity of Christ.[4]

1.9   Pilgram Marpeck, "Defence," Loserth, *Marbeck*, 298

It must now therefore be quite clear what we mean when we talk about the Word through which the children of God are born. We mean one single Word of the Father which is brought to us in the Gospel through the hominized[5] Word, the Lord Jesus Christ, by himself and his apostles like a flowing stream coming from the fountain or eternal[6] Son (the stream and the fountain and Son are one). Even today [this Word] speaks in the hearts of the believers through his Holy Spirit as a living Word or speech of God as also Peter testifies when he says: And this is the Word by which the gospel is preached to you, namely none other than the only Word of the Father, for that is God and Jesus Christ himself. . . .

That true gospel and Word of the Father (by which one becomes a Christian or born again) was preached and proclaimed to human persons by the human person[7] Jesus Christ, himself the Word, through himself and his apostles, but only with the human and physical voice and not by means of angels. He adhered to that order (as a God of order) that the physical must preach to the physical. . . .

1.10   Bernhard Rothmann, "Restitution," 1534, *SBR*, 237

Whenever we thus earnestly present the teaching of Christ to men we teach that one must remain constant in it otherwise the end would be worse than the beginning. To which some are accustomed to answer and say: Since it is so strict with you it would be better for us to stay away from it. To this we reply: Man is by nature in death, and if he is not redeemed by Christ he remains in death. There is no other way to life but the narrow, strait way through Christ. If now you are set upon this way and ready to walk on it but decide not to, you remain in death. If however you enter upon it you are on the way and have a hope of arriving at blessedness provided you continue and do not wantonly fall away. For Christ desires to help you. Therefore do not be discouraged to start on the way of righteousness, for while we do not have in us the ability to carry it out we are all able in him who strengthens us, even Christ. Without him we can do nothing.

1.11   Bernhard Rothmann, "Confession of Faith," 1534, *SBR*, 197

We also believe that almighty God allowed the eternal Word, his Son, through whom he made man and all things, Col. 1, [16], to become flesh, Jn. 3, [16]. This happened after man fell into death[8] out of that Word through the poison of wickedness[9] of the old serpent so that death embraced the whole human race through one man. The Son was given for man into death in order that those who believe on the Son should not perish but have eternal life, Jn. 3, [16]. Thus we believe in Jesus Christ the Son of the living God who for us poor sinners became man and suffered death on the tree of the cross for us and the whole world, in order that we, free from sin, should henceforth walk in purity and without spot as befits our calling.

1.12   Bernhard Rothmann, "Confession of Faith," 1534, *SBR*, 199

It is enough that we confess our faith in simplicity and leave the judgment to pious and good-hearted people. We believe that there is one Christ, not born of Mary's flesh and blood, but rather as the article of faith says, he was conceived of the Holy Ghost and born from Mary, the Virgin. Mary did not receive it from her own flesh and blood but she conceived the living Word of God by the Holy Ghost. This Word of God, as John says in chapter one, became flesh and dwelt among us. The Holy Ghost did not find that from which Christ was conceived and born, in Mary. Rather, the Son of Man descended from heaven as Paul says in Cor. 10: the first man was an earthly man from the earth, but the second is a heavenly man from heaven. In summary, the Son and the Word of God has become man and Mary conceived him by the Holy Ghost. This is what the Scripture as well as the creed says and so we believe. We know that the gates of hell have no power against such belief. Mt. 16 [16]. For since God's Son became man and was for us surrendered to death by the Father, even so, without a doubt, he will give us all things with him. Rom. 8 [32], Jn. 3 [16]. However if it had been Mary's flesh that died for us, my God, what comfort and courage could we derive from that? That would be like paying for one sin with another and to wash and cleanse one uncleanness with another. Only mistrust and contempt could follow from this in the long run, indeed mockery against the love and mercy which God has shown toward us sinners.

1.13   Dirk Philips, "The Incarnation of Jesus Christ," 1557, "The True Knowledge of Jesus Christ," 1558, Kolb/Klaassen, *Philips*, 97-100, 109, 136-137

We believe and confess that Jesus is our Lord and Saviour (Jn. 1:13, 14; 3:16; 1 Jn. 4:9), the first-born and only begotten Son of the eternal and almighty Father and of the living God (Mt. 16:16), the brightness of his glory, and the express image of his essence (Heb. 1:2, 3); divine from the beginning of the world and from eternity, and inexpressibly born of the Father, and one Being with the Father, in such manner that they are one God and Lord, having equal power, might, love, glory, work, and will together eternally (Mic. 5:2-4; Is. 53:12; Jn. 5:19-27; 8:14-19; 9:4; 10:15-18; 13:3; 14:6-10; 15:1; 17:3-22).

But because the Son of God is called the Word (Greek, Logos; Latin, Sermo or Verbum), it is by no means to be understood that every word that God utters is his Son (Jn. 1:1). Oh, no! For the Son is not a spoken word, but an existent Word (1 Jn. 1:1), of whom all the words by God (which is the Holy Scripture) bear testimony (2 Pet. 1:20, 21; 2 Tim. 3:16). The Son of God is called the Word for the following reason (according to the understanding of many learned men), and has this significance (so far as we can comprehend the Scriptures): that the Son is the express image of the nature of the

Father (Heb. 1:3), proceeding out of the mouth of the Most High (Mt. 4:4). We maintain, that he proceeded as material Word, and as a natural Son of God, one in essence, kind, and nature with the Father (Jn. 10:35; 13:3). Indeed, into the same the Father poured his essence and reflected it in him in a visible way. That is why the apostle says that God who in time past spoke by the prophets, afterward spoke to us by his Son, the incarnated Word (Heb. 1:13, 2: Col. 1:15). Thus the Son is not a spoken, but a speaking Word. By this Word, that is, by the Son's word of power, all things are upheld (Heb. 1:3) and have their being. Therefore John declares that the Son is the Word of life, from whom the apostles saw and heard all the things which they have proclaimed to us (1 Jn. 1:1-3).

. . . .

Therefore we believe and confess that Jesus Christ is our Redeemer, Saviour, and Mediator (1 Tim. 2:5, 6; Gal. 1:4), truly God and man. He is truly God from everlasting, and born of the Father before the foundation of the world (Mic. 5:1, 2). But he became truly man in these last days. How his incarnation was brought about the evangelists and apostles describe to us in clear and express language. . . [he cites a number of Scripture passages].

Now if the body of Christ had been formed by Mary (as the world thinks and says with such want of understanding), there would be no difference between the body of Christ and that of Adam, because as Christ was conceived of the Holy Ghost in Mary (Lk. 1:31, 35; Mt. 1:20), so also Adam was made by God, and had no other father than God. What difference would there be, then, between the body of Christ and the body of Adam, if the body of Christ had been made of the earth, the same as the body of Adam (Gen. 1:27)? The body of Christ would necessarily have been made of the earth if it had been formed of human seed, for because of the body all men are dust and earth (Gen. 2:7). It should, however, be remembered that Adam was made of pure earth by God. But after that the earth was made unclean by sin, and all men were laid under the curse and became corrupt in their nature (Rom. 3:10; Gal. 3:10). How, then, should Christ have a pure body, if he had been formed of human seed which is unclean (Jn. 14:4)? Far from it! God, the heavenly Father, prepared a body for Jesus Christ, his only begotten son (Heb.

10:5), not of unclean human seed, with which he impregnated Mary, the pure virgin, through the power of his Holy Spirit, to which the aforequoted statements of the evangelists and apostles clearly testify (Mt. 1:20; Lk. 1:31).

. . . .

Since then these brothers and sisters[10]—children of Christ—have flesh and blood, Christ also partook of the same in the same way, that is, he became man, even as his brothers, sisters, and children are (Heb. 2:14). But the apostle does not say—nor does he mean—that he became man of our human flesh and blood, and it cannot be truthfully proven from his words. For Christ is the spotless Lamb of God (Jn. 1:36; 1 Pet. 1:19; Rev. 5:6), and without sin. But his brothers, sisters, and children are, according to the flesh, sinful by nature. What dwells in their flesh Paul clearly shows in his epistle to the Romans when he says: "I know that in me, that is, in my flesh, dwelleth no good thing" (Rom. 7:18). Hence the holy flesh of Christ, which is meat indeed (Jn. 6:55) and makes alive, did not originally come from our flesh and blood, but he, Christ, was graciously given to us and begotten by God, our heavenly Father, as a gift and proof of his everlasting love and unfathomable mercy, and was made man (Is. 7:14) like as we are. How, by what means, and whence this came to pass has been sufficiently stated and declared above.

. . . .

The doctrine of Jesus Christ is the word of the heavenly Father (Jn. 7:16; 3:11; 8:28; 12:49; 14:10, 24). The teaching of the Son and the testimony of the Holy Spirit is superior to all the teachings of the prophets, and it contains all that serves and promotes godliness. Nor can the will of the heavenly Father be found and confessed anywhere so clearly as in the words of Jesus Christ, by whom the Father has in these last days spoken, made known his will, and fully expressed it (Heb. 1:2). Hence all that is contrary and not conformable to the words of Christ, is not God's word or will: for no other foundation can be laid, than that is laid, which is Jesus Christ (1 Cor. 3:11).

. . . .

Hence no doctrine has any status that does not harmonize with the teaching of Christ and his apostles. Man does not live by other

38

words which proceed from the will of man, but alone by the words of God (Mt. 4:4), which have been made known to us by Jesus Christ and his apostles. Here is the bread of heaven; here is the water of life.

1.14 Menno Simons, "Triune God," 1550, *CWMS*, 492-493

Dear brethren in the Lord, we believe and confess that this same eternal, wise, almighty, holy, true, living, and incomprehensible Word, Christ Jesus, which was in the beginning with God and which was God, incomprehensible—born of the incomprehensible Father, before every creature—did in the fullness of time become, according to the unchangeable purpose and faithful promise of the Father, a true, visible, suffering, hungry, thirsty, and mortal man in Mary, the pure virgin, through the operation and overshadowing of the Holy Spirit, and so was born of her. We confess that he was like unto us in all things, sin excepted; that he grew up as do other men; that at the appointed time he was baptized and entered·upon his preaching task, and office of grace and love which was enjoined upon him from the Father, and which he obediently fulfilled. He erased the handwriting, that is, the law, which was against us; and has at last, through the eternal Spirit of his heavenly Father, offered himself in this human flesh, nature, and weakness, in which he sighed, wept, and prayed unto the Father, and sweat water and blood, and thus purified our hearts of dead works that we should serve the true and living God. All who believe on him and through him received grace, mercy, forgiveness of sins, and eternal life, and that by means of his crimson blood which he has in his great love sacrificed and shed on the cross for us poor sinners, according to the good pleasure of the Father. And so he has become our only and eternal High Priest, Atoner, Mercy Seat, Mediator, and Advocate with God his Father.

For even as God, the Almighty Father, through his Almighty Word, Christ Jesus, had created Adam and Eve, so also when they and their descendants were seduced by the serpent he restored them so that we should give no one the praise for our salvation, neither in heaven nor on earth, but the only and eternal Father through Christ Jesus, and that through the illumination of the Holy Spirit. This is enough of the incarnation.

For further reading:

Beachy, *Grace* 79-86, 208-213.
Cornelius J. Dyck, "The Christology of Dirk Philips," *MQR* XXXI (July 1957), 147-155.
Estep, *Anabaptist Story,* 133-140.
Friedmann, *Theology,* 53-56.
Keeney, *Dutch Anabaptist,* 89-99.
William E. Keeney, "The Incarnation, a Central Theological Concept," Dyck, *Legacy,* 55-68.
Walter Klaassen, "The Bern Debate of 1538: Christ the Center of Scripture," *Mennonite Quarterly Review* XL (April 1966), 148-156.
Klassen, *Covenant Community,* 61-66, 130-135.
Krahn, *Dutch Anabaptism,* 196-198.

II

The Work of God in Man

This section includes statements on justification, faith and works, free will, original sin, predestination, and the gospel of the creatures. These are grouped here because of their inner relationship.

Anabaptists were one and all agreed that the process of salvation begins with God's gracious act in Jesus Christ. There can no longer be any question about this. Once Luther's formulation on faith and works is seen as one way of several to set out the problem, our minds can be more open to consider the Anabaptist view. Anabaptists, too, believed that man is saved by grace and not through any merits of his own.

But they were equally certain that man was not saved in spite of himself. God has graciously provided a way of salvation, but in order to benefit from it man must freely choose it for himself. This implied that man could choose, and it was a rejection of the Protestant doctrine of the bondage of the will. The will was set free by God's grace and then man could choose to do the good that God desires for man.

They also rejected the doctrine of predestination, understood as the sovereign designation of some to salvation and others to damnation. To Anabaptists this appeared to charge God with evil and to rob man of the liberty to make choices for or against God.

The emphasis on man's ability to choose and the rejection of predestination inevitably assigned to man a function in the process of salvation. God's grace "goes before" but man could resist it or he could surrender to it. By surrendering and choosing he was contributing to the process. There was definitely an element of synergism[11] present which related the Anabaptist view of justification more to the late medieval than to the Protestant view.

41

We also encounter, especially in Denck and Hut and Hut's followers, a cross mysticism. There we hear about the purgation that is necessary before faith can come. It is a process of emancipation from dependence on created things to complete dependence upon God alone. This process is the human experience of the cross which everyone must endure to be saved.

The teaching about "the gospel of the creatures" also had mystical origins. The idea is basically that knowledge of God comes to man first through the created world which prepares the way for the gospel of Christ. But it is also more than that; the suffering of Christ was seen to be already inherent in the processes of nature which require suffering and death that there may be life. Again, it is the idea of "the Lamb slain from the foundation of the world."

Anabaptists simply refused to accept Luther's separation of works from faith, or action from confession. Works, they argued, were a part of faith, and without them faith was not faith. Much Scripture even in the New Testament called for evangelical obedience and if God called for it, Anabaptists argued, it must be his will and it must be possible to do it. Works were the outward expression of faith and not simply the fruit of faith as Luther said.

This same emphasis emerges in several discussions of Christ's work on the cross. Christ, it is argued, made atonement for the sins of the whole world, but it could become operative only if there was obedience which was expressed in works of faith. Thus there was no effective atonement or justification without obedience.

Finally, we find, among the Dutch especially, the conviction that once God works in human life by his Spirit an ontological change takes place. They are changed into divine beings after the image of Jesus. There is therefore also a rejection of Luther's view that even a Christian is at the same time a sinner and justified.

2.1   Balthasar Hubmaier, "The Summary of a True Christian Life," 1525, Davidson/Klaassen, *Hubmaier*, 59-60

The Samaritan must come—that is Christ—who brings medicine with him, wine and oil, and pours it upon the wounds of the sinner. Wine represents man's repentance for his sins, and the oil anoints his sores and mollifies them. Christ says: believe in the gospel which states clearly that I am the physician that has come into the world to make the sinner righteous and godly. The gospel teaches also that I am the only gracious, reconciling, interceding mediator and peacemaker with God our Father. He who believes on me shall not be damned but has eternal life. Through such comforting words the sinner is quickened, comes to himself, becomes joyful, and entrusts himself to his physician. He commits and entrusts his sickness to the physician, surrenders as much as a wounded man can, and calls to him for healing. The physician helps, advises, and promotes whatever the wounded man cannot do in his own strength so that he can follow his word and commandment.

Now all the teachings which diagnose diseases and point to the physician are only "the letter that kills" before they are believed. But in faith God makes them to live, wax green, and bear fruit. Thus by faith, water became wine at the wedding. One must put on the rough coat of John the Baptist before one can receive the soft, mild, and meek lamb, Jesus Christ. Then a man surrenders himself sincerely from the heart and purposes to lead a new life, according to the rules and teachings of Christ, the physician, who has made him whole, and from whom he derives his life. So Paul acknowledges openly that it is not he that lives, but Christ that lives in him. Christ is the life in him. Outside of Christ, he confesses that he and his works are vain, of no account, and an accursed sinner.

2.2 Balthasar Hubmaier, "Justification," 1526, Westin, *Quellen*, 461-462

Faith alone and by itself is not sufficient for salvation. This article will first be tested in the writings of Paul. With the heart man believes to righteousness and with the mouth confession is made to salvation (Rom. 10). Now we do not wish to be mouth Christians only, to boast and say: O yes, we believe that Jesus Christ suffered agony and death for us. Rather, faith must express itself also in love to God and the neighbor. Thus John teaches us when he says: Little children, let us not love in word or speech but in deed and truth. By this we shall know that we are of the truth (1 Jn. 3). Faith must be active in love (Gal. 5). Therefore faith by itself alone is like a green fig tree without fruit, like a cistern without water, like a cloud without rain.... O, we wish to be good evangelical Christians; we boast about our great faith, but have never touched the works of the gospel and faith with the smallest finger. Therefore we are, as stated above, nothing but mouth Christians, ear Christians, and paper Christians, but not action Christians. About these St. James severely admonishes us in his Christian and useful epistle when he writes: What does it profit, my brothers, if a man says he has faith but has not works? If a brother or sister is ill-clad and in lack of daily food, and one of you says to them: Go in peace, be warmed and filled, without giving them the things needed for the body, what does it profit? So faith by itself, if it has no works, is dead. You have faith and I have works. Show me your faith apart from your works, and I by my works will show you my faith. You believe in the one God; you do well. Even the devils believe and shudder (Jas. 2). I confess this article with all my strength: that faith by itself alone is not worthy to be called faith, for there can be no true faith without the works of love.

2.3   Balthasar Hubmaier, "Justification," 1526, Westin, *Quellen*, 468-469

Whoever denies the free will of man and says that "free will" is nothing but an empty and useless term without any reality, the same slanders God as a tyrant. He charges God with injustice and gives manifold cause to the wicked to remain in their sins. Indeed, he overthrows more than half of the holy Scriptures. The proof of this article: If man were robbed of his free will God could never justly condemn the sinner for his sins. For he condemns him for reasons about which man can do nothing. God forbid! Moreover Christ would be robbed of his just accusation which he will bring against sinners on the last day saying: I was hungry and you did not feed me. I was sick and in prison and you did not come to me, etc. (Mt. 25). Certainly sinners could excuse themselves with good reason and say: It was impossible for us to feed and visit you since we have no free will. Indeed, because of your eternal foreknowledge and judgment we must go with the devil into eternal fire in order to fulfil your eternal foreknowledge. It follows moreover from this destructive teaching that man may justifiably put his guilt on God and say: my stealing and my robbing was not my fault but God's will which no one can resist (Rom. 9). Without his will I could not have done it. Because of my will I had to do it because it is bound and imprisoned. Through this error all those Scriptures would be overthrown which speak about willing and doing. . . .

2.4   Balthasar Hubmaier, "Discussion of Zwingli's Baptism Book," 1525, Westin, *Quellen*, 203

Zwing: The children of Christians are certainly and undoubtedly children of God.

Bal: There you attack God's judgment and grant to physical birth what belongs alone to the spirit and the Word of God. For God alone makes children of God. Children however are the inheritors of sin and wrath which we inherit from father and mother be they Christian or unchristian. We were all conceived and born in sin.

2.5   Balthasar Hubmaier, "Justification," 1526, Westin, *Quellen*, 473

Original sin is not simply a fault or a shortcoming as some say, but a sin which condemns those who are not in Christ and who walk after the flesh. It is the mother and root of all sin.

To prove this article it is written that King David makes a grave lament precisely because of original sin and calls to God: Behold, I was conceived in sin, and in sin my mother gave me birth (Ps. 50 [51]). Similarly Job cursed the day on which he was born and the night which said: A man is conceived (Job 3). Paul says: I can will what is right, but I cannot do it. For I do not do the good I want, but the evil I do not want is what I do. Now if I do what I do not want, it is no longer I that do it, but sin that dwells within me (Rom. 5). Through sin death has entered the world (Rom. 5). We have all sinned in Adam (1 Cor. 15), and have become children of wrath (Eph. 2).

45

Many other Scriptures like Gen. 3 and 8 and Rom. 8 could be cited here. But enough for now. Whoever says that original sin is no sin presumes to teach Paul and to instruct him in what is and what is not sin. That is a blasphemous presumption. . . .

2.6   Hans Denck, "Recantation," 1527, Fellmann, *Denck I*, 107-108

God will give to each according to his work. The evil eternal punishment according to his justice; the good eternal life according to his mercy. It is not that someone earns something from God or that God should owe man something since he deals with us specifically and severely, but he pays us according to the promise which he has previously given us. He looks to faith and good works; he is pleased and rewards them. Not that they originate in us but rather that we do not in vain receive or perhaps completely reject the grace which he has offered us. It all comes from the one treasure which is truly good, namely the Word that was with God from the beginning and has in the last times become flesh. Well for that man who does not reject the gifts of God.

Faith is the obedience to God and the confidence in his promise through Jesus Christ. Where this obedience is absent there all confidence is false and a deception. This obedience must be genuine, that is that heart, mouth and deed coincide together. For there can be no true heart where neither mouth nor deed is visible. And where the heart is not honest all words and works are nothing but deception. An evil heart betrays itself with pride and impatience. A good heart proves itself with humility and patience.

Whoever has recognized the truth in Christ Jesus and obeys it from the heart is free from sin, although he is never free from temptation. It is impossible for him to walk firmly in the way of God unless he be strengthened by God. Whoever runs, more or less lacks in truth, obedience and freedom.

In summary, whoever submits his will to the will of God, he is free for good and imprisoned for good. Whoever does not so submit his will is free for evil and imprisoned for evil. Whoever is one's master frees one to do in his service whatever he desires. God coerces no one to remain in his service whom love does not coerce. The devil, however, is unable to force anyone to stay in his service, who has once seen the truth.

It, therefore, makes no difference whether one speaks of the free or the bound will; one must understand the difference on both sides. The word itself is not worth the discord.

2.7 Hans Denck, "The Contention That Scripture Says," 1526 Fellmann, *Denck I*, 37

He proved his full perfection in that he offered up his life without contradiction and took it again without glory through the power of the Father. In all of this he never hesitated one moment but completed everything in its time, nothing too early and nothing too late. No one else has done this, and whatever anyone has done, he has received it from Christ, that is justification by grace. He, however, received it from no one than from the Father. That is grace by justification.

2.8 Hans Denck, "The Order of God," 1527, Fellmann, *Denck I*, 92

This work is done by the Word of God that preaches to man in condemnation and says clearly: you are yourselves to blame, therefore you may not put on someone else the guilt and the suffering which you yourself have willed and which you suffer justly. As soon as man becomes aware of the Word of God, he becomes partly free (Jn. 8) to continue in his wickedness or to sacrifice himself in suffering. The more he resists suffering the more he condemns himself until finally he sinks into death. But the more he surrenders and humbles himself under the mighty hand of God (1 Pet. 5) the better the Lord can do his work. But man thinks he will be destroyed. When the work begins in him he becomes empty and hungry but not satisfied (Amos 8). Then he looks from afar into the bosom of Abraham (Lk. 16). He knows that he is receiving justice, but does not know that God is so near to him (Jer. 23) and merciful toward all flesh (Ecclus. 18).

2.9   Hans Denck, "The Contention that Scripture Says," 1526, Fellmann, *Denck I*, 33

By your lack of serene surrender you prove that you seek yourself rather than God for his own sake, since you are constantly looking for hiding places in order to evade the hand of God. For since you are a poor little plant and he an enormous stone you are always anxious that he will crush you if you hold still for him. For that is the way flesh and blood perceives [God's work] before man surrenders. When he seeks for blessedness there seems to be only condemnation and man's perverted nature does not enjoy that. If only a man would hold still the time would have come for the spirit of the Lamb to give witness and tell him that to lose oneself is the only way to blessedness. . . . This witness is in all men and speaks to each one personally according to the degree to which he listens.

2.10   Jacob Kautz, "The Seven Articles," 1527, *Quellen: Baden und Pfalz*, 114

Jesus Christ of Nazareth has not suffered for us or made satisfaction for us in any way unless we stand in his footsteps, walk the way he blazed before us, and follow the command of the Father as the Son, everyone in his measure. Whoever speaks, understands, or believes differently about Christ makes an idol out of Christ, which all the scribes and false evangelists and the whole world do.

Even as the external eating of the forbidden fruit by Adam harmed neither him nor his descendents if the inner acceptance had not been there, so also the physical suffering of Jesus Christ is not the true satisfaction and atonement toward the Father without inner obedience and the greatest pleasure to obey the eternal will of God.

2.11   Hans Hut, "The Mystery of Baptism," 1526-1527, Rupp, *Patterns*, 383-388

First then, Christ says, "Go into all the world and preach the gospel of all creatures [aller creaturen]." Here the Lord shows how man shall come to the knowledge of God and himself, namely through the "gospel of all creatures." But we must first of all learn and

48

know what is this "gospel of all creatures." For, God have mercy, the whole world is utterly ignorant of it, and it is also never preached in our age. And though it be preached and spoken by the poor in spirit, despised of the world [die der welt veracht], as it should be, to those to whom it is revealed, yet to the soft and carnal men, especially the hireling preachers, who none the less boast that they preach the gospel, it is the very greatest folly and fanaticism, and those who so preach are railed at as the most scandalous false prophets and lying spirits. Ah well, they have their little day, and, as Paul has so well said, the word of the cross is foolishness to them that are perishing; but to those who shall be saved (that is, us) it is the power of God.

In the "gospel of all creatures" is nothing else signified and preached than simply Christ crucified, but not Christ alone as Head, but the whole Christ with all members, this is the Christ which all creatures preach and teach. The whole Christ has to suffer in all members, and not as our Scribes preach Christ (who nevertheless want to be the best, as we hear daily from them), that Christ as the Head has borne and accomplished everything. But then what happens to the members and the whole body in which the suffering of Christ must be fulfilled? Of this Paul bears witness, when he says, "I rejoice in my suffering, for I fulfill what is lacking in the suffering of Christ in my body." And therefore, in a short time, which has already begun, they must with their wisdom be turned into fools, for it is God's good pleasure through foolish, silly, and fanatical preaching, as the clever ones call it, to save those who believe it, though these rage against it never so much. So they must in a short time, for all their wisdom and pride, give way to the poor in spirit who, as Paul says, are simply fanatics to them. Now this you are to understand with diligence, my dearly beloved brethren, and mark the word which Christ calls "the gospel of all creatures" [das evangelion aller creaturen]. For it is not here to be understood as though the gospel is to be preached *to* the creatures, cats and dogs, cows and calves, leaves and grass, but as Paul says, the "gospel which is preached to you, in all creatures."[12] This he also shows when he says that the eternal power and divinity will be perceived when a man truly recognizes it in the creatures or works from the creation of the world[13]. . . .

Thus it is nothing else, as he expounds it in another place, than a power of God which saves all who believe in it. But if a man will understand and confess God's eternal power and divinity, or his invisible being, by the works or creatures from the creation of the world, he must then mark and consider how Christ always showed the kingdom of heaven and the power of the Father to the common man in a creature, through a parable, through handicrafts, in all manner of works with which men are occupied. He did not direct the poor man to books, as now our senseless scribes do, but he taught them and showed them the gospel by means of their work, the peasants by their field, seed, thistle, thorn and rock. In the prophets God says men are not to sow amongst thorns, but are first to clear the ground, plough it or turn it up, and then plant afterwards. The power of God, as it is shown us here, is God's work towards us, that God's power must be exercised towards us, as the work of the peasants towards the field. This Christ shows with the field, and Paul says, "you are God's husbandry." As the peasant does with his field, before he sows seed in it, so does God also with us, before he plants his Word in us, that it may grow and bear fruit. He teaches the gardener the gospel from his trees, the fisherman from his catch, the builder from his house, the goldsmith by the testing of his gold, the housewives from their dough, the vinedresser by his vineyard, vine and shoots, the tailor by the patching on an old garment, the merchant by the pearls, the reaper by the harvest, the woodcutter by the axe laid to the tree, the shepherd by his sheep, the potter by his pottery, the steward and the bailiff by their accounts, the pregnant woman by her childbearing, the thresher by his winnowing fan, the butcher by his slaughtering. Paul illustrates the body of Christ in and through a human body, and so Christ always preached the gospel of the kingdom of God by the creatures and in parables and without a parable he did not preach to them. And so David says "I will open my mouth and speak in parables."

From such parables men are diligently to mark how all the creatures have to suffer the work of men, and come through the suffering to their end, for which they were created, and also how no man can come to salvation, save through suffering and tribulation which God works in him, as also the whole Scripture and all the creatures show

50

nothing else but the suffering Christ in all his members.

That is why the whole of the Scriptures is described simply through creatures. And therefore did God give the children of Israel to understand his will through creaturely and ceremonial works, and announced, preached, and described them through Moses. God commands that oxen, sheep, he-goats, rams, and bullocks shall be sacrificed. Through Isaiah he testifies that he does not will such, as he says, "The sacrifice of bulls, the blood of sheep, calves and goats have I not chosen," and through David he says, "I will not take any bullock out of thy house, nor he-goats out of thy folds." Therefore God's commandment does not consist in the letter [red] but in the power [kraft] which the Spirit gives, and the spiritual force of such commandment will always hold good for men—that man is in relation to God as such sacrifice is in relation to men. That is why David sacrifices to God a burnt offering of rams, oxen and goats, and offers a calf for himself. Such ceremonial sacrifices are therefore signs and witness that men are to offer themselves as living sacrifices. Accordingly God commands [Lev. 11, Deut. 14] that men shall eat clean animals, the [spiritual] force of which is that men are to give themselves to God to suffer the will of God, as such animals have to suffer our will, and he forbids the eating of unclean beasts, the [spiritual] force of which is that we are not to keep company with impure men, who are compared with such animals. For it is written [Acts 10:15] there is nothing unclean and all is good. These ceremonies point out what is the will of God, and are intended for us as truly as for the children of Israel.

That is why Christ always spoke through parables, and these consist not in the speaking, but in the power and the meaning. All animals are subject unto man; if a man needs one he must first prepare, cook and roast it, and the animal must suffer. So it is with God and man: if God is to make use of us or enjoy us, we must first be justified by him, and cleansed within and without: inwardly from desire and lust, outwardly from all improper behaviour and misuse of creatures. The peasant sows no corn amongst thistle, thorns, sticks and stones, but he first weeds them out and then sows afterwards. So does God with us: he sows his Word not in a man who is full of thistles or thorns or has desire and affection only towards creatures;

that anxiety about bodily welfare which God forbids, must first be rooted out. The builder does not make a house out of whole trees, but first cuts them down and then fashions them as he wills, and afterwards makes a house out of them. In this way we are to learn God's Work and will towards us, which is as a man behaves with a house before he lives in it, which house (Paul says) we are.

Man is often called a tree in the Scriptures: if he is to be turned into a house he must be cut off from the world with all lusts. Then as on a tree one branch sticks out, now in one direction and now in another, so is it too with the desires of men, one branch stretches towards possessions, another towards wife and children, a third towards money, a fourth towards fields and lands, to pomp and temporal honour.

Therefore all the works which we accomplish with the creatures should be our Scriptures which we closely mark. For the whole world with all creatures is a book, in which is to be seen in act all those things which are read in the written book. For all elect men from the beginning of the world until Moses have studied in the book of all creatures, and have taken knowledge of it by reason, as it is written from nature by the Spirit of God in the heart, because the whole law is expressed in creaturely works. And all men are in this wise concerned with the creatures, as the law shows, even the heathen who have not the law of Scripture, and yet do the same thing which they do who have the scriptural law. The law of Scripture prescribes how a man must kill a beast before it is offered to God, and only after this was it eaten; even so do the heathen who have the law of nature, and who eat no animal alive. So we must first die to the world and live in God....

As therefore the law is inscribed in all creatures and shown forth there, we read it in our daily work. In this book we are occupied daily, and the whole world is full, yes, full of the will of God so expressed, of which our own hearts bear witness if we keep them from the coarsening of worldly disorder and lust, and so men can perceive the invisible being and eternal power of God in the works of the creatures, and see how God works with men and prepared them for the end of their perfection which can only take place through the cross of suffering according to his will. That is why all creatures are subject to man, to rule over them, and as the whole Bible is written in terms of all creatures, so Christ too spoke, or preached and declared, the "gospel in all creatures" in a parable, as he himself did when he preached it to the poor. So he did not point them to the chapters of a book, as our Scribes do, for all that a man can show through the creatures is all confirmed [?: the original is *beweiset*] in the Scriptures, and Christ needs no Scriptures except for the sake of the scribes, to convince them with it. When the gospel in all creatures is thus preached according to the commandment of the Lord, and man is brought thereby to understand that reason in a natural and real way is included in his own works which he does over and in the creatures, in which he acknowledges God's will towards him, and gives himself into joyful obedience to Christ, he sees that no man can be saved in any other way than by suffering the will of God in body and in pain, as it may please God.

2.12   Leonhard Schiemer, "Letter to the Church at Rattenberg," 1527, Müller, *Glaubenszeugnisse*, 65

As soon as they become aware of this light they are terrified in their hearts because of the Word of God; they bend all their energies to resist sin. They pray, hear much preaching, read a lot, and ask many questions, all with a sincere heart. Although they are the enemies of sin nevertheless they cannot resist sin in their own power and are often overcome by the flesh. However they are immediately sorry for it, suffer on account of it, and humble themselves faithfully. To them God gives grace upon grace. He wishes to be gracious and merciful to them for the Lord says: I will look upon him who is humble and who is shocked by my Word. David also says: a broken and a humble heart, you O God, will not despise. Christ says: come to me all who labour and are heavy laden and I will quicken you. Elsewhere it is written: The Spirit of the Lord is upon me because the Lord has anointed me. He has sent me to bring good news to the poor, to bind up the broken hearts, to preach release to the captives, and to open the prison of the prisoners, and to comfort all who mourn. Truly these have lamentation, restlessness and heartache so that no writing or teaching can comfort them except God's Word.

This fire burns them, and gives them no rest until God enlightens them about the means or the ways through which they might escape from sin. They can tell you something about hell, and their inner sorrow weighs on them so that externally they cannot be really happy in their actions and words.

2.13 Leonhard Schiemer, "Letter to the Church at Rattenberg," 1527, Müller, *Glaubenszeugnisse*, 65-67

Blessed are those who hunger and thirst after righteousness, that is how they may be made righteous, for they will be satisfied. Blessed are those who mourn and weep for they shall be comforted. The second grace is called righteousness. It is a great work of God to create man out of nothing, but it is an equally great work to justify a sinful man. But that can in no way happen outside of the conception, birth, death, and resurrection in us of Christ who is our righteousness. Whoever will be my disciple, says Christ, must follow me. Again he says that without me you can do nothing. Peter says: whoever suffers in the flesh ceases from sin. The first light has been our schoolmaster until the other, that is Christ came, who is the light of the world. When his spirit enters me I am no longer under the schoolmaster but under grace. There the law of works, sin, death, and members ceases, and the law of the Spirit, faith, life, and the heart commences. But this Spirit is given to no one except he first submit himself to the cross and the chastisement of the Lord.... For it is impossible for the omnipotence of God to save me except through the cross. For this is blessedness and God himself that I love nothing save God alone and seek joy and comfort, security and life in nothing else than in the one God alone, and that my heart no longer depends in anything on the creatures.... Now if we are no longer to love any creature that we have loved before there is only one thing for God to do and that is to prune our branches: that is to say, he takes the creatures from us, and sets us naked and exposed into the second birth, gives us his Spirit and teaches us to know and love him. This however does not take place without pain, suffering, and anguish.... Thus when God sends us the loss of wife, children, father, mother, brother, sister, property, wealth, health in body or even life it is our unbelief that gives us pain. We cannot firmly believe that it happens for our good and that something better awaits us in the future.... But there is an even greater unbelief that tortures us, namely godless thoughts such as: God will forget me. He will not remain faithful to me. He is a respecter of persons and will not help me as he has helped others. Unbelief cannot be more stupid than to think: if I surrender to God I surrender security. I will perish. If, however, I remain with the world I will soon be safe and not perish so foolishly. If I become or remain a Christian God will not feed me but if I remain a heathen I will freely feed myself. If I become a Christian my children will die of hunger; if not they will be safe. To all this I say: clearly you are not yet a Christian but an evil heathen. It is painful until faith is separated from unbelief. It takes a good smeltinghouse, a strong test, a pungent acid,[14] for an uncrucified Christian is like untested ore and like a house the wood of which is still in the tree. Only the fact that we do not know him prevents the love of God in us. Since he is the greatest good it is impossible not to love him alone and above all things if one knows him. Whoever truly knows God loves him so much that it would be impossible to love anything besides him even if it were commanded on pain of eternal damnation. Indeed, if I truly knew God my spirit and soul would be so overjoyed that this joy would penetrate into the body and it would become unfeeling,[15] impassable, immortal, and glorified. Therefore if man is cleansed from all love of the creatures and even his own life, God brings about [this bodily change] through that sleep which all the saints share until the resurrection of the dead.[16] Thus we cannot know God until the cover, which hides the divine light in us, that is the creatures, is removed. And the more the creature is withdrawn from us for the sake of Christ, the more the light and the Word of God shines forth. Whoever therefore submits himself to God under the cross is a child of God.

2.14   Leonhard Schiemer, "Letter to the Church at Rattenberg," 1527, Müller, *Glaubenszeugnisse*, 49

In the marvelous creation of heaven and earth and the other creatures God may be known. Paul says that God's invisible essence and his everlasting power and deity can be known, if one comprehends it, ever since the creation of the world. He also says that God has created the visible things in order that through them the invisible may be known. Further he says that the gospel that I have preached to you is being preached in all the creatures. In five days God created all creatures. However, because on the sixth day, the day on which man was created, they become beneficial to man, the creation comes to its rest. Man too is not created in order that on the sixth day he remain a man, but in order that he comes into the seventh day, indeed that he becomes deified and comes to God. That is man's true rest and the true holy day.... The means by which the creatures benefit man is suffering. Man kills, cuts, and prepares them, and the creatures quietly endure it and suffer for the sake of faith. And even as an animal cannot benefit man as food unless the lamb die, no man will be saved unless he die for the sake of Christ.

2.15   Michael Sattler (?), "On the Satisfaction of Christ," before 1530, *Legacy*, 115-116

How then has Christ worked satisfaction for our sins? Answer: Not alone for our own, but for the sins of the whole world, insofar as the world believes in him, and follows after Him according to the requirement of faith, as has been said. Yea, he as the head of his church, has done enough; yet he will nevertheless day by day again do enough in his members and for them, until the end of the world, just as he had done from the beginnings [of the world] until his appearance. Therefore, when one speaks of justification through Christ, one must also speak of that faith, which cannot be without works of repentance, yea, not without love, which is an anointing. For such an anointed faith, which is given to one from the resurrection of the dead, is the only Christian faith, and is reckoned unto righteousness (Rom. 4).

Again when one speaks of works, one must preach not, after the manner of the work-righteous, the works of law but the works of faith; that is a turning away from works, creatures, and your own self, through faith in Christ the crucified one, not as what man can

56

do from himself, but what he really can do in the power of faith; which thereby are not man's works but God's, since the willing and the ability to turn to God are not of man but the gift of God through Jesus Christ our Lord.

Verily, blessed be he who remains on the middle path, who turns aside neither to the work-righteous (who promised blessedness or the forgiveness of sins, through works done without faith, i.e., through that which, in one's works one thinks is one's own; thus they turn aside to the left and lead others that way,) preaching works in such a way that they think no more of faith, and wish neither to see nor to hear anything about faith, that it is necessary for salvation, so that all their works are like wild plums, i.e., ceremonies without faith. Nor to the side of the scribes, who although they have forsaken works, then turn aside to the right, and teach in the name of "gospel" a faith without works, and take the poor obedient Christ (who had no place to lay his head—Lk. 9.—who speaks without complaint or self-defense, Lk. 22, "nevertheless, Father, not my will but thy will be done") as their satisfaction, but will not hear what he says, Lk. 9: "Come, follow me." Item, Lk. 14: "He who does not forsake all that he possesses, cannot be my disciple." Item, Mk. 8: "He who would follow me, let him deny himself and take up his cross and follow me." Yes, the Father must also be a fanatic to them, when he says, "That is my beloved Son, in whom I take satisfaction; hear him."

2.16   Pilgram Marpeck, "Confession," 1532, *The Writings*, 145-146

In contrast, the true assurance of God and Christ which is received with certainty and which is written in the heart, believed and trusted even to death, characterizes the birth of the Spirit, of which water baptism is only a witness. As Paul says [Gal. 5:22], being made alive in the Spirit was a clear revelation apprehended in peace, joy, comfort, confidence, and true love, with a clean heart and sincere faith, with patience, meekness and lowliness of heart, with mercy and peacemaking, friendliness and true godliness, with the whole heart, which is kindled by the fire of the Holy Spirit, with a burning love for God and the brothers, with faithfulness even unto death which witnesses, reveals itself, and believes all the words of Christ to the pleasure and praise of the Father. For it is the Spirit which testifies to Christ [Rom. 8:16] and reveals the gifts of the service of the body of Christ and the whole world; he does not strive to rule but denies himself. He divests himself and surrenders everything at the feet of Christ, and is given only to service. Although in Christ he is a Lord and child of all, he does not consider all things as things to be grasped; rather, he humbles himself for servanthood, for Christ the Son of God did not consider his divinity as spoil but served friend and foe, did good and loved even to death [Jn. 13:1]. In summary, the Spirit's witness, life, and birth is of Christ, and hidden with Christ in God, to the eternal praise of the Father.

2.17 Melchior Hoffman, "Ordinance of God," 1530, Williams, *Spiritual*, 201-202

Therefore faith cannot make one justified, if one does not bring in therewith his fruits. As Christ also says [Mt. 7:16 ff.] of all such strong belief, of all such who [will] confidently believe and confess him to be a Lord and say that they had prophesied in his name and cast out devils and had done many mighty acts—these he will nevertheless not recognize. Such faith does not [by itself] bring about justification, nor again [that of] those who there [in Mt. 26:37 ff.] said: Lord, where have we seen you and not served you? The same also believed, but that is all in vain. Of the same kind Saint Paul also writes [1 Cor. 13:1 ff.] that even if one had such faith that he could move mountains, yea, and spoke with the tongues of angels, and understood all mystery, and gave all his goods for God's sake, and let his body be burned—in all such cases belief would have absolutely no worth, if love were not present therein. For what kind of faith would that be in the case of a woman with her husband, to whom she publicly adhered and confessed to be her lord and bridegroom, and nevertheless continuously went out to commit adultery and illicit love-making with others? . . .

2.18 Melchior Hoffman, June/July, 1533, *Quellen: Elsass II*, 105

Thirdly it was his witness from proof of holy Scripture that according to the true illumination of God's Word man has a free will to choose good or evil even as Adam had. For as the Son of Man has made free through the Word, so man is truly free, Jn. 8. And when the birth through God's Word has taken place so that man can distinguish between good and evil, then life and death is placed before him . . . and he is told as in Mt. 19: if you would enter life, keep the commandments; you are made well, sin no more, Jn. 15. For whoever after receiving salvation remains faithful to the end, shall be saved, Mt. 10 and 24. For when man is born as a new creature he receives the power to become a child of God, Jn. 1. This can also be seen in Jn. 3 when the Lord says: this is the condemnation that they love the darkness more than the light. According to that, man has the freedom of choice but he has chosen unrighteousness rather than righteousness. This is shown also in Mt. 22 and Lk. 14. Those who were invited to the feast were well able to come, but they did not want to since they loved something else more. The biblical Scriptures are full of such freedom.

Further he has also witnessed that man has no free will to do the good while he is imprisoned in blindness and in the bonds and power of Satan. However when he is set free through the light of the divine Word he has been saved from the first death as it is written: when your Word goes forth it illuminates and gives the simple understanding. However if he is to be condemned he must freely choose the second death. Such death takes place of his own choice. For God's will will not burn in hell, only selfwill. And no one will be condemned for the first death but all will be saved. Condemnation is the second death.

2.19 Melchior Hoffman, June/July, 1533, *Quellen: Elsass II*, 104-105

Secondly it was his witness from proof of Holy Scripture that God did not create a single person from the beginning of the world until the last day for condemnation. All are created for eternal salvation, and the Son of God suffered for all. As the whole seed of Adam without their own fault was condemned in Adam so also they are again made blessed, redeemed, and purchased from death through Jesus Christ freely and without any merit of their own. For as in Adam all die, so in Christ shall all be made alive.... And as the curse came through Adam on all men, so the blessing came again on all men through Jesus Christ. Rom. 5. For the promise of God must remain firm to the whole seed. Rom. 5 and 2 Cor. 5. Heb. 2 and 1 Tim. 2 are clear witness that Jesus Christ died for all, not one excepted. As also the holy apostle witnesses in 1 Jn. 2 that he is an atoner not only for the sins of the believers, but for the sins of the whole world, that is, for the whole seed of Adam. God also swore to Abraham that in his seed, which is Christ the eternal Word, Gal. 3, all the peoples on the earth should be blessed.... To this also the holy Paul witnesses in Rom. 11 that God will have mercy on all. Of such witness the biblical Scriptures are full that Christ Jesus did not suffer for half a world but for the whole world, that is the whole seed of Adam.

2.20   Jakob Hutter, "Plots and Excuses," ca. 1535, Müller, *Glaubenszeugnisse*, 187-188

Thus the godless say to the godly: O yes, you boast about your good works, act like the hypocrite in the temple, and think that therefore you are without sin. To this we reply that we can take no credit for good as natural men, but we give all glory and praise to God to whom it rightfully belongs. For it is obvious that man in himself cannot think anything good, let alone do it, as Paul says. For because of the grace of God we know that the works which we do and carry out as men count for nothing before God on that day. Inasmuch, however, as God does them in us through his grace and his spirit by whom all the believers are governed, they are good, just, pleasing and acceptable to God.

They also charge and say that we wish to be without sin and they quote the passage from John which says: If we say we have no sin, we deceive ourselves and the truth is not in us. But they neglect to continue when John says: If, however, we confess our sins, he is faithful and just to forgive our sin and cleanses us from all unrighteousness. Consequently we have acknowledged our sin and regretted and wept over it before God. Through faith in Christ we have been cleansed and justified through his grace. By his filial spirit we have been assured that we are the children of God, true heirs, and fellow-heirs with Christ provided we suffer with him in order that we may also be glorified with him. We therefore no longer serve sin.... Nor do we follow carnal Israel and today's hypocrites who seek to establish their own righteousness but will not be subject to the righteousness which counts before God.

...All those who live and walk in the spirit do not fulfill the lusts of the flesh. For through the spirit they mortify the works of the body and are no longer debtors to the flesh. For they no longer serve God in the old manner of the letter but in the new manner of the spirit. Thus the godly have sin but they do not consent to it nor do they carry out its bidding. Although the evil inclination and wicked lust do spring up and stir in all the godly, yet they do not consent to it. It is a source of pain to them and they resist it with all their might. They restrain it and force it down through the power of the spirit.

2.21   Bernhard Rothmann, "Restitution," 1535, *SBR*, 234-235

The Scriptures say: In view of the fact that you, like all men, are by nature a child of wrath, subject to sin, death, devil, and hell, that is, since you lie in such a prison, you cannot help yourself, nor can anyone else but Christ alone. Now Christ comes and proclaims to you that he has purchased and redeemed you. In your place he has paid for death who is your jailer. Now if you, who were imprisoned and to whom such a proclamation is made, receive and believe the good news of Christ, you are free and blessed. If you do not believe, you are in death. But whenever you hear this good news of Christ no matter where you are and no matter how sinful, you will be cleansed of all things and receive power to become a child of God, provided you honestly receive Christ. To ascribe to him only the redemption from original sin (as the Papists do) is not receiving Christ honestly. For when he comes he redeems us from all ignorance and blindness of heart in which we were imprisoned through Adam's fall. It is also not receiving Christ honestly when we believe his redemption and accept it and then forthwith remain in our former life. This is the problem with the evangelicals. It is to receive Christ rightly and to learn that in Christ there is an upright life. As soon as we have heard of him and confessed him we put off the old man with the former life, are renewed in our spirits, and put on the new man who is created in God in true righteousness and holiness. Who thus receives Christ and his redemption receives it honestly. And if he stays with it and holds to it and continues in it he is truly redeemed and saved. But whoever does not so accept the redemption of Christ, but after he has received Christ and the knowledge of him falls back again, still lusting after the old life, and is won over by the allurements of this world, that is, the works of the flesh, in him the redemption of Christ is lost, and his condemnation is just.

2.22 Pilgram Marpeck, "Judgment and Decision," 1542, *The Writings*, 352-353

Gospel of the Creatures

The gospel of the creatures is that the gospel may be preached through discerning the nature of the divine creation by which the Creator is known. Carnal reason, however, has no right to use the witness of the creatures of the gospel; reason errs in its use, an error which has beset all the philosophers in this world. Paul warns us (Col. 2 [4]) not to become their prey. But carnal man, who as yet has no understanding of the law of God, must first, by means of the creatures, be led into a knowledge of God; Christ the Lord talked to the people about the kingdom of God by means of many parables of nature. Paul also had to use nature to introduce the Gentiles to the gospel, for natural, carnal man knows nothing of God. For him the creation of God is a true gospel only until such time as he knows God the Father in the Son, the Lord Jesus Christ, and the Son in the Father. According to the flesh, the Son is a creature of all creatures, since all things exist for him. All these things will be fully known beyond this time. For this reason we all have to remain and work in partiality and fragmentation until completeness comes, since, as Paul says, all our knowledge is only fragmentary.

2.23 Pilgram Marpeck, "Judgment and Decision," 1542, *The Writings*, 341-342

God is a God of order and not of disorder, and he has firmly united his own omnipotence to his will and order. It is not as the predestinarians[17] and others say, without any discrimination, that God has the right to all salvation and damnation. He has, certainly, but not outside of his order and will, to which his power is subordinated. Otherwise, one may claim his divine power on behalf of all[18] as, indeed, Satan and his prophets are doing. Wherever the omnipotence and might of God serves their purposes, they imperiously and indiscriminately use it, without the will of his[19] Father, as Luther does with the sacrament, child baptism, infant faith, and such like. Whenever they find themselves at their wits end they save their theology by appealing to the omnipotence of God. There is no sharper nor more deceitful article of false teaching than to use and preach the power and omnipotence of God outside of the order of God's Word.[20]

Further, it is the greatest blasphemy against God and the word of his truth, by which he has ordered all things in heaven and on earth, in which order they shall remain in eternity. For God himself is the wisest order in and through his Word, that is, Jesus Christ his only begotten from eternity. Whoever manipulates the omnipotence of God outside of this order is a deceiver and seducer. Again, whoever establishes, commands, or prohibits any order outside of the divine order and omnipotence he denies God's power and glory.

2.24 Peter Riedeman, *Account*, 1542, 46-48

WHAT FAITH IS

Faith is not the empty illusion that those men think who only bear it about with them in their mouths, and know no more about it; who think that Christianity is in words only, and therefore hold and regard each and all as Christians, no matter how they live, if they but confess Christ with the mouth.

True and well-founded faith, however, is not of men but a gift of God, and is given only to those who fear God. Therefore Paul says,

"Not every man hath faith." For such faith seeks that which does not appear, and grasps the invisible one and only mighty God, and makes us at one and at home with him, yea of his nature and character. It dispels all wavering and doubt, and makes our heart hold surely, steadfastly and firmly to God, through all tribulation.

Therefore it makes us certain and well assured of all God's promises, just as—to speak in parables—a man who takes an object in his hand and holds it, as long as he does hold it, is certain that he has it. In the same way faith grasps the promise of God which is invisible, and cleaves and holds to the same as though it saw it.

Therefore faith is a real divine power, which renews man and makes him like God in nature, makes him living in his righteousness, and ardent in love, and in keeping his commandments.

In order to make no one uneasy, we want to say why we give or ascribe such power to faith. This we do because faith is God's gift, and given to men that they might thereby seek and find God; who, when he has been found, stirs up and works all things in them through faith, so that in believers, in proportion to their faith, nothing takes place save what God works in men, as Paul says, "Not I, but the grace of God," and again, "Not I live now, but Christ lives in me."

Thus faith is also given victorious strength, as it is written, "And our faith is the victory that overcometh the world," as indeed God does in us through faith. Thus faith does and works all things, and makes man pleasing to and loved by God.

FROM WHENCE FAITH COMES

According to the words of Paul, this faith comes from a diligent hearing of the preaching of the word of God, which is proclaimed by the mouth of God by means of those whom he sends. Here, however, we speak not of the literal, but of the living word that pierces soul and spirit, which God has given and put in the mouth of his messengers. The same word makes wise unto salvation, that is it teaches to know God; and from the knowledge of God faith springs up, grows and increases, and with faith knowledge. These entwine and grow together and lead man to God, and plant the same in God, so that he that has such faith lives and walks in God, and God in him.

64

The more zealously we hear and receive the word, the more knowledge grows. The more knowledge grows, or the more we know God, the more do faith and trust in him grow. And the more we believe in him, the more he shows himself to us, and gives himself to us to know. Where, however, such faith which does all this in man is not present, there is no faith but an empty delusion and darkness, by means of which men betray and deceive themselves. We have now made confession of our faith, and want next to give a faithful account, according to the grace God gives us, of what we teach.

2.25   Peter Riedeman, *Account*, 1542, 59-62

CONCERNING REMORSE

Now those who seek further counsel as to how to free their souls from the eternal destruction and death into which they are led by sin; desiring to free themselves from their sins, which are the snares of the devil, and partake of the grace of Christ—such we teach, together with John, the preacher of repentance, Peter and the apostles, that they must repent. But he who would truly repent with all his heart must first feel real remorse for his sin. But if he is to feel remorse for his sins he must first recognize how wrong, evil, harmful and destructive they are. Without this, remorse and repentance cannot endure—still less can he receive grace. For true remorse follows the recognition of sin. The man feels real repugnance, hatred and horror of his sin, yea, real loathing of himself for having so long obeyed it, for having suffered himself to be guided and controlled by it and led away from the God for whose sake he has being.

CONCERNING REPENTANCE

Thus remorse leads to true repentance, that is real humiliation and abasement before God because of the transgression. For repentance means to humble and abase oneself before God, and to be ashamed before him because of one's vice; which shame brings a real turning point, so that the man runs with haste, calls, cries and prays to God for forgiveness and grace, and begins at the same time to bring the flesh into subjection, to slay and kill it, to break it in, bridle it and feed it with hyssop. For recognized sin fills the conscience with fear and leaves it no peace. But the uneasy conscience seeks, searches and asks where help, counsel and healing may be found, as David says, "I lifted up mine eyes unto the hills to see from whence help would come to me, even so cometh my help from the Lord who hath made heaven and earth." Every anxious, troubled, fearful, broken and contrite heart, if it flee to him, will find with him peace and comfort. As it is written, "Upon whom shall I look but upon him who is of a broken and contrite spirit."

We point out also thereby that no such death-bed remorse and repentance as the world has, which says to-day, "I am sorry for my sin" and yet does the same again to-morrow, can stand before God and receive grace; but only that which proceeds from a sincere heart. To such an one will God draw nigh, and will both begin and bring to perfection his work in him.

MAN IS GRAFTED INTO CHRIST

To such a fearful and anxious heart, that is sorry for its sin and knows not where to turn in its distress, so that the world itself is too strait for it and it lifts up its heart to God alone—to such an one will God show himself, and will comfort him in his sorrow, showing him his Son who says, "Come unto me all ye that are heavy laden, and I will refresh you. Take my yoke upon you for it is easy and light." He calls to us in this way, however, through the servants whom he has chosen from the world to be his witnesses. Those who hear his voice and come to him he will in no wise cast out.

We teach further, that Christ came into the world to make sinners blessed, as it is written, "This is the Father's will, that every one which seeth the Son and believeth in him should not be lost but have everlasting life"; and that man through faith might be planted and grafted into Christ. This, however, takes place as follows: as soon as the man hears the gospel of Christ and believes the same from his heart, he is sealed with the Holy Spirit, as also Paul says, "After that ye believed, ye were sealed with the Spirit of the promise, that is with the Holy Spirit, which is the pledge of our inheritance, the pledge of the redemption of us, who are his property, for the praise of his glory." This Spirit of Christ which is promised and given to all

66

believers makes them free from the law or power of sin, and plants them into Christ, makes them of his mind, yea, of his character and nature, so that they become one plant and one organism together with him: he the root or stem, we the branches, as he himself says, "I am the true vine, ye, however, are the branches." Thus we are one substance, matter, essence, yea, one bread and body with him—he the head, but we all members one of the other. Now, because Christ is the root and the vine and we are grafted into him through faith, even as the sap rises from the root and makes the branches fruitful, even so the Spirit of Christ rises from the root, Christ, into the branches or twigs to make them all fruitful. Hence the twigs are of the same character as the root, and bear only corresponding fruit, as Christ himself says in the parable, "No man gathereth figs from thistles, or grapes from thorns. No good tree can bring forth evil fruit, neither can a corrupt tree bring forth good fruit, but each tree bringeth forth fruit of its own kind." Now since Christ is a good tree and vine, nothing but what is good can or may grow, flourish and be fruitful in him.

2.26 Dirk Philips, "Regeneration and the New Creature," 1556, Kolb/Klaassen, *Philips*, 296-298, 308

Through this promise, yea, through this gracious gospel of Jesus Christ, man is again comforted, yea, renewed in the image of God, and is born again to eternal life. In the beginning God desired to have people who are made in his image, and still does. Therefore he created man in his image and in his likeness in the beginning, as it is written: "God created man for eternal life in his image that he should be as he (that is God) is" (Wis. of Sol. 2:23).

After man was created by God the Father after his own image and likeness, that is, in the image and likeness of Christ, and after restoring him from the fall in mercy by the obedience and righteousness of the Son of God (Rom. 5:18), every person (after having come to the age of discretion, and able to distinguish good from evil) must by the enlightenment, operation, and declaration of the Holy Spirit be born again into a new divine being, yea, into the fellowship and likeness of Jesus Christ. He must be transfigured into the same image, from glory to glory, yet all by the Spirit of the Lord (2 Cor. 3:18), and thus by the Holy Spirit created anew in the image and likeness of God through Jesus Christ.

. . . .

From the foregoing we learn that regeneration of man takes place by the word of truth, and his renewal by the Holy Spirit in such a way that all, who through hearing of the gospel and the cooperation of the Holy Spirit believe in Jesus Christ the only begotten Son of the living God, our Lord and Saviour, are born of God, enlightened and taught by the Holy Spirit, and are children of God, as Paul confesses in these words: "Ye are all the children of God by faith in Christ Jesus."

. . . .

From all this it is evident that regeneration is really the work of God in man, by which he is born again of God through faith in Jesus Christ in the Holy Spirit. For the heavenly Father begets or brings forth the new creature, but the Word of the heavenly Father is the seed from which the new creature is born (Jas. 1:18, 1 Pet. 1:23). The Holy Spirit renews, sanctifies and keeps the new creature in the divine life (1 Jn. 3:9; Tit. 3:5). Therefore this regeneration is a mighty and fruitful work of God that emanates from the almighty and most high God through Jesus Christ, in the Holy Spirit.

. . . .

But this glorification of Christ through the Holy Spirit is properly accomplished in his disciples who accept and keep his word in true faith, as he himself says: "I am glorified in them" (that is, in my disciples) (Jn. 17:10). Christ is glorified in his disciples in the same way as the Father is glorified in him; but the Father is glorified in Christ in this that he revealed his Father's name to his disciples, spoke his Father's word, did his will, and finished his work. As he himself says: "I have glorified thee on the earth, O Father: I have finished the work which you gave me to do (Jn. 17:4). Hence his disciples also must keep his teaching, do his will and finish his work, that Christ may be glorified in them. But this is the beginning and the end of the teaching of Jesus Christ (as said above), that we sincerely repent, believe the gospel, are baptized upon our faith in the

68

name of the holy Trinity, that is, in the name of the Father, and of the Son, and of the Holy Spirit, and are diligent by the grace of God to observe all that Christ has commanded us (Mt. 28:20).

2.27   Menno Simons, "Distressed Christians," 1552, *CWMS*, 504, 505-506

Those who accept this announced Christ by a true faith which, according to the doctrine of Paul, was given us of the Father unto wisdom, righteousness, sanctification, and deliverance, are in a state of grace for Christ's sake and have God as their Father; for by faith they are born of him. He forgives them all their sins; has compassion on all their human shortcomings and weaknesses. He turns them from the curse, wrath, and eternal death. He accepts them as his beloved children, and grants them Christ Jesus together with all his merits, fastings, prayers, tears, sufferings, pain, cross, blood, and death. Besides this, he grants also his Spirit, inheritance, kingdom, glory, joy, and life. And this we say, not by our own merits and works, but by grace through Christ Jesus. As Paul says, God, who is rich in mercy, for his great love wherewith he loved us, even when we were dead in sins, hath quickened us together with Christ (by grace ye are saved); and hath raised us up together, and made us to sit in heavenly places in Christ Jesus; that in the ages to come he might show the exceeding riches of his grace, in his kindness toward us through Christ Jesus. For by grace are ye saved through faith; and that not of yourselves; it is the gift of God; not of works, lest any man should boast. For we are his workmanship, created in Christ Jesus unto good works, which God hath before ordained that we should walk in them. Eph. 2:4-10.

. . . .

Since then they believe God's Word which says, To be carnally minded is death, If you live after the flesh, ye shall die, and adulterers, fornicators, drunkards, the avaricious, the proud, and all liars shall not inherit the kingdom of God, and since they believe that he will save none contrary to his Word; that he will judge in accordance with his Word, that he is the truth and cannot lie, as the Scriptures testify; therefore it is that they sincerely fear the Lord, and by that fear die unto their flesh, crucify their lusts and desires, and shun and abhor the unclean, ungodly works which are contrary to the Word of the Lord.

Besides this, they acknowledge the abundant grace, favor, and love of God toward us as shown in Christ Jesus, and therefore they love their God in return, for he first loved us as John says. And they are ready by this love to obey in their weakness his holy Word, will, commandments, counsel, doctrine, and ordinances, according to the talent received. They show indeed that they believe, that they are born of God and are spiritually minded; that they lead a pious, unblamable life before all men. They have themselves baptized according to the commandment of the Lord as proof that they bury their sins in the death of Christ and seek to walk with him in newness of life. They break the bread of peace with their dear brethren as proof and testimony that they are one in Christ and his holy church, and that they have, or know no other means of grace and remission of their sins, neither in heaven nor on earth than the innocent flesh and blood of our Lord Jesus Christ alone, which he once by his eternal Spirit in obedience to the Father sacrificed and shed upon the cross for us poor sinners. They walk in all love and mercy and serve their neighbors. In short, they regulate themselves in their weakness to all words, commandments, ordinances, Spirit, rule, example, and measure of Christ, as the Scripture teaches; for they are in Christ and Christ is in them; and therefore they live no longer in the old life of sin after the earthly Adam (weakness excepted), but in the new life of righteousness which comes by faith, after the second and heavenly Adam, Christ, as Paul says, I do not now live, but Christ liveth in me; and the life which I now live in the flesh, I live by the faith of the Son of God, who loved me, and gave himself for me. Gal. 2:20. Christ says, he who loves me keeps my commandments. John 14:15.

For further reading:

Beachy, *Grace*, 28-29, 67-78.
Richard C. Detweiler, "The Concept of Law and Gospel in the Writings of
    Menno Simons," *MQR* XLIII (July 1969) 191-212.
Cornelius J. Dyck, "Sinners and Saints," Dyck, *Legacy*, 87-102.
Estep, *Anabaptist Story*, 145-147.
Friedmann, *Theology*, 78-100.
Keeney, *Dutch Anabaptist*, 66-73.
Oyer, *Lutheran Reformers*, 218-223.
Wenger, *Even Unto Death*, 93-97.
George H. Williams, "Sanctification in the Testimony of Several So-Called
    Schwärmer," *MQR* XLII (January 1968), 5-25.

III

The Holy Spirit

Virtually all Anabaptist statements regarding the Holy Spirit are orthodox. They identify him as the third person of the Trinity. How is it then, that Anabaptists have so often been labelled spiritualists, people who preferred the direct inspiration of God to the words of Scripture? The reason is that the Anabaptists talked more about the Spirit than others did. They believed that they were living in the age of the Spirit, the time when every child of God would have the Spirit. They often spoke, almost naively, about being led by the Spirit, and being given divine illumination.

It is true that there were cases of illuminism, of rejecting the Word in favour of the Spirit. Certainly this tendency is noticeable again in the early South German Anabaptism of Denck, Kautz, Hut, and Bünderlin. Even these men always depended on the Bible, but they accepted Scripture because the Spirit in them testified to its truth.

But most Anabaptists managed to maintain the tension between Word and Spirit, holding clearly and firmly to both. They claimed that every believer had the Spirit and was capable, therefore, of understanding Scripture and participating in its interpretation.

They rejected both the Catholic and the Protestant views which implied, practically, that only some in the church, the clergy and teachers, had the Holy Spirit.

The man who gave most attention to the relation of the invisible Spirit to the visible church was Pilgram Marpeck. With untiring effort he tried to articulate his view of the unity of outer and inner Word, of the work of God the Spirit in individual and church and what he called "the external apostolic service of the church." The Spirit, he writes, moves with the external service, but it may not therefore be concluded that if the service is performed the Spirit is there. The Spirit works only where there is faith and obedience.

Apart from these emphases we find the usual ones, based on Scripture, of the Spirit as the illuminator of Scripture, as the one who brings to remembrance all that Jesus taught, as the one who transforms believers from sinners into saints, and as the one who comforts the believer, especially in times of suffering and martyrdom.

3.1   Hans Denck, "Concerning the Law of God," 1526, Fellmann, *Denck I,* 59

Whoever has received God's new covenant, that is, whoever has had the law written into his heart by the Holy Spirit is truly righteous. Whoever thinks that he can observe the law by means of the Book ascribes to the dead letter what belongs to the living Spirit. Whoever does not have the Spirit and imagines that he will find him in Scripture looks for light and finds darkness, looks for life and finds only death, not only in the Old Testament but also in the New. . . . Whoever has really laid hold of truth can assess it without Scripture.

3.2   Hans Denck, "Concerning the Law of God," 1526, Fellmann, *Denck I,* 63

All commandments, customs, and laws insofar as they are written in the Old and New Testaments are suspended for the true disciple of Christ since he has a word written in his heart, that is that he loves God alone. By this he orders everything that he does even if he has nothing written. If there is a part in the whole that he cannot understand he does not despise the witness of Scripture but he searches diligently and compares them with each other. But he does not accept the Scripture before it has been interpreted for him through the anointing of the Spirit. When he does not understand he suspends his judgment and waits for God's revelation. For a belief or a judgment that has not been revealed by the key of David may not be accepted without great error.

3.3 Balthasar Hubmaier, "Twelve Articles," 1526-1527, Davidson/Klaassen, *Hubmaier*, 219

I believe in the Holy Spirit who proceeds from the Father and the Son, and yet is one with them, very God. He hallows all things and without him nothing is holy. In him I place all my trust that he will teach me all truth, increase my faith, and kindle the fire of love in my heart by his holy inspiration, that my heart may burn with true, unfeigned and Christian love toward God and my neighbors. This I beg of you with all my soul, my God, my Lord, my Comforter.

3.4 Hans Hut, "A Christian Instruction," 1527, Müller, *Glaubenszeugnisse*, 35-36

And now, what does he see through the Holy Spirit in truth? The Father in the power of his omnipotence by whom he has been made. He also knows the Son in whom he was tested, cleansed, justified, and circumcised a true child of God. He has open access to the Father and has become one with Christ and all his members. They are one community and one body in Christ. All the members of this community are enemies of sin and enjoy and love righteousness. And even if such a person sins and falls it is not done with pleasure. Therefore also he is not cast out, for the Lord holds him in his hand and his sins are forgiven and not counted as sin to him.... Now everything is all graciousness, mercy, praise, glory and honour in the Holy Spirit. Everything is in common; nothing is one's own. That is the way it has been from the beginning of the world until now but it has never been universal. The prophets witness that the Lord will pour out his Spirit over all flesh and all men will be taught of God eternally, live according to the will of God, and filled with all goodness. That cannot take place universally until the whole world has been humbled in tribulation and anguish.

74

3.5 Leonhard Schiemer, "A Letter to the Church at Rattenberg," 1527, Müller, *Glaubenszeugnisse*, 56

This is the secret, subtle, hidden, true power of the almighty God and well known only to the true surrendered children of God and hidden and unknown to all the children of this world. Those who do not feel in themselves a power about which they have to say that things that were once impossible are now possible are not yet born again of water and spirit, even the Holy Spirit. Those who do not have assurance, that is that they are so certain of their faith that they could not be made more certain by any man, do not have the Holy Spirit. The Spirit is given to no one unless he first submit himself to the cross and to brotherly love. He who does not have him cannot believe in him, but believes externally and can never enter into eternal life. He is called by many names in Scripture such as Word, light, grace, a wind, water, a vine, oil, bread, meat, blood, comforter, anointing, and master. Whoever is not taught by this master under the cross in brotherly love and life, to him the Scripture is sealed.

3.6 Leonhard Schiemer, "A Letter to the Church at Rattenberg," 1527, Müller, *Glaubenszeugnisse*, 70-71

The anointing which you have received from God remains with you and therefore you have no need to have anyone teach you. Rather, what the anointing teaches you is the truth and no lie. Remain in what she has taught you. About this oil the Lord speaks thus: the comforter, the Holy Spirit, which the Father will send you in my name will teach you all things, and will bring to your remembrance all that I have told you. This oil is the Holy Spirit. He, however, teaches no one who has not first despaired of all human comfort and wisdom and has lifted his heart to God alone. He comforts and strengthens no one who has not first been terrified and estranged from all human comfort and strength. Therefore the Lord says you should not allow yourselves to be called master. Now this master Christ receives no one as his student or disciple who has not rejected and hated everything that he has, and follows him and carried his cross. One must sit still and wait for the comfort of the Lord as the Scriptures show in many places especially in the Psalms and in the prophets. Isaiah and the laments of Jeremiah especially show that the Christian's strength consists alone in being still and not to fall away from or despair of the word of the Lord. Rather he is to be long-suffering and patient and to await the comfort of the Holy Spirit in great desolation and tribulation. That is the true illness about which the Scriptures speak, especially Paul when he says: when I am ill, then I am strong. He also says that if we suffer much for Christ we will also be comforted much through Christ. That is what Christ means when he says: for a little while you will see me, and then for a little while you will not see me. When the apostles asked him to explain this he answered: truly, truly, I say to you. You will weep and lament but the world will be glad. And if they kill you they will think that they do God a service. . . . I will not leave you alone; I will come to you, etc. The life of the world has a happy beginning but an eternally sorrowing end. Our life has a sorrowful beginning, but soon the Holy Spirit comes and anoints us with the oil of unspeakable joy. Still we should not wait only for the comfort of God, but one Christian should speak to and comfort the other in tribulation. . . . Concerning this oil James says: If anyone is sick, let him call for the elders of the church, and let them pray over him, anointing him with oil in the name of the Lord. And the prayer of faith will heal the sick man. The Lord will raise him up, and if he has committed sins he will be forgiven. Here James does not refer to Italian olive oil. The elect saints who in these days praised God in their holy martyrdom at Salzburg[21] and elsewhere could have been bathed in tubs full of oil had they not remained steadfast in their faith. But the comfort of the Holy Spirit eased their suffering. With this oil the apostles anointed and so do we to this day.

3.7   Jacob Hutter, "The Fourth Epistle of Jacob Hutter," 1535, Müller, *Glaubenszeugnisse*, 154

You have also heard and understood that the Lord has long gone before you during the day in the cloud, that is his servants and preachers. But the night will come when the cloud will no longer be visible. Then the Lord will no longer go before us in the pillar of cloud, but in the pillar of fire will God go before his own. That is the light and brilliance of his Holy Spirit and through God's word, which word and spirit is in all godly, Christian hearts who by it are ruled, instructed, taught and led in all truth and through a true Christian well-grounded faith. That is the pillar of fire in our hearts. Happy is he in whom the light glows and shines for he will not fall nor be confounded even in the night as the Scriptures testify.

3.8   Peter Riedeman, *Account*, 1542, 36-38

WE ACKNOWLEDGE THE HOLY SPIRIT

Since the strength, power, nature, character, and essence of the godhead are illustrated for us and to be recognized in the creation, the work of God's hand, we say that just as, when one speaks, one exhales and emits breath with the word, so that from both the speaker and the spoken word a living breathwind blows and voice proceeds and is uttered, even so the Holy Spirit comes from the Father and the Son, or from the Truth and the Word. But as the Son or the Word proceeds from the Father and yet remains in him, the Holy Spirit proceeds from them both and remains in them both for ever and ever.

Thus we acknowledge him, with the Father and the Son, to be God. The names are three, but there is but one God, rich above all who call to him, yea who call to him with trust. For even as fire, heat and light are three names and yet one substance, one nature and essence, even so are God, the Father, Son and Holy Spirit three names and yet one being. And even as fire, heat and light do not separate or depart one from the other (for where one is, there are all three, and where one is lacking, none is present), even so the Father, Son and Holy Spirit: where one of them is, there they are, all three; but whosoever has one of them not, lacks all three. For just as little as one can take heat and light from fire and yet leave fire, even so and still less can one take the Son and the Holy Spirit from the Father.

Just as the breath determines the word and gives it shape and sound, even so the breath, wind and spirit of God makes the word living and active within us and leads us into all truth. This, yea even this, is the power of God that does, works and perfects all things, confirms all things, joins, comforts, teaches and instructs; and through this, his working in us, assures us that we are children of God.

We believe that in the Holy Spirit we have all comfort, delight and fruitfulness and that he confirms, brings to pass, carries out and perfects all things; that he also teaches, directs and instructs us, assures us that we are children of God, and makes us one with God, so that through his working we thus become incorporated into and partakers of the divine nature and character. And this his work—God be praised!—we experience within ourselves in truth and power in the renewing of our heart.

In God we have absolute certainty that he has drawn our heart to him and made it his dwelling place, and removed and cut out from our heart evil, sin and the lust to sin, so that he has made our heart hang upon his word, to seek, love and with diligence to hear, and not only to hear but also to keep and with all diligence to follow, the same. But all this the one Holy Spirit, we believe, does and works in us.

3.9   Pilgram Marpeck, "Concerning the Lowliness of Christ," 1547, *The Writings*, 453-457

Therefore, all external service of Christ, and of those who belong to him in the time of this mortal life, serves and prepares the way for the Holy Spirit. [This external service consists] of the external preaching, teaching, miracles, baptism, foot washing, the Lord's Supper, discipline, chastisement, and admonition. Such service also includes the ban of exclusion and separation from the fellowship of the body of Christ. In order to preserve the true fellowship of all the faithful, we are commanded to keep the ban, together with the Lord's Supper, in remembrance of the true love of Christ and his gracious deed in his death. In the time of his mortal life, Christ did not rule; he served. He sent his own to serve, not to rule. Man is to be served by Christ and his own, and man is to be prepared for the Holy Spirit. Some spirits either regard such preparation as unnecessary, or else they regard it too highly. But wherever this service of Christ is not carried out in all its provisions, there the Holy Spirit cannot do his work. To believe, like Peter, that such a Lord should not wash one's feet, and to refuse to have the act performed on the basis of such carnal reasoning, is to rely on private invention rather than the Holy Spirit. Even today, Christ says to these individuals that they can have no part in his kingdom. For the Holy Spirit may not, and cannot, function, nor find an abiding place without the preparatory teaching. Service is commanded by Christ, and it is the means by which, according to the command of Christ, men are prepared. Moreover, the Key of David is also a means, for it is the key of the understanding with which earthly man's mind is opened. Then, the Holy Spirit, as true God with Father and Son, can move where he will, namely, in those whom the Father draws to Christ, to the same apostolic church and bodily service, preaching and teaching, baptism, foot washing, and the Lord's Supper. Men submit to this service in the obedience of faith in Christ and under the discipline of the Spirit.

When we as men are renewed, and born again of the Holy Spirit, the Holy Spirit becomes the pledge and the third witness of salvation. The apostolic service of the church is properly carried out, in accordance with the commands of Christ, when it prepares, cultivates, fertilizes, and, as God's helper, breaks again[22] the hearts of men. When this new breaking occurs, the church seeds and plants, in the heart, the word of truth, which is to be believed, and it waters the heart with the water of baptism. But even if all external service is done according to the command of Christ, the earthly Man, the Spirit still moves in glorious liberty wherever he will, and he gives the increase and the growth to whomever he will. Such is the prerogative, in eternity, of the Godhead, and it belongs to the Father and the Son.

It is sheer fabrication and deception when some insist that the Holy Spirit moves apart from the apostolic service of the church, that such service, commanded by Christ, is unnecessary. On which Holy Spirit, then, did the Lord base his teaching, Word, and work? If not the actual spoken words, commands, and laws of Christ, reminded and taught by the Spirit, what other teaching words or work can, or may, the Holy Spirit teach, remind, and lead us into as the truth? For the Lord himself promised that the Holy Spirit would remind us of all that Jesus said or commanded. Certainly, a spirit who teaches contrary to the Son of Man, who taught men with a human voice, is a deceiving spirit.

Again, they deceive themselves who think that, when they serve, teach, and baptize, simply because the apostolic service is performed, it follows that the Holy Spirit also moves and teaches. Nor is the church of Christ merely where the external service is properly done. *Not so!* If the inner, through the Holy Spirit, does not witness to the external, through faith, everything is in vain, for where the carcass is, the eagles gather. The true community and gathering of Christ cannot be identified with a place, nor can it be called a human name. Wherever such a gathering is, according to the Word of the Lord, there Christ is with the Father and the eternally abiding Holy Spirit. They love him who keep his Word and commandment. To them, he and the Father will come and dwell.

Therefore, whoever says that Christ is anywhere else than living on earth, as in heaven, in the power and clarity of the Spirit in the heart of each faithful believer, he is a deceiver. Whoever does not find Christ dwelling in his own heart, eternally will not find him elsewhere.

However, where such hearts as temples and dwellings of God are built into a spiritual dwelling for the Lord, these places are named and identified only as long as the faithful live there.[23] Thus, that place is holy for the sake of the saints, even as God sanctified the figurative temple. When it was destroyed, its place was profaned. The same is true of a place without saints. Where they do not dwell, it is a curse and malediction; it is desecrated, destroyed, and profaned before God. At this time we see it clearly in the whole world.

Because of their sectarian, external, coerced religion, by which they deceive themselves, the whole world imagines that it has Christ living here or there. Since the earthly and true service of Christ did not come into force in the hearts of the apostles without the moving of the Holy Spirit, how can the forced and coerced faith, or the faith based on old custom, stand before God? This forced and coerced faith, based as it is on sophistic interpretation of Scripture or on ancient custom, is not from God, nor is it taught by the Holy Spirit and his manner, birth, artistry, and wisdom; [it is unrelated to the Spirit's] reminding and leading us into truth. Rather, it is from the generation and will of the flesh of man (Jn. 1 [13]) who is steeped in his earthly, fallen nature and human reason, sophistry, and wisdom.

Thus, even if, in the power of the Spirit before man, one should preach and teach the apostolic service and teaching of Christ which flows out of the inmost being of the believers as the fountain flowing into eternal life, still, the teaching of the Spirit, which alone reminds and leads us into truth, and which teaches the divine artistry of wisdom, has always and must always accompany it. Those who are thus taught are not taught by any man, but by God.

All the others continually learn from, and are taught by, men. But these others never come to the knowledge of the truth, which is eternal life (Jn. 17 [3]). They never know God the Father as the true God, and Jesus Christ as the One whom the Father has sent. Therefore, the Lord says that not everyone who cries "Lord, Lord" will enter the kingdom of heaven. Only he will enter who does the will of the heavenly Father. Since no one knows the Father but the Son and him to whom the Son reveals the Father (Mt. 11 [27]), no one but the Son could do the will and pleasure of the heavenly Father. Thus, no one but only the Father knows the Son.

3.10   Pilgram Marpeck, "To the Church at St. Gall and Appenzell," 1551, *The Writings*, 505

Thus it behooves us that we carefully examine and test all things, and that we do not judge, reject, misinterpret, nor falsify what we do not understand, in order that in so doing we do not condemn ourselves and be plunged into error. For the gifts of the Holy Spirit are weighty. He moves us, when and where he wills, giving them to whomever he desires, through Scriptures, speech, discipline, fear, tribulation, and judgment as he desires and pleases. He gives through profound and mediocre understanding, in length and breadth, in height and depth. Everything is his. He is Lord and Sovereign over all, over written and spoken Scriptures which men test, learn, experience, witness to, and judge to the praise of God and their own salvation, and from them to judge themselves and others.

Therefore whoever despises and scorns the written and spoken aid of the Holy Spirit as though it would do more harm than good, and it were better not to write or speak so much and things would thus be better all round, accuses the Holy Spirit and the aid of his gifts. He scorns and mocks what he has never known and what serves his salvation. He expects to learn about the Holy Spirit and his gifts by putting himself in the place which belongs to God the Holy Spirit alone.

3.11 Dirk Philips, "The Church of God," Kolb/ Klaassen, *Philips*, 382-383

The Holy Ghost is the third name, person, power, and activity in the Godhead, of one divine essence with the Father and the Son (Mt. 28:19). He proceeds from the Father through the Son and acted with them in the creation. He is the Spirit of truth, a Comforter of the conscience (1 Jn. 5:8; Jn. 16:13), and a Dispenser of all spiritual gifts, which are poured by God the Father through Jesus Christ into the hearts of believers (1 Cor. 12:11). By him they are enlightened, renewed and sanctified (Tit. 3:6; 1 Cor. 3:11), and become a possession of God (Eph. 1:14) and new creatures in Christ. By him they are kept to everlasting life, and without him no one knows God or believes in Jesus Christ. All good gifts come from the eternal Father through Jesus Christ (2 Cor. 5:16, 17; Jas. 1:17; 1 Cor. 4:7), and are divided to us by the Holy Spirit (Mt. 7:11).

3.12 Menno Simons, "Reply to Gellius Faber," 1554, *CWMS*, 760

Reader, understand my meaning. I never entertained the thought that God's Holy and eternal Spirit was not God in God, and God with God. Yet, Gellius would accuse us, who are not guilty, of denying the sanctification, grace, fruit, and power of the Holy Spirit, because some, who have been expelled by us, have erred in this respect, and probably still err; although he sees with his eyes and feels with his hands the sanctification and power of the Holy Spirit in our people, namely, that they restrain the old man with his lusts and destroy the sins in their flesh, a thing which he calls the sanctification of the Holy Spirit, as has been heard.

3.13 Menno Simons, "Triune God," 1550, *CWMS*, 495-496

We believe and confess the Holy Ghost to be a true, real, and personal Holy Ghost, as the fathers called him; and that in a divine fashion, even as the Father is a true Father and the Son a true Son. Which Holy Ghost is a mystery to all mankind, incomprehensible, ineffable, and indescribable (as we have shown above of the Father and the Son); divine with his divine attributes, proceeding from the Father through the Son, although he ever remains with God and in God, and is never separated from the being of the Father and the Son.

And the reason that we confess him to be such a true and real Holy Spirit is because we are brought to this by the Scriptures, for he descended upon Christ at the baptism in the bodily shape of a dove, and appeared unto the apostles as cloven tongues like as of fire; because we are baptized in his name as well as in the name of the Father and of the Son; because the prophets have prophesied through him, performed miracles, had dreams and saw visions; because he is a dispenser of the gifts of God, and that (take note) according to his own will. He moved Zacharias, the son of Barachiah; he moved John the Baptist while yet in his mother's womb, and He said to Simeon, That he should not see death before he had seen the Lord's Christ. The Holy Ghost said, Separate me Barnabas and Paul. And to Peter, Behold, three men seek thee. He guides us into all truth; he justifies us. He cleanses, sanctifies, reconciles, comforts, reproves, cheers, and assures us. He testifies with our spirit that we are the children of God. This Spirit all they receive who believe on Christ. Paul admonishes us not to grieve him. Whosoever sins against the Spirit, says Christ, unto him it shall not be forgiven. David desired that God might not take from him this Spirit, for all that have not this Spirit are not of Christ.

For further reading:

Beachy, *Grace*, 153-155, 156-158.

Walter Klaassen, "Some Anabaptist Views on the Doctrine of the Holy Spirit," *MQR* XXXV (April 1961), 130-139.

————, "Spiritualization in the Reformation," *MQR* XXXVII (April 1963), 67-77.

Klassen, *Covenant and Community*, 67-76.

IV

CROSS, SUFFERING,
AND DISCIPLESHIP

The following selections should be read together with those in chapter 2, since there are very close inner ties between them. Christ's atonement on the cross, and the justification, sanctification, and perfection of the disciple are seen as one inseparable process. If in Catholicism the cross was made contemporary in the mass, and if in Protestantism it happened through the faithful dispensing of Word and sacrament, the cross became contemporary in Anabaptist thought in its function in the lives of the disciples.

Riedeman in 4:13 states the basic facts of God's act of salvation in Christ. All the other selections concentrate on the cross as the daily experience of the disciple.

The Anabaptist churches were suffering churches, especially in the years covered by this source selection. The experience of intense suffering seems to have forced this aspect of the biblical view of God's people to the forefront. The real physical and spiritual suffering served as a theological integrator, prompting the rediscovery of the early church's view of Christ's suffering continuing in his members.

Old themes from the church's life reemerge. Again and again it is affirmed that suffering is the true sign of being a Christian and of being a member of the true church (4.10. See also selections in chapter 5). Suffering for Christ's sake is identified as the nearest, most direct way of gaining eternal life (4.4). This is a view that developed out of the martyr experience of early Christianity and had been preserved especially in the ascetic tradition in monasticism.

The suffering of the disciple is seen as the suffering of the cross of Christ in a very direct and immediate sense. It is therefore not accidental or haphazard but is part of the movement of history by which God will eventually be victorious. The cross with its humiliation, obedience, patience, and forgiveness stretches from its point in history both backward—all the elect of God have suffered from the beginning of the world—(4.10) and forward. It is one great redeeming and liberating movement of God.

It is therefore not surprising to read that both the internal suffering which is caused by the slow liberation from dependence on created things (4.7) and the external suffering of persecution are understood as part of the cross of Christ, not something done for Christ, but something done with Christ. The disciple shares in the cross as a co-sacrifice (4.14).

Even less surprising are the frequent affirmations that this suffering, inasmuch as it is the suffering of Christ, liberates from sin, yes, destroys sin (4.8) and "adds to the piety of the pious" (4.16). Thus suffering is understood as the expected and natural lot of the disciple because of the oneness of the disciple with his Lord (4.8).

Selection 4.12 is included as a specific case of bearing the cross. Endres Keller was an ordinary man, and the fact that he eventually gave up does nothing to discredit the strength and pathos of his testimony.

4.1 Hans Denck, "Recantation," 1527, Fellmann, *Denck I*, 106

The suffering of Christ is sufficient for the sins of all men even if no man were ever saved. For no one can comprehend [the suffering] except he who has the spirit of Christ. The spirit equips and arms the elect with the mind and thoughts of Christ. But whoever depends upon the merits of Christ and nevertheless continues in a carnal, beastly way of life, he thinks of Christ as in ancient time the pagans thought of their gods. It is as though he did not esteem the merits of Christ. That is a blasphemy of which the world is full. For whoever believes that Christ has liberated him from sin can no longer be the slave of sin. But if we continue in the old life we do not truly believe. . . .

4.2 Hans Denck, "The Contention that Scripture Says," 1526, Fellmann, *Denck I*, 39-40

Since love was perfect in him, and since love hates or envies no one but rather receives everyone, even though we were all his enemies, he would not exclude anyone. Had he excluded someone his love would have been unsound and a respecter of persons. That cannot be. Is it odd that we rejected him even as before we rejected the Father? Should it not be true that he died for all simply because not all are saved? Is it untrue that the Father created all men good because they did not remain good? God forbid! Indeed, Christ was so fully surrendered (although he loved everyone without measure) that he would have suffered for nothing had that pleased the Father. That is why this sacrifice was so pleasing to God that it would have been sufficient for all guilt even if there had been a thousand times as many worlds. But when the Scripture says he died for many and then again he died for all, is not a contradiction, but is written because not all accepted the light, although it shone for all. Many deny the Lord, even though he purchased them as the Scriptures richly testify.

4.3 Hans Denck, "The Contention that Scripture Says," 1526, Fellmann, *Denck I*, 45, 50

But the medium is Christ whom no one can truly know unless he follow him in his life, and no one may follow him unless he has first known him. Whoever does not know him does not have him and without him he cannot come to the Father. But whoever knows him and does not witness to him by his life will be judged by him.... Woe to him who looks elsewhere than to this goal. For whoever thinks he belongs to Christ must walk the way that Christ walked.

4.4 Balthasar Hubmaier, "A Christian Instruction," 1526-1527, Davidson/Klaassen, *Hubmaier*, 323-324

Leon: What is the nearest way by which one can go to eternal life? Hans: Through anguish, distress, suffering, persecution and death, for the sake of the name Christ Jesus. He himself had to suffer, and thus enter into his glory (Lk. 24). St. Paul also says: all who will live godly in Christ must endure persecution (2 Tim. 3). Where Christ is and lives, he bears his cross upon his shoulders, and gives to each Christian his own little cross to bear, and with it to follow him. We should wait for the little cross, and when it comes receive it willingly, with joy and patience, and not choose our own chips and scraps of wood in imagined spirituality, and lay them on ourselves without divine understanding.

4.5 Jörg Wagner, "Wer Christo jetzt will folgen noch," 1527, *Ausbund*, 1564, translated by David Augsburger, 1962

He who would follow Christ in life
Must scorn the world's insult and strife,
And bear his cross each day.
For this alone leads to the throne;
Christ is the only way.
   Christ's servants follow him to death,
   And give their body life and breath
   On cross and rack and pyre.
   As gold is tried and purified
   They stand the test of fire.
Renouncing all, they choose the cross,
And claiming it, count all as loss,
E'en home and child and wife.
Forsaking gain, forgetting pain,
They enter into life.

4.6 Michael Sattler, 1527, *Ausbund*, No. 7, 46-48[24]

When Christ with his true teaching came
And gathered up his flock so fair,
He taught them all to follow him
And patiently his cross to bear.
   He said, You my disciples true

Must watch and be alert each day,
Love nothing more upon this earth
Than me and all my words alway.
The world will seek to do you harm
With mocking and with hate and shame.
They'll scatter you and slander you
And brand you with the devil's name.
And when for my sake and the Word
They persecute, revile, and kill,
Rejoice! for your reward is great
Before God's throne on Zion's hill.
O Christ be pleased to aid your own
Who dare to follow and confess,
That through your lowly bitter death
They may be saved from all distress.

4.7 Hans Hut, "A Christian Instruction," 1527, Müller, *Glaubenszeugnisse*, 34

If a man is to come to the knowledge of the living Son of God he must await the work of God through the cross of Christ which we must carry and follow in the footsteps of Christ. At those places Christ shows us the seriousness and righteousness of God the Father which the Father exercises through Christ. And all who desire to grow in the body of Christ in which the Son of God is known and through which we become God's children and joint heirs with Christ as Paul witnesses to the Romans (Rom. 8:17) [must] also suffer with him and grow into the image of the Son of God through the justification of the Father. And whoever will not follow the footsteps and ways [of Christ] and will not carry the cross of Christ he does not have or know the Son. And whoever does not have or know the Son does not have or know the Father, and cannot be illuminated by the graciousness of the Holy Spirit who dwells in us.

Thus in the other part is shown only the means, work, truth and righteousness of the crucified Son of God. In him we must be incorporated to participate in the unity of the Trinity. This is revealed to us in the deepest suffering. Against this the fear and enmity of the whole Word is directed. A man must endure in himself all the articles if he is to come to a knowledge of the highest good. The Word must be received in him with a true heart through the Holy Spirit and become flesh in us. That happens through great terror and trembling as with Mary when she heard the will of God from the angel. The Word must be born in us too. That can happen only through pain, poverty, and distress inside and out, etc. And where the Word has been born and become flesh in us so that we praise God for such a favour, our heart has found peace and we become Christ's mother, brother, and sister. These people who are now satisfied with God become a derision and stumbling block to the whole world. With Christ they are called enthusiasts and Beelzebub. Everything he says is stamped as a lie by the world, and he himself is called a lying spirit because he admonishes the world about its ways and will not conform to them.

4.8   Leonhard Schiemer, "A Letter to the Church at Rattenberg," 1527, Müller, *Glaubenszeugnisse*, 51-52

As soon as a man wants to begin to live as a Christian he will experience exactly those things that Christ experienced.... That is the lot of all Christians for the disciple is no greater than the master. For it is grace if someone for the sake of conscience suffers godly sorrow.... For it is grace with God when you patiently suffer for doing good. For to this you were called, since Christ also suffered for us and left us an example that you should follow in his footsteps. He committed no sins neither was deceit found in his mouth. Christ suffered in the flesh. Arm yourselves with the thought that whoever suffers in the flesh ceases from sin.... It is given to you that you not only believe in Christ but also suffer for him and fight the same battle. Paul says that you are heirs of God and joint heirs with Christ if you suffer with him in order that you may be exalted with him in glory. For we must be conformed to the image of his Son.... It is true, Christ's suffering destroys sin but only if he suffers in man. For as the water does not quench my thirst unless I drink it, and as the bread does not drive away my hunger unless I eat it, even so Christ's suffering does not prevent me from sinning until he suffers in me.

4.9   Hans Schlaffer, "Brief Instruction," 1527-1528, Müller, *Glaubenszeugnisse*, 90

Those are Christians who are minded as Christ was so Paul says. They arm themselves for suffering, do not entangle themselves in the ways of the world, have no fellowship with the works of darkness but rather with the works of light, are not ashamed of their master Christ and his words, and follow him in the same (each according to the measure of grace awarded). Therefore he will not be ashamed of them before God his heavenly Father and all his angels as he himself says, and then continues: Whoever loves his life will lose it, and whoever hates and denies his life in this world for my sake will preserve it for eternal life. Whoever would serve me must follow me, where I am there my servant must also be, and whoever serves me will be honoured by my Father. If anyone wants to follow me, says the Lord, let him deny himself, take up his cross daily, and follow me. To sum up, a Christian is a follower of Christ. That cannot be changed even if the whole world should end in ruins, which it will certainly do (and I believe soon). For a thousand years are as one day with God, says Peter. For this reason the Christians lift up their heads and expect their redemption with joy. It will come in the return of Christ to judge the living and the dead.

4.10   Jacob Hutter, "Letter to the Prisoners at the Hohenwart," 1535, Fischer, *Huter*, III, 22-23

Therefore be comforted and be of good courage, for God leads [his own] into hell and out again, he makes them sorrowful and then glad again, he gives death and also life, and after the storm he restores the sun. Therefore be long-suffering and wait patiently for the redemption of your bodies. Do not become slack or tired in the race and do not look behind you. Beware that the love in your hearts does not grow cold or be totally extinguished. Do not be ashamed of the bonds and suffering of Christ, but rejoice greatly in your hearts, for

91

you know that nothing else has been promised you for your life on earth except suffering and death, tribulation, anxiety, distress and great persecution, pain, torture, insult and shame at the hands of godless men. That is the true sign and seal of all the pious children of God, the sign of Christ or the Son of Man and all his members which must appear at the last time according to the word of the Lord. Yes, cross and tribulation truly adorns all the children of God. It is a beautiful honour in the sight of God and all the saints; a deserved glory and wreath of joy from them. For this was the way of the holy prophets and patriarchs and of Christ the holy Lord and all his disciples, in fact of all the elect from the beginning of time. When therefore we endure for the sake of truth we must remember that it does not mean that we are the enemies of God but his friends and dear children. . . .

4.11 Bernhard Rothmann, "The Hiddenness of Scripture," 1535, *SBR*, 316-317

Observe therefore, that although Christ was a lord of all things, he left his glory and had to struggle and fight as a servant in order to enter again upon the glory which he had left. We say this in order that it may be better and more clearly understood what and who the real Christ is and in order that those of good will may the better learn the real Christ. For the Papists and the Lutherans and whoever else they may be do not know Christ truly. For they say that Christ's flesh and body was derived from Mary's flesh and body.[25] The Son of God, so they say, assumed Mary's sinful flesh. Thus they make a plaything out of the passion. The Son of God himself did not suffer, they say, but stood by and watched it. They also do not know how Christ is our example and that we must follow his footsteps honestly. They claim that there were two distinct natures in Christ at the same time, the one divine, and the other human. Similarly they make a Christ out of baked bread. The Papists say: As certainly as he hung on the cross, etc. But the Lutherans so confine Christ to the bread that he cannot be outside of it. Whenever they have so confined him they say: Ha, there I have you! If these knaves knew who and what Christ is we judge that they would treat him more worthily and not juggle with him. That they do not really know him is revealed in that they do not walk as he walked. For to know Christ truly means to keep his commandments and follow his footsteps. Such a knowledge of Christ justifies, as the prophet says, and it is eternal life. Whoever says: I know Christ Jesus, but does not keep his commandments, is a liar and the truth is not in him.

4.12 Confession of Andres Keller, 1536, Schornbaum, Quellen: Bayern II, 200-201

I hope, dear lords, that you will not act rashly against me. I say this not from deceitful motives, but because I do not want you to incriminate yourselves by doing me violence. What good is it to you to reduce me to this miserable condition? I am distressed beyond misery, I am poverty-stricken and robbed of my ability to work, all of which I can not overcome in my lifetime. I have been starved so that I cannot now eat or drink, and my body is broken. How would you like to live for five weeks with only boiled water and unflavoured[26] bread soup? I have been lying in the darkness on straw. All this would not be possible if God had not given me an equal measure of his love. I marvel that I have not become confused or even mad. I would have frozen if God had not strengthened me, for you can well imagine how little a bit of hot water will warm one. In addition to this I suffered great torture twice from the executioner, who has ruined my hands, unless the Lord heals them. I have had enough of it to the end of my days.

However, I know that God never forsakes me if I suffer for the sake of his word. I know full well that I have experienced with great pain the Enemy's temptations against you. May God forgive you and all the dear people who have falsely accused me before you. Many things done long ago I have now been charged with.

However, I know that God works with me for good and that my tribulation is a sign of his love for me. David says: Blessed is the man whom you, Lord, chastise. You teach him your law so that he may have patience (Ps. 94: [12]). The wise man says: The Lord quickly punishes and chastises him whom he loves (Heb. 12:6), for he gives him his favour, even as a father his child. Therefore, dear Lords, you will find in me nothing but patience in word and deed. I will obey you till I die and I will obey God till I die. But I will not build on this commandment of men, which is against God, as long as there is breath in me. I will not be a hypocrite, either to curry favour or to avoid suffering, but will seek the truth with all my heart.

4.13   Riedeman, *Account*, 1542, 28-31
SUFFERED UNDER THE POWER OF PILATE, CRUCIFIED, DEAD AND BURIED

We confess also that, after he had finished the Father's work for which he was sent and had declared to men the Father's name and taught them repentance and faith in God, by the considered counsel of the Father he was given over into the hand of sinners, who, after greatly dishonouring and torturing him, put him to the most disgraceful death, namely that on the cross.

We confess with Peter likewise, that he was put to death in the flesh, that is, in so far as he came of the seed of David, and of Mary, but was made alive in the Spirit; and we say that it was not the divine but the human nature of Christ that died—the divine, that is his nature in so far as it came from heaven, forsook and left the human, that the Scripture might be fulfilled which saith, "Thou didst make him for a little while suffer want of God, and didst crown him again with glory and honour." The apostle likewise speaks the same saying, "For we see that it is Jesus who for a little while suffered the want of angels or of God, and through suffering and death was crowned with glory and honour, for through the grace of God he tasted death for us all." Now, since our transgression and sin so moved the Father that he laid the same upon him and for them gave him into death, we confess that our sins have crucified him. Therefore all who still continue in sin cease not to crucify and mock the Son of God. For he came to take away our sin and destroy the work of the devil. Those, however, who permit not the same to be taken from them, but remain for ever therein, mock his coming into the world and count the blood of the covenant of God an unholy thing; for this reason is his suffering and death no comfort to them but a cause of eternal judgment.

94

Again, he was taken down from the cross and laid in a grave, that the word which was spoken by him might be fulfilled: "Except a corn of wheat fall into the ground and die, it abideth alone: but if it fall into the ground and die, it bringeth forth much fruit." And for this reason was he laid in the earth and rose again—that all who have fallen asleep and lie in the earth might through him arise and come forth; as it is written: "The hour is coming, in the which all that are in the graves shall hear his voice and shall come forth; they that have done good, unto the resurrection of life; and they that have done evil, unto the resurrection of judgment and of damnation."

DESCENDED INTO HELL

That he might fulfill all things, we confess that he also went down to the lowest parts of the earth (namely to the place of captivity, where they are kept who aforetime believed not the word which was spoken to them) and proclaimed to the spirits in prison that the word of salvation had now been sent, which had previously been resolved upon by God and promised to men, that all who believe it wholeheartedly might thereby be set free; and that he had now, in accordance with the promise given to the fathers, destroyed the power of death, hell and the devil, which had for so long betrayed and deceived them.

ON THE THIRD DAY ROSE FROM THE DEAD

We confess also that, after he through his death had destroyed the power of death, he rose again from the dead through the power of the Father, and became the first-fruits of them who are to inherit blessedness, for it was impossible for death to hold him. As David says of him, "I have set the Lord always before my face, for he is at my right hand that I might not be moved. Therefore is my heart glad and my tongue rejoices, for my flesh also shall rest secure and in hope. For thou wilt not leave my soul in hell; neither wilt thou suffer thine Holy One to see corruption."

Thus we confess him to be risen from the dead; and that he died and rose again, that he might be Lord of the dead and living. For after he had overcome the devil and death and had risen again, he was given by the Father power, might and royal dignity, as he himself also says, "All power is given unto me in heaven and on earth."

He was also seen for several days of his disciples, who had before been chosen to be his witnesses, and after his resurrection he ate and drank with them, and gave them command to gather his bride, community and church, to proclaim repentance and the forgiveness of sins to all nations and to establish the obedience of faith in his name.

4.14 Pilgram Marpeck, "Concerning the Love of God in Christ," *The Writings*, 547-548

Thus many of the ancients (Job and others) overcame evil by means of good deeds through patience in tribulation, who afterward overcame everything in and through patience and waited for the redemption of Christ.

With gentle patience, love, and truth he overcame evil with all goodness, love, faithfulness, truth, and mercy, and [for evil] returned passionate intercession for his enemies, and surrendered his human life and eternal bliss on the cross in unbroken patience, a submissive and silent Lamb of sacrifice for the sins of man and his salvation. This is the universally hallowed cross of Christ—and no cross of guilt—by which in the innocence of Christ all the followers of Christ overcome, and through which they have free access in and to God, provided their hearts do not accuse them in guilt.

For they are washed from their sins through the innocence of Christ to be a pure and sanctified co-sacrifice pleasing and acceptable to God, as Paul says, which is the reasonable service of God. In it the highest joy can be expected and had, namely that one does not have to suffer as a debtor or an evildoer, but may praise God in the matter according to the words of Peter: "Let no one among you suffer as a murderer, thief, evildoer, or a covetous one." If someone suffers as a Christian, however, he should not be ashamed; let him praise God in the matter. For it is time that judgment begins on the house of God (1 Pet. 4:16 ff.). Furthermore, those who suffer, commit their souls to the faithful Creator with good works. Thus the cross of Christ is a holy, innocent cross if one suffers innocently as a witness of God in the truth and for the truth to the praise of God. To this holy cross of Christ, our highest shelter and shield, we have surrendered with holy patience (not obliged or forced patience) to overcome all our enemies in the victory of Christ.

4.15 Dirk Philips, "A Loving Admonition," Kolb/ Klaassen, 1558, *Philips*, 422

Be diligent therefore, my most beloved, by the grace of God, to bear the cross of Jesus Christ with patience, and look with the eye of faith to the joy and glory which is prepared for you. Walk continually worthy of the gospel and of your calling, according to the rule of apostolic teaching, in one Spirit and mind. Beware of the false prophets, which preach to you smooth things and lead you into all manner of carnal license by which the offence of the cross is removed, and observe what is true Christian liberty, namely, as Jesus says in the Gospel: "If you continue in my word, then are ye my disciples indeed; and you shall testify to the truth, and the truth shall make you free" (Jn. 8:31, 32).

4.16 Menno Simons, "Cross of the Saints," ca. 1554, *CWMS* 614, 618-619, 620

When we consider, worthy brethren, our very weak and sinful nature, how that we are prone to evil from our youth, how that in our flesh no good thing dwelleth, and how that we drink unrighteousness and sin like water, even as Eliphaz the Temanite said to Job, and when we consider how that we have a tendency at all times (although we do seek and fear God) to mind earthly and perishable things, then we see that the gracious God and Father, who through his eternal love always cares for his children, has left behind in his house an excellent remedy against all this, namely, the pressing cross of Christ. Thus we who now through Christ Jesus are taken up to eternal grace to the glory of the Father, who with a pure heart believe on Christ Jesus whom we love in our weakness, may, through the aforesaid cross, that is, through much oppression, tribulation, anxiety, apprehension, bonds, seizure, and so forth, let go of all the transitory things of earth, and that which delights the eyes. And so we die unto the world and unto the flesh, love God alone, and seek the things that are above where Christ sitteth at the right hand of God, as Peter also says, For as much then as Christ hath suffered for us in the flesh, arm yourselves likewise with the same mind, for he that hath suffered in the flesh hath ceased from sin, that he no longer should live the rest of his time in the flesh to the lusts of men, but to the will of God.

. . . .

We know very well dear brethren, how that this cross seems to be to the flesh grievous, harsh, and severe, and in the present is not considered a matter of joy, but rather of sorrow, even as Paul says. But since it contains within itself so much of profit and delight, in that it constantly adds to the piety of the pious, turns them away from the world and the flesh, makes them revere God and his Word, as was said above, and since it is also the Father's holy will that by it the saints should be approved, and the pretender exposed in his hypocrisy, therefore all the true children of God are prepared to love, to do the will of the Father, rejoicing in it. As Paul says, God forbid that I should glory save in the cross of our Lord Jesus Christ by whom the world is crucified unto me and I unto the world. Similarly, the apostles departed from the presence of the council rejoicing that they were counted worthy to suffer for his name.

. . . .

You see, my worthy brethren, if you conduct yourselves after this manner in your oppression and trials, if you drink with patience the cup of the Lord, give testimony to Christ Jesus and his holy Word in word and deed, if you allow yourselves as meek lambs for the testimony of Christ to be led with perfect constancy to the slaughter, then in you the name of God will be praised and made holy and glorious, the name of the saints will be revealed, the kingdom of heaven extended, the Word of God made known, and your poor weak brethren in the Lord will be strengthened and taught by your courage.

98

4.17　Menno Simons "The New Birth," ca. 1537, CWMS, 101

By this counsel we are all taught that we must hear Christ, believe in Christ, follow his footsteps, repent, be born from above; become as little children, not in understanding, but in malice; be of the same mind as Christ, walk as he did, deny ourselves, take up his cross and follow him; and that if we love father, mother, children, or life more than him, we are not worthy of him, nor are we his disciples.

4.18　Menno Simons, "Foundation," 1539, CWMS, 225

I confess my Saviour openly; I confess him and dissemble not. If you repent not, and are not born of God, and become not one with Christ in Spirit, faith, life, and worship, then is the sentence of your condemnation on your poor souls already finished and prepared.

All who teach you otherwise than we have here taught and confessed from the Scriptures deceive you. This is the narrow way through which we all must walk and must enter the strait gate, if we would be saved. Neither emperor nor king, duke nor count, knight nor nobleman, doctor nor licentiate, rich nor poor, man nor woman, is excepted. Whosoever boasts that he is a Christian, the same must walk as Christ walked. If any man have not the Spirit of Christ, he is none of his. Whosoever transgresseth and abideth not in the doctrine of Christ, hath not God.

4.19　Menno Simons, "Hymn of Discipleship," ca. 1540, CWMS, 1066

I'd rather choose the sorrow sore,
　And suffer as of God the child,
Than have from Pharaoh all his store,
　To revel in for one brief while;
　　The realm of Pharaoh cannot last
　　Christ keeps his kingdom sure and fast;
　　Around his child his arm he casts.

In the world, ye saints, you'll be defamed,
   Let this be cause for pious glee;
Christ Jesus too was much disdained;
    Whereby he wrought to set us free;
      He took away of sin the bill
      Held by the foe. Now if you will
      You too may enter heaven still!

If you in fires are tested, tried,
   Begin to walk life's narrow way,
Then let God's praise be magnified,
    Stand firm on all he has to say;
      If you stand strong and constant then,
      Confess his Word in the sight of men,
      With joy he extends the diadem!

For further reading:

Beachy, *Grace*, 124-128.

Harold S. Bender, " 'Walking in the Resurrection'—the Anabaptist Doctrine of Regeneration and Discipleship," *MQR* XXXV (April 1961), 96-110.

_____, "The Anabaptist Vision," Hershberger, *Anabaptist Vision*, 29-54.

J. Lawrence Burkholder, "The Anabaptist Vision of Discipleship," Hershberger, *Anabaptist Vision*, 135-151.

Friedmann, *Theology*, 27-35, 130-133.

Keeney, *Dutch Anabaptist*, 114-144, 181-190.

Franklin H. Littell, "The Discipline of Discipleship in the Free Church Tradition," *MQR* XXXV (April 1961), 111-119.

Wenger, *Even Unto Death*, 99-102.

John C. Wenger, "Grace and Discipleship in Anabaptism," *MQR* XXXV (January 1961), 50-69.

V

The Church

Anabaptists worked out their doctrine of the church in the light of an ancient tradition. Hubmaier, Sattler, Schiemer, Rothmann, Stadler, Simons, and Philips had all been priests in the church of Rome. Some had also been Protestant clerics, notably Hubmaier and Rothmann. Roman Christianity had long assumed the validity of the Volkskirche, that is, that with the exception of heretics and Jews everyone in Europe belonged to it by virtue of baptism. The papal church had also developed into a massive centralized institution, which, even in the sixteenth century, had vast political power.

Protestantism in Wittenberg and Zürich, and later also in Geneva, England, and Scotland, developed variations of the traditional view. Although the geographic scope in each case was more limited, each country had an official faith of which all citizens were assumed to be adherents.

Anabaptism broke completely with this pattern after initial uncertainty. By 1527 the vision in Switzerland was clear. The church was now identified as the gathered congregation of believers who have voluntarily entered it by baptism upon confession of faith (5.3, 5.5). Only those can be members who are obedient to Christ (5.5). Love is the chief mark of the church (5.2). That love expresses itself, according to the Hutterite Stadler, in complete self-denial, meaning especially the surrender of all private property. It is a community of mutual aid in which nothing is held back from those in need (5.6). Peter Riedeman contributes his fine passage about the church being a lantern in a dark place, a beacon to light the way to those in the darkness of this world (5.9).

Several things are of special note. Hubmaier writes very clearly

101

about the church's mandate to forgive and retain sin. The church literally has this power and its decision will be honoured in heaven (5.1). Anabaptism transferred what in Catholicism were sacerdotal powers, to the whole Christian congregation (see selections in section 8).

Of considerable interest is Dirk Philips' description of the church. In selection 5.10 he identifies the whole divine community of angels and redeemed humanity in heaven and on earth as the church. This was a traditional Catholic way of denoting the church's borders. He also says that the true church is to be found wherever the Word is preached truthfully and where the sacraments are administered according to the Word. That is the classic Protestant definition of the church. But he adds to these the Anabaptist emphasis on the visibility of the church. It is seen because its members live public lives of obedience to Christ.

Of note finally is the description of the church by Bernhard Rothmann. It is well thought out and clearly presented, and varies in no important point from the rest of Anabaptism. This evangelical description surely sheds some light on the seriousness and sanity with which the Münster Anabaptists went about their experiment.

5.1 Balthasar Hubmaier, "Twelve Articles," 1526-1527, Davidson/Klaassen, *Hubmaier*, 219-222

I also believe and confess the existence of the holy, universal Christian church. That is, a community of saints, a brotherhood of many pious and believing men, who with one accord acknowledge one God, one Lord, one faith and one baptism. They are called together, regulated and ruled here on earth through the only and living Word of God. This church is beautiful, without spot, unerring, pure, without wrinkle, unblamable.

I also profess openly that you, my Lord Jesus Christ, have hallowed the church to yourself through your rose-coloured blood. You are her head and bridegroom; you will be with her even to the end of the world. O my God, let me and all Christian men be found in this church at last.

May we be one with her in faith and doctrine, and hold all that you have commanded us in your Word, and root up all that you have not planted.

May we not be led astray by any human invention, opinion, teaching of the Fathers or popes, councils or universities, nor ancient usages, nor be brought into error by them.

O my Lord Jesus Christ, reestablish the two bonds, that is baptism and the Lord's Supper, with which you have girded and bound your bride, the church. For unless these two be set up again according to your arrangement and ordinance, and be used accordingly, we shall have neither faith, love, churches, vows, brotherly admonition, ban, nor excommunication. And without these, things can never prosper in your church.

I believe and profess the remission of sins. The church has received the keys—that is, the power—from Christ to open to the sinner the gates of heaven as often as he feels sorrow and repentance for his sins, and to receive him into the sacred community of Christian believers, as the Prodigal Son and the contrite Corinthian.

But where a man will not heed the threefold fraternal admonition, nor desist from his sins, I believe in my heart that the church has the power to exclude such a one, and to regard him as a publican and a heathen. This I believe and profess openly, my Lord Jesus Christ. When the church looses a man on earth, he is truly loosed and released from his sins also in heaven. But, on the other hand, he whom the church has bound and excluded from her fellowship on earth, he is also bound before God in heaven, and excluded from the one Christian church (outside of which there is no salvation). For Christ has given to his spouse, the church, the keys; he gave such a commandment when he was yet on earth.

5.2   Michael Sattler, "Letter to the Church at Horb," 1527, *Legacy*, 59-60

Further, dear fellow members in Christ, you should be admonished not to forget love, without which it is not possible that you be a Christian congregation. You know what love is through the testimony of Paul our fellow brother; he says: Love is patient and kind, not jealous, not puffed up, not ambitious, seeks not its own, thinks no evil, rejoices not in iniquity, rejoices in the truth, suffers everything, endures everything, believes everything, hopes everything. If you understand this text, you will find the love of God and of neighbor. If you love God you will rejoice in the truth and will believe, hope, and endure everything that comes from God. Thereby the shortcomings mentioned above can be removed and avoided. But if you love the neighbor, you will not scold or ban zealously, will not seek your own, will not remember evil, will not be ambitious or puffed up, but kind, righteous, generous in all gifts, humble and sympathetic with the weak and imperfect.

Some brothers, I know who they are, have fallen short of this love. They have not wanted to build up one another in love, but are puffed up and have become useless with vain speculation and understanding of those things which God wants to keep secret to himself. I do not admonish or reject the grace and revelation of God, but the inflated use of this revelation. What is the use, says Paul, if one speaks with all sorts of tongues of men and angels? And knows all mysteries, wisdom, and has all faith, he says, what is all that worth if the one and only love is not exercised? You have experienced what such puffed up speech and unwisdom have brought to birth. You still see daily their false fruits, whether they have abandoned themselves completely to God.

5.3   Leonhard Schiemer, "A Letter to the Church at Rattenberg," 1527-1528, Müller, *Glaubenszeugnisse*, 56

Church or ecclesia is a gathered congregation of people which is built on Christ and not on the pope, emperor, etc. Nor are the stone houses and towers church. Paul says you are no longer pilgrims and strangers but fellow citizens and members of the household of God built on the foundation of the apostles and prophets. For the prophets all had the spirit of Christ. That is why Christ is the cornerstone, whom the builders of the house of God cast out as a prophet. But this true sign of the holy Christian church is spoken against everywhere.

Paul says: whoever speaks or preaches another gospel than that of the apostles, let him be damned and cursed. Among us you will find the life of the church of the apostles. But whenever it is found it is called a new sect, and its members are killed even as they did the apostles. Many lies are invented against them. However this is testimony to their salvation. Without it they would not be Christians. This church you will find clearly described in Acts 2, 4, and 5.

5.4   Bernhard Rothmann, "Confession of Faith," 1533, *SBR*, 192

The church of Christ is a gathering of the believing children of God who praise the name of God. No one else belongs in it. Since all people by nature do not understand the things of God they are taught the true faith and the knowledge of God through the Word. Moreover the Scriptures offer us no other way. Therefore the first thing which all people and each one in particular who are to be brought into the knowledge of God and the holy church of God (so far as it is proper for us to judge this) must encounter is the preaching and the hearing of the divine Word. It is the source of faith. Immediately such a person is regarded as God's child and may then and there be reckoned a member of the holy church. Christ is the foundation on which the holy church is erected and built. This foundation must be laid before the church is built on it; it must be laid through the proclamation and witness of the gospel. The true witnessing to Christ and the preaching of the gospel is the first means by which the church is prepared. The church is gathered, erected and built of those who believe. They will be led into unity and sanctification as Christ prayed—John 17—and be preserved by the Father. Why then do we waste many words on this? The Scriptures richly testify that faith comes from hearing the Word and that the holy church be built only of those who believe. It cannot be denied that the true proclamation of the holy gospel started the holy church.

The second thing through which the holy church is built is holy baptism. Baptism is the entry and gateway to the holy church; therefore according to God's order no one may be allowed into the church except through baptism. That is the common usage of baptism.

5.5   Bernhard Rothmann, "Restitution," 1534, *SBR*, 241-242

The true Christian congregation is a gathering large or small that is founded on Christ in the true confession of Christ. That means that it holds only to his words and seeks to fulfil his whole will and his commandments. A gathering thus constituted is truly a congregation of Christ. But if this is missing a gathering cannot in truth be called a congregation of Christ even if it has the name a hundred times. That this is true and that the proper knowledge of Christ is that he is the true Lord and only Saviour and Redeemer and that this is the basis of the Christian gathering, the Scriptures confirm in abundance.... It is necessary to remain on this foundation. That we adhere solely to the words of Christ and do his will, to this he himself witnesses when he said to his disciples: If you keep my words you are truly my disciples, and again: You are my friends if you do what I command you. But whoever concerns himself with other teachings and commandments cannot be a disciple or friend of Christ, nor do they belong in the church of Christ. To it belong only the disciples and friends of Christ who keep his teaching and commandments. When Christ sent out his apostles to gather his church he spoke to them and gave them this commandment: Go and teach all nations, baptize them in the name of the Father, the Son, and the Holy Ghost, and teach them to observe everything that I have commanded you. The first teaching is that they present to them the basics of God's will in Christ. If then they accept the teaching and wish to become disciples of Christ they shall baptize them so that they may put on Christ and be incorporated in his holy church. Finally, in order that they may remain friends of Christ, the ones baptized should be taught everything that Christ commanded. All this can be clearly seen in the apostolic writings. Behold, this is the true church of Christ from the beginning and still is. For although many others claim to be the church of Christ, as for example the anti-Christian papal crowd do, it is a vain claim. Not all that glistens is gold.

5.6 Ulrich Stadler, "Cherished Instructions," ca. 1537, Williams, *Spiritual*, 277-279

There is one communion (*gmain*) of all the faithful in Christ and one community (*gmainschaft*) of the holy children called of God. They have one Father in heaven, one Lord Christ; all are baptized and sealed in their hearts with one Spirit. They have one mind, opinion, heart, and soul as having all drunk from the same Fountain, and alike await one and the same struggle, cross, trial, and, at length, one and the same hope in glory. But it, that is, such a community (*gmain*) must move about in this world, poor, miserable, small, and rejected of the world, of whom, however, the world is not worthy. Whoever strives for the lofty things [of this world] does not belong. Thus in this community everything must proceed equally, all things be one and communal, alike in the bodily gifts of their Father in heaven, which he daily gives to be used by his own according to his will. For how does it make sense that all who have here in this pilgrimage to look forward to an inheritance in the kingdom of their Father should not be satisfied with their bodily goods and gifts? Judge, O ye saints of God, ye who are thus truly grafted into Christ, with him deadened to the world, to sin, and to yourselves, that you never hereafter live for the world or yourselves, but rather for him who died for you and arose, namely, Christ. [They] have also yielded themselves and presented themselves to him intimately, patiently, of their own free will, naked and uncovered, to suffer and endure his will and, moreover, to fulfill it and thereafter also to devote themselves in obedience and service to all the children of God. Therefore, they also live with one another where the Lord assigns a place to them, peaceably, united, lovingly, amicably, and fraternally, as children of one Father. In their pilgrimage they should be satisfied with the bodily goods and gifts of their Father, since they should also be altogether as one body and members one toward another.

Now if, then, each member withholds assistance from the other, the whole thing must go to pieces. The eyes won't see, the hands won't take hold. Where, however, each member extends assistance equally to the whole body, it is built up and grows and there is peace and unity, yea, each member takes care for the other. In brief, equal care, sadness and joy, and peace [are] at hand. It is just the same in the spiritual body of Christ. If the deacon of the community will never serve, the teacher will not teach, the young brother will not be obedient, the strong will not work for the community but for himself and each one wishes to take care of himself and if once in a while someone withdraws without profit to himself, the whole body is divided. In brief, *one, common* builds the Lord's house and is pure; but *mine, thine, his, own* divides the Lord's house and is impure. Therefore, where there is ownership and one has it, and it is his, and one does not wish to be one (*gmainsam*) with Christ and his own in living and dying, he is outside of Christ and his communion (*gmain*) and has thus no Father in heaven. If he says so, he lies. That is the life of the pilgrims of the Lord, who has purchased them in Christ, namely, the elect, the called, the holy ones in this life. These are his fighters and heralds, to whom also he will give the crown of life on the day of his righteousness.

Secondly, such a community of the children of God has ordinances here in their pilgrimage. These should constitute the polity (*policeien*) for the whole world. But the wickedness of men has spoiled everything. For as the sun with its shining is common to all, so also the use of all creaturely things. Whoever appropriates them for himself and encloses them is a thief and steals what is not his. For everything has been created free in common (*in die gmain*). Of such thieves the whole world is full. May God guard his own from them. To be sure, according to human law, one says: That is mine, but not according to divine law. Here in this ordinance [in our community] it [the divine law] is to be heeded (*gilt es aufsehens*) in such a way that unbearable burdens be not laid upon the children of the Lord, but rather ones which God, out of his grace, has put upon us, living according to which we may be pleasing to him. Thus only as circumstances dictate will the children of God have either many or few houses, institute faithful house managers and stewards, who will faithfully move among the children of God and conduct themselves in a mild and fatherly manner and pray to God for wisdom therein.

5.7 Menno Simons, "The New Birth," ca. 1537, *CWMS*, 94-95

These are the holy Christian church which has the promise; the true children of God, brothers and sisters of Christ. For they are born with him of one Father, they are the new Eve, the pure chaste bride. They are flesh of Christ's flesh and bone of his bone, the spiritual house of Israel, the spiritual city Jerusalem, the spiritual temple and Mount Zion, the spiritual ark of the Lord in which is hidden the true bread of heaven, Christ Jesus and his blessed Word, the green, blossoming rod of faith, and the spiritual tables of stone with the commandments of the Lord written on them. They are the spiritual seed of Abraham, children of the promise, in covenant with God and partakers of the heavenly blessing.

These regenerated people have a spiritual king over them who rules them by the unbroken sceptre of his mouth, namely, with his Holy Spirit and Word. He clothes them with the garment of righteousness, of pure white silk. He refreshes them with the living water of his Holy Spirit and feeds them with the Bread of Life. His name is Christ Jesus.

They are the children of peace who have beaten their swords into plowshares and their spears into pruning hooks, and know war no more. They give to Caesar the things that are Caesar's and to God the things that are God's.

Their sword is the sword of the Spirit, which they wield in a good conscience through the Holy Ghost.

Their marriage is that of one man and one woman, according to God's own ordinance.

Their kingdom is the kingdom of grace, here in hope and after this in eternal life.

Their citizenship is in heaven, and they use the lower creations such as eating, drinking, clothing, and shelter, with thanksgiving and to the necessary support of their own lives, and to the free service of their neighbor, according to the Word of the Lord.

Their doctrine is the unadulterated Word of God, testified through Moses and the prophets, through Christ and the apostles, upon which they build their faith, which saves our souls. Everything that is contrary thereto, they consider accursed.

Their baptism they administer to the believing according to the commandment of the Lord, in the doctrines and usages of the apostles.

Their Lord's Supper they celebrate as a memorial of the favors and death of their Lord, and an incitement to brotherly love.

Their ban or excommunication descends on all the proud scorners—great and small, rich and poor, without any respect of persons, who once passed under the Word but have now fallen back, those living or teaching offensively in the house of the Lord—until they repent.

They daily sigh and lament over their poor, unsatisfactory evil flesh, over the manifest errors and faults of their weak lives. Their inward and outward war is without ceasing. Their sighing and calling is to the Most High. Their fight and struggle is against the devil, world, and flesh all their days, pressing on toward the prize of the high calling that they may obtain it. So they prove by their actions that they believe the Word of the Lord, that they know and possess Christ in power, that they are born of God and have him as their Father.

5.8 "Bern Colloquy," 1538, Haas, *Quellen*, 281, 293

We do not insist that there was no one that pleased God even in the blindness and darkness. We commit that to God; he will have known them. Since, however, that papal church was founded on error, and since the basis of that church was nothing but error, we cannot admit that this church was the true Christian church. For it cannot be that there was a church of which no one knew and that was not recognized. Rather, in this matter one must go back to the foundation of the apostles. Thus we were compelled to start such a true church. Some things we have received from you the preachers, but not everything. . . .

. . . .

We are not convinced when you say that the holy Christian church has continued from its beginning. Nor have we any assurance about your sending by this true church. We insist that faith precede and repentance follow from it. All that was hidden under the papacy; there were no Christians. Everybody walked in darkness. Therefore the true church came to an end at some time, and we have made a new beginning upon the rule from which others had departed.

5.9   Riedeman, *Account*, 1542, 38-40
THROUGH WHOM IS GATHERED TOGETHER ONE HOLY, CHRISTIAN CHURCH

We confess also that God has, through Christ, chosen, accepted and sought a people for himself, not having spot, blemish, wrinkle, or any such thing, but pure and holy, as he, himself, is holy. Therefore is such a people, community, assembly or church gathered and led together by the Holy Spirit, which from henceforth rules, controls and orders everything in her, leading all her members to be of one mind and intention (so that they want only to be like Christ, to partake of his nature, and diligently to do his will), cleaving to him as a bride and spouse to her bridegroom, yea, as one body with him, one plant, one tree, bearing and giving one kind of fruit, as Paul says, "As many as are led by the Spirit of God, they are the children of God," and again, "The same Spirit assureth us that we are children of God."

Since, then the church is an assembly of the children of God, as it is written, "Ye are the temple of the living God," as God has said, "I will dwell in them and walk in them; and I will be their God and they shall be my people," "Wherefore come out from among them, and be ye separate, says the Lord, and touch no unclean thing; and I will receive you, and will be your father, and ye shall be my sons and daughters." The children of God, however, become his children

111

through the unifying Spirit. Thus, it is evident that the church is gathered together by the Holy Spirit: also that she has being and is kept in being by him, and that there is no other church apart from that which the Holy Spirit builds and gathers.

Therefore is the assembly of the unjust and sinners, whores, adulterers, brawlers, drunkards, the covetous, selfish, vain and all those who lie in word and deed, no church of God, and they belong not to him; as Paul says, "If any man have not the Spirit of Christ he is none of his." Thus is not only their assembly not a church of Christ, but none of them can be or continue therein unless he repent of his sins, as David says, "The sinner shall not stand in the congregation of the righteous." After him John also says, "There shall in no wise enter into it anything that defileth, neither that worketh abomination and lies; but they which are written in the living book of the Lamb. But outside are dogs, sorcerers, and whoremongers, idolators, murderers, and whosoever loves and makes a lie."

WHAT THE CHURCH IS

The church of Christ is the basis and ground of truth, a lantern of righteousness, in which the light of grace is borne and held before the whole world, that its darkness, unbelief and blindness be thereby seen and made light, and that men may also learn to see and know the way of life. Therefore is the church of Christ in the first place completely filled with the light of Christ as a lantern is illuminated and made bright by the light: that his light might shine through her to others.

And as the lantern of Christ has been made light, bright and clear, enlightened by the light of the knowledge of God, its brightness and light shines out into the distance to give light to others still walking in darkness, even as Christ himself has commanded, "Let your light shine before men, that they may see your good works and praise God, the Father in heaven." Which thing, however, cannot be other than through the strength and working of the Spirit of Christ within us. As, however, the outward light sheds a ray and beam, in accordance with its nature, to give light thereby to men, even so the divine light, wherever it has been lit in a man, gives forth its divine ray and beam. The nature of this light, however, is true, divine

112

righteousness, brightness and truth, which is shed abroad by the lantern which is the church of Christ, more brightly and clearly than by the sun, to give light to all men.

Thus the church of Christ is, and continues to be, a pillar and ground of truth, in that the truth itself shows and expresses itself in her, which truth is confirmed, ratified, and brought to pass in her by the Holy Spirit. Thus, whosoever endures and suffers the working of the Spirit of Christ is a member of this church; but whosoever does not suffer this work but allows sin to have the rule over him belongs not to the church of Christ.

5.10   **Dirk Philips, "The Church of God," 1562, "Sending the Preachers," 1559, "Refutation of Two Letters of Sebastian Franck," after 1563, Kolb/ Klaassen, *Philips*, 369-370, 375-376, 203-204, 483-484**

The church of God was originally begun by God in heaven with the angels, who were created spirits and flaming fire (Ps. 104:4; Heb. 1:7), to stand before the throne of God praising and serving him.

. . . .

Afterward the church of God was begun in Paradise with Adam and Eve, who were created in the image and likeness of God (Gen. 5:2), upright, good, and pure creatures of God, incorruptible and immortal (Gen. 2:7; Wisd. of Sol. 2:23). They were endowed with a virtuous nature, divine attributes, and true knowledge, love, and fear of God so long as they remained in the original creation and ordinance of God, and bore the image of God (Sir. 10:12, 13).

Therefore, the church of God is a church of holy beings, namely, of the angels in heaven and of the believing reborn men on earth, who have been renewed in the image of God. These are all united in Jesus Christ (Eph. 3:6; Col. 1:27), as Paul explains in his epistles, especially to the Hebrews, when he writes: "You have come to Mount Zion, to the city of the living God, to the heavenly Jerusalem, to the company of many thousand angels, to the church of the firstborn, which are written in heaven, to God, the Judge of all, to the spirits of perfect righteousness, and to Jesus the Mediator

113

of the new covenant, and to the blood of sprinkling, that speaks more eloquently than the blood of Abel" (Heb. 12:22-24).

From these words we may clearly understand that the company of many thousand angels, the church of the firstborn, which are written in heaven, and the spirits of perfect righteousness, together with all believers which have been added to it, all together comprise the church of God, over which God, the righteous Judge, rules, of which Christ is the Head, and in which the Holy Spirit dwells (Eph. 1:22, 23; 1 Cor. 3:16; 6:19; 2 Cor. 6:16; Eph. 2:21, 22, etc.).

. . . .

But how this came to pass, and how the building of the church of Jesus Christ was accomplished, the Scripture shows us with great clarity, namely by the right teaching of the Word of God, by the faith that comes by the hearing of the Word of God (Rom. 10:18), and the enlightenment of the Holy Spirit. But no one can enter into the kingdom of God, into the heavenly Jerusalem, that is, the church of Jesus Christ, unless he heartily amends his ways, sincerely repents, and believes the gospel (Mt. 3:2; Gal. 4:6-9). Indeed, just as God founded his church on earth in Paradise with pure and holy people, who had been created in his image and after his likeness (Gen. 1:26; 2:8), so he still desires to have in his church such as are created in Jesus Christ and have been renewed by the Holy Spirit. For although the salvation promised to man has been purchased by Jesus Christ the Saviour, and although the forfeited life has been redeemed by the blood of the one offering, and is offered to all mankind in the gospel (Tit. 2:13; Heb. 2:2, 3; 3:12-15; 5:1-3; 10:18-20), nevertheless not all men enjoy this eternal salvation and eternal life, but those alone who in this life are born again by the Word of Jesus Christ. It is those who allow themselves to be sought and found by the light of the Word of God, who obey the voice of their Shepherd (1 Pet. 1:23-25; Jas. 1:18, 19; Jn. 3:3; 8:32; 12:46), who are enlightened with the true knowledge of God and his will and in sincere faith accept the righteousness that is in Christ.

. . . .

Herewith is shown sufficiently that the church of God is not only invisible, but also visible, and in part manifest to the world. Moreover it is not in one particular place or location, like the figura-

114

tive Jerusalem, which was at no other place but in the land of Judah alone. But the heavenly Jerusalem is wherever God's Word is rightly taught, believed and obeyed, and the sacraments of Christ are rightly observed according to the word.

. . . .

The church of the Lord, although existing in spirit and in truth, is nevertheless also visible, as I explained in my book on The Sending of Preachers, and still declare. The reasons are as follows: 1. The name church or congregation indicates that it is not only invisible, but also visible, for the term used is ecclesia, that is, a gathering or congregating together, and he who addresses the congregation is Ecclesiastes. Hence Solomon is called Ecclesiastes, because he spoke to the congregation or church of Israel. Now, it is certain and incontrovertible that as Solomon was, as a preacher, visible, so the church also was visible to whom he addressed his words. 2. Christ Jesus himself chose his apostles (Jn. 15:16), and gathered them together as a church, and was not always invisible in Jerusalem and Judea. 3. The apostles, according to the command of the Lord, through the preaching of the gospel, in faith and truth, and by proper Christian baptism, and the power and unity of the Holy Spirit, gathered a church (Mt. 28; Mk. 16). This was not an invisible body, for they did not write nor send their epistles in a general or indiscriminate way to all people, but specifically denominating the believers and God-fearing people, designating the places and calling many persons by name. How is it possible for all this to be invisible?

5.11 Menno Simons, "Reply to Gellius Faber," CWMS, 742-743

With this I will terminate the doctrine of the churches, and conclude this subject with the following questions and answers, which I trust, by the grace of God, will give the industrious reader no little gain and bring great clarity.

Question. What is the church of Christ?
Answer. A community of saints.

115

Q. *With whom did she originate?*
A. With Adam and Eve.

Q. *Of whom is she?*
A. Of God through Christ.

Q. *Of what kind of servants is she begotten?*
A. Of those who are irreproachable in doctrine and life.

Q. *Whereby do they beget her?*
A. By the Spirit and Word of God.

Q. *To what purpose do they beget her?*
A. That she may serve, thank, and praise God.

Q. *Of what mind is she?*
A. In her weakness, of Christ's mind.

Q. *What kind of fruits does she bring forth?*
A. Fruits which are conformable to the Word of God.

· ·

The True Signs by Which the Church of Christ May Be Known
    I. By an unadulterated, pure doctrine. Deut. 4:6; 5:12; Is. 8:5; Mt. 28:20; Mk. 16:15; Jn. 8:52; Gal. 1.
   II. By a scriptural use of the sacramental signs. Mt. 28:19; Mk. 16; Rom. 6:4; Col. 2:12; 1 Cor. 12:13; Mk. 14:22; Lk. 22:19; 1 Cor. 11:22, 23.
 III. By obedience to the Word. Mt. 7; Lk. 11:28; Jn. 7:18; 15:10; Jas. 1:22.
  IV. By unfeigned, brotherly love. Jn. 13:34; Rom. 13:8; 1 Cor. 13:1; 1 Jn. 3:18; 4:7, 8.
   V. By a bold confession of God and Christ. Mt. 10:32; Mk. 8:29; Rom. 10:9; 1 Tim. 6:13.
  VI. By oppression and tribulation for the sake of the Lord's Word. Mt. 5:10; 10:39; 16:24; 24:9; Lk. 6:28; Jn. 15:20; 2 Tim. 2:9; 3:12; 1 Pet. 1:6; 3:14; 4:13; 5:10; 1 Jn. 3:13.

For further reading:

Beachy, *Grace*, 87-98.
Harold S. Bender, "The Anabaptist Vision," Hershberger, *Anabaptist Vision*, 29-54.
Estep, *Anabaptist Story*, 179-194.
Keeney, *Dutch Anabaptist*, 145-174.
Cornelius Krahn, "Menno Simons' Concept of the Church," Dyck, *Legacy*, 17-30.
Franklin H. Littell, "The Anabaptist Concept of the Church," Hershberger, *Anabaptist Vision*, 119-134.
_____, "Spiritualizers, Anabaptists, and the Church," *MQR* XXIX (January 1955), 34-43.
Nanne van der Zijpp, "The Conception of Our Fathers Regarding the Church," *MQR* XXVII (April 1953), 91-99.
Wenger, *Even Unto Death*, 69-91.
Frank J. Wray, "The Anabaptist Doctrine of the Restitution of the Church," *MQR* XXVIII (July 1954), 186-196.

VI

Church Order

The fluid, charismatic phase[27] of primitive Anabaptism in Zürich and Zollikon gave way very quickly to the development of elements of order. In 1531 Hans Pfistermeyer said, "I freely concede that Christians need to establish some order in the church since not all have the same function" (6.6). This had already been clearly acknowledged in article five of the Schleitheim Confession in 1527 (6.2) as well as in section two of the earliest known Anabaptist congregational order (6.1). Various functions in the congregation were recognized, which those who had the requisite gifts were called on to carry out.

The Reformed theologians in Switzerland and the Netherlands denied Anabaptism the right to be called a church because the pastors were not chosen according to proper church order.[28] Hence we have lengthy statements on this subject from several writers. They reject the arguments that sacramental ordination, apostolic succession, or education are proper legitimations for holding the office of pastor. Only a man who lives an upright Christian life and who has been taught by the Holy Spirit can be considered as a pastor. Anabaptists of all varieties assumed that one could have no confidence in the teaching of a man who was not stringently obedient to the moral dictates of Scripture. Furthermore, only those pastors had unquestioned legitimacy as God's spokesmen who had been chosen by a congregation that was equally obedient. In Anabaptism holiness denoted ethical and moral, not sacramental, purity.

It was also recognized that a man could not appoint himself as a "servant of the Word." This always came at the initiative of the congregation. The functions of the pastor were primarily baptizing,

118

preaching and teaching, presiding at the Lord's Supper, administering church discipline, and exercising general oversight over the church.

Orders for the administering of baptism and the Lord's Supper also developed early (6.3, 6.4, 6.11, 6.15) in various centres, although none of them became normative. These orders apparently developed in order to insure always a biblical view of the church.

Concern for the place of children in the church, which resulted from careful listening to the arguments for infant baptism, is expressed in Pilgram Marpeck's order for dedication of infants, the only one of its kind in Anabaptist writings (6.7).

We also get some insights into congregational meetings in selections 6.5, 6.9, 6.10, 6.13. What is especially striking is the rejection of the preacher's monologue and an uncompromising emphasis on congregational participation, especially in selections 6.5 and 6.9. This emphasis may be in some conflict with the high role allotted to the pastor in selections 6.2 and 6.13.

Pilgram Marpeck, who even though he was not a trained theologian, nevertheless often penetrated more deeply into theological issues than university trained leaders, also gave attention to the observance of Sunday. He understood the value of a special Lord's day, but rejected all legalistic observance and pointed to the broad symbolic significance of the institution (6.14).

The selections on baptism and Lord's Supper should be read together with the theological discussions of the subjects in chapters 8 and 9 respectively.

6.1   "Congregational Order," 1527, *Legacy*, 44-45

Since the almighty eternal and merciful God has made his wonderful light break forth in this world and [in this] most dangerous time, we recognize the mystery of the divine will, that the Word is preached to us according to the proper ordering of the Lord, whereby we have been called into his fellowship. Therefore, according to the command of the Lord and the teachings of his apostles, in

119

Christian order, we should observe the new commandment in love one toward another, so that love and unity may be maintained, which all brothers and sisters of the entire congregation should agree to hold to as follows:

1. The brothers and sisters should meet at least three or four times a week, to exercise themselves in the teaching of Christ and his apostles and heartily to exhort one another to remain faithful to the Lord as they have pledged.

2. When the brothers and sisters are together, they shall take up something to read together. The one to whom God has given the best understanding shall explain it, the others should be still and listen, so that there are not two or three carrying on a private conversation, bothering the others. The Psalter shall be read daily at home.

3. Let none be frivolous in the church of God, neither in words nor in actions. Good conduct shall be maintained by them all also before the heathen.

4. When a brother sees his brother erring, he shall warn him according to the command of Christ, and shall admonish him in a Christian and brotherly way, as everyone is bound and obliged to do out of love.

5. Of all the brothers and sisters of this congregation none shall have anything of his own, but rather, as the Christians in the time of the apostles held all in common, and especially stored up a common fund, from which aid can be given to the poor, according as each will have need, and as in the apostles' time permit no brother to be in need.

6. All gluttony shall be avoided among the brothers who are gathered in the congregation; serve a soup or a minimum of vegetable and meat, for eating and drinking are not the kingdom of heaven.

7. The Lord's Supper shall be held, as often as the brothers are together, thereby proclaiming the death of the Lord, and thereby warning each one to commemorate, how Christ gave his life for us, and shed his blood for us, that we might also be willing to give our body and life for Christ's sake, which means for the sake of all the brothers.

120

6.2   Michael Sattler, Schleitheim Confession, 1527, *Legacy*, 38-39

V. We have been united as follows concerning shepherds in the church of God. The shepherd in the church shall be a person according to the rule of Paul, fully and completely, who has a good report of those who are outside the faith. The office of such a person shall be to read and exhort and teach, warn, admonish, or ban in the congregation, and properly to preside among the sisters and brothers in prayer, and in the breaking of bread, and in all things to take care of the body of Christ, that it may be built up and developed, so that the name of God might be praised and honored through us, and the mouth of the mocker be stopped.

He shall be supported, wherein he has need, by the congregation which has chosen him, so that he who serves the gospel can also live therefrom, as the Lord has ordered. But should a shepherd do something worthy of reprimand, nothing shall be done with him without the voice of two or three witnesses. If they sin they shall be publicly reprimanded, so that others might fear.

But if the shepherd should be driven away or led to the Lord by the cross, at the same hour another shall be ordained to his place, so that the little folk and the little flock of God may not be destroyed, but be preserved by warning and be consoled.

6.3   Balthasar Hubmaier, "Baptismal Order," 1527, *Armour*, 143-144

BALTHASAR HUBMAIER'S BAPTISMAL ORDER
AS FOLLOWED AT NICOLSBURG

Whoever desires to receive water baptism should first present himself to his bishop so that he may be tested as to whether he is sufficiently instructed in the articles of the law, gospel, and faith, and in the doctrines which pertain to a new Christian life. Also he must give evidence that he can pray, and that he can intelligently explain the articles of the Christian faith. This must all be ascertained about the candidate before he can be permitted to be incorporated into the church of Christ through external baptism unto the forgiveness of his sins.

If he meets these requirements, the bishop then presents him to his church. He admonishes all the brethren and sisters to kneel and with hearty devotion to pray to God, that God may graciously grant to the candidate the grace and power of his Holy Spirit, and that he will bring to pass that which he has begun in him through his Holy Spirit and divine Word.

The administration of baptism is then to proceed thus: The bishop shall say: Come, Holy Spirit; fill the hearts of thy believers and enkindle in them the fire of thy love: thou who hast assembled the peoples of many tongues in the unity of faith. Hallelujah! Hallelujah! Praise be to God! Praise be to God!

Then the bishop proffers the baptismal vow to the candidate thus:

The Bishop: Believest thou in God the Father Almighty, Maker of heaven and earth?

The Candidate: (in words for all to hear): I believe.

The Bishop: Believest thou in Jesus Christ, his only-begotten Son, our Lord; who was conceived of the Holy Ghost; born of the Virgin Mary; suffered under Pontius Pilate; was crucified dead and buried; that he also descended in his spirit and preached the gospel to the spirits who were in prison; on the third day he was reunited with his body in the grave and rose in power from the dead; after forty days he ascended unto heaven, where he sits at the right hand of his Father Almighty; thence he shall come to judge the living and the dead; believest thou this?

The Candidate: I believe.

The Bishop: Believest thou also in the Holy Spirit; and believest thou in one Holy Universal Christian church, one communion of the saints which has the keys to remit sin; believest thou also in the resurrection of the flesh, and in eternal life?

The Candidate: I believe.

The Bishop: Wilt thou also in the power of Christ renounce the devil, all his works, legions, and pomps?

The Candidate: I will.

The Bishop: If thou hereafter sinnest and thy brother knoweth it,

122

wilt thou accept from him the first and the second steps of fraternal discipline, and then, if necessary, willingly and obediently allow thyself to be disciplined before the church?

The Candidate: I will.

The Bishop: Dost thou now desire, upon this profession of faith and pledge, to be baptized in water according to the institution of Christ, and thus to be incorporated and enrolled into the external Christian church unto the forgiveness of thy sins?

The Candidate: I desire this in the power of God.

The bishop then baptizes:

The Bishop: I baptize thee in the name of the Father, and of the Son, and of the Holy Ghost, unto the forgiveness of thy sins. Amen. May it thus be true.

The bishop admonishes the church a second time to pray for the one newly baptized. They are to pray that God will increase his faith, and the faith of all Christian men, and will grant us all power and perseverance, so that we finally may be found and be preserved in one Christian faith.

When the church has finished praying the bishop lays his hands upon the head of the one newly baptized and says:

I give thee witness and authority, that thou henceforth shalt be numbered among the fellowship of Christians; that as a member of this fellowship thou shalt participate in its keys, and thou shalt break bread and pray with the other Christian sisters and brethren. God be with thee and with thy spirit. Amen.

6.4   Interrogation of Ambrosius Spitelmaier, 1527, Schornbaum, *Quellen,* 26

Sixthly, he says that they use no other words than these: I baptize you in the name of the Father, the Son, and the Holy Spirit. Then they take some water in a bowl or a pitcher, dip two fingers in the water and make the sign of the cross upon the forehead. That is the form and manner of their baptism. But before this the Word of God in the creatures is preached. If he believes the words that they are so, he may be baptized, but without compulsion.

6.5 Interrogation of Ambrosius Spitelmaier, 1527, Schornbaum, *Quellen*, 35-36

Asked where they come together and what they do Spitelmaier answered:

They have no special gathering places. When there is peace and unity and when none of those who have been baptized are scattered they come together wherever the people are. They send messages to each other by a boy or girl. When they have come together they teach one another the divine Word and one asks the other: how do you understand this saying? Thus there is among them a diligent living according to the divine Word.

6.6 "Conversation with Pfistermeyer," 1531, Haas, *Quellen*, 41, 43

I have been offended by their [the clergy's] remuneration since it has its source in usury. I know full well that he who serves with the gospel is entitled to a sufficient living from it. However, it may not come from interest or from usury. It is unrighteous gain to live from interest and from the proceeds of offerings to idols. To preach against such abuse and to live off it at the same time means that he will not be listened to. If he accepts it, how can he condemn it?

. . . .

I freely concede that Christians need to establish some order in the church since not all have the same function. Nevertheless, the preachers must be supported by resources a Christian can justify. Thus it would happen that once those in need had been looked after, the balance would be used for support of the preachers. Anything left over after that would be distributed to the poor. But if the preacher lives on the proceeds of usury, he cannot chastise nor condemn it.

6.7 Pilgram Marpeck, "Confession," 1532, *The Writings*, 147

Third, the infants shall be named before a congregation and God shall duly be praised for them; thanks and blessing shall be

124

given to his fatherly goodness that, through Christ Jesus our Lord and Saviour, he has also had mercy on the innocent creatures and that, without discrimination, he has taken them in his hands and assured them of the kingdom of God. We rightfully owe him gratitude at all times for his goodness. In the liberty of the Spirit and Word of Christ, we should pray for everyone, and also for the child, that God would also in future give us knowledge of his gracious will, etc. We admonish the parents to cleanse their conscience as much as lies in them, with respect to the child, to do whatever is needed to raise the child up to the praise and glory of God, and to commit the child to God until it is clearly seen that God is working in him for faith or unfaith.

6.8 Hans Hotz in "Bern Colloquy," 1538, Haas, *Quellen*, 287-288, 296, 301

Concerning our calling and commission to the ministry of preaching we answer as follows. A Christian community must be pure and holy. If she detects gifts and virtues in a member as Paul speaks about it, then she has the authority to send them to preach the gospel.... Before there can be Christian preaching there must first be a change of life, improvement, and the new birth. Then, if the virtues are detected in such a person, the commissioning follows as Christ called the apostles to follow him. They had to become subject to his righteousness and abstain from sin. Only then he sent them and commanded them to preach the good news.... [At this point the speaker, presumably Hans Hotz, says that he joined the Anabaptists because he saw true improvement of life there.] There has grown a true Christian community who commissioned us as servants and disciples of the church of Christ and who committed to us the office of preaching.

. . . .

Through our faith we have received grace and the apostolic office from God. However, we do not believe that all who believe and receive the faith in Christ should therefore be preachers. For there are different offices which are distinguished from each other but all belong to the one body.

. . . .

We also confess that not everyone who is called to the godly life should teach. We believe that there is a variety of gifts and offices. A person may not appoint himself; he must be chosen by the church. I too, for my own part, did not preach until the faithful, who are called to a Christian life through the teaching of Christ, and gathered through a penitent life, called me to do so.

6.9   "Some Swiss Brethren," 1532-1540, Peachey, *Answer*, 11

That all things may be done in the best, the most seemly and convenient manner when the congregation assembles, which congregation [*gemein*] is a temple of the Holy Spirit (1 Cor. 6) where the gifts of inner operation of the spirit in each one (note, in *each* one) serve the common good (1 Cor. 12, Eph. 4). Note, for the *common* good. How could this more suitably be applied, offered or employed for the common good than in the coming together precisely for this common good and edification, as stated in chapter 14: When such believers come together, "Everyone of you (note, *every* one) hath a psalm, hath a doctrine, hath a revelation, hath an interpretation," etc. And he enjoins them thereupon to permit all this to be done, that is, to apply or to use, to the edification of the congregation which comes together, so that it may be a bright light in spite of the presumptuous attacks of the adversaries. And it is Paul's intention that if one sitting by or listening receives a revelation or is moved to exercise his spiritual gift or to prophesy, then the first shall hold his peace; and Paul says that all may prophesy, one after the other, and wants that at all times the spirit of the one who prophesies, or teaches, or preaches first, shall be subject to, and silent before, the one from among those seated or listening who has something to prophesy, and shall not show himself discordant or unpeaceful, as some, especially among their preachers, presume that they need yield to no one, either to be silent or to speak, especially not to us. Out of this [situation] discord and sects follow, contrary to the above-mentioned words of Paul, yes, contrary even to their own glosses which they have placed at this point in several German testaments.

126

So Paul in the end of the chapter commands that they shall not forbid to speak in tongues, which, according to the beginning of the chapter serves to the edification of the congregation. How much less authority has one to forbid prophesying, teaching, interpreting, or admonition to the edification of the congregation? When some one comes to church and constantly hears only one person speaking, and all the listeners are silent, neither speaking nor prophesying, who can or will regard or confess the same to be a spiritual congregation, or confess according to 1 Cor. 14 that God is dwelling and operating in them through his Holy Spirit with his gifts, impelling them one after the other in the above mentioned order of speaking and prophesying?

6.10 Leopold Scharnschlager, "Mutual Order," 1540, Fast, *Der Linke Flügel*, 131-133

Since manifold deceptions gain ground everywhere it is important that the called, surrendered and obligated members of Jesus Christ, wherever they are in the world and in distress, should not forsake their gatherings (Heb. 10:25). Rather, according to the opportunities provided by place and persecutions they should come together for the sake of Christ's love, wherever and however they may, whether there be few or many.... Such gathering should take place with wisdom, moderation, good sense, discipline, friendliness, and a quiet manner, all the more so because we can see that the day of the Lord is near at hand....

When they come together and they have no appointed leader, they should admonish one among them whom they regard as capable in a friendly and pleasant manner to read or speak to them according to his God-given gift. Or else someone may personally offer himself for service out of love. One after another should be allowed to speak—depending upon whether something has been given to him as Paul teaches (1 Cor. 14)—and offer his gifts for the improvement of the members in order that our congregation be not like those falsely claiming to be such where only one and no one else may speak. But before they begin to speak they should fall on their knees (1 Tim. 2:1) and faithfully call on the Lord that he will grant them to speak fruitfully. At the conclusion they should diligently admonish one another to walk by the mind of the Lord and steadfastly to remain in him, faithfully to wait and watch for the Lord until he comes. . . . When they depart, they should once again call and pray to the Lord for all the members and their needs and for all men according to the instruction of our dear brother Paul (1 Tim. 2:1 ff.). Further they are to thank God for all his gifts and goodness (1 Thess. 5:17 ff.), and, according to the opportunity before they leave to break bread with one another in memory of the death of the Lord (1 Cor. 11:24).

Whenever they have thus come together an elder, or if there is none, a senior brother, should, for the Lord's sake, be concerned for the poor members. This should be done with wise, sincere, gentle, not offensive nor aggressive, but earnest, emphatic words that their hearts may be moved to willingness and mercy and that the way and power of love grows according to God's pleasure. Above all a brother should always have a box or bag nearby with the knowledge of the church members, so that every member knows that a free offering or thanksgiving may be put into it if the Lord so admonishes either during the meeting or after. This must be done in order that, whenever necessary, the poor may be given something according to the necessity of each and the amount available. The brother who is in charge of the money is to distribute it with diligent care in a good conscience and the fear of God. It is not to be done as the world does it with its poor without investigation or examination of life, whether it is necessary or not, whether the recipient is a miser or not. For it is a holy office (Acts 6:1 ff.).

6.11   Peter Riedeman, *Account*, 1542, 79-81

THE MANNER OF BAPTIZING, OR HOW ONE BAPTIZES

If one is to baptize, it is necessary that there be at least two persons, namely, he that baptizes, and he that is baptized. He that baptizes, however, first calls and cries out that one must repent, points out to the man his sin, how he may come to God and find grace with him, and how baptism is a bond with God; in this way he shows him the benefit of baptism, through which the man is moved to desire baptism. Thus, he who is to be baptized must first request, ask for, and desire it.

Then, when he desires baptism, he who baptizes asks him if he believes in God the Father, Son and Holy Spirit. Thus, he who is to be baptized must confess his faith. He that baptizes asks him further who desires baptism if he reject the world, sin and the devil. These he must reject. Further, he that baptizes asks if he desires to yield himself to God with all his heart and all his soul and all his members, henceforth to live no more to himself but to God and his church and to suffer God, only, to rule over, and use all his members. If this is his desire, the baptizer asks further whether he be well assured of all this and certain in his heart that this is the truth, and that there is no other way to life than is shown him in Christ. And if he likewise confess this, the baptizer asks if he desires to bind himself to God and be baptized. If he so desires, the baptizer tells him to humble himself with bent knees before God and his church and kneel down, and he takes pure water and pours it upon him and says, "I baptize you in the name of the Father and of the Son and of the Holy Spirit, who, in accordance with your faith, has forgiven your sins and drawn and received you into his kingdom, wherefore sin henceforth no more, lest a worse thing befall you."

Now, since in baptism the man's sins are left behind and forgiven, and the church has the key, this should take place before the church, who, together with him who baptizes and him who desires baptism, kneels down and asks God to forgive his sins before baptism takes place. Where, however, this cannot be and the church cannot be reached, the baptizer may do it apart, or alone.

WHO CAN SO BAPTIZE AND TEACH

It is not for all and sundry to take upon themselves such an office, namely that of teaching and baptizing; as James declares, saying, "Dear brothers, let not each strive to be a teacher, for we all sin much, and shall then receive all the greater condemnation." For which reason none must take upon himself or accept such power, unless he be chosen properly and rightly by God in his church and community, as the apostle shows the Hebrews, saying, "Let no man take this honour unto himself, but he that is chosen of God as was Aaron.

For also Christ glorified not himself to be made an high priest."
Thus, his ministers likewise must not press themselves forward and
come to the fore, but wait until God draws them out and chooses
them.

CONCERNING ELECTION

If the church needs one or, indeed, more ministers, she must
not elect them as pleases herself, but wait upon the Lord to see
whom he chooses and shows them. Therefore they should continue
in earnest prayer and petition to God that he might care for them,
answer their need and show them whom he has chosen for his
ministry. After continuing thus earnestly in prayer, those who have
been recognized through God's counsel to be suitable are presented
to all. If there be many of them we wait to see which the Lord shows
us by lot; if, however, there be only one or just as many as are
needed, then we need no lot, for the Lord has shown us him,
therefore we accept him or them in the fear of God as a gift and
present from God. His appointment to the office is then confirmed
before the church through the laying on of the elder's hands.

None, however, is confirmed in his office except he be first
proved and revealed to the church, and have the testimony of a good
life and walk, lest he fall into the snare of the wicked. Now, however,
many say, "Who then chose the first one?" To which we say, "God."
For in the Old Testament when Israel had turned away from him,
God showed his grace again and again and gave them a saviour out
of their midst, who set them once more in the right way; that he
might prove that he was Israel's God.

Thus also has he done anew, since the people had fallen away
and estranged themselves from him or had departed and forsaken
him. Nevertheless, for the sake of those remaining, he turned not
away his mercy, but, when the time had come when he desired to
have compassion upon us once more, that the wicked might have
less cause to rejoice, he clothed with the power of his Spirit one who
had held the office of preacher among those who with their mouth
professed to be Christians but denied this in power, that he might
bring them back. For this reason also he laid his word in his mouth,
and himself gave witness to the same in the power of his working;

130

and has opened for us the hearing ear to heed it, and also, himself, made it fruitful in us to his praise.

6.12   Peter Riedeman, *Account*, 1542, 123-124

CONCERNING SINGING

Paul says, "Sing and make melody in your heart to the Lord, with psalms and hymns and spiritual songs." For this reason we say that to sing spiritual songs is good and pleasing to God if we sing in the right way, that is, attentively, in the fear of God and as inspired by the Spirit of Christ.

For it is for this reason that they are called spiritual songs: namely, that they are inspired and made and composed by the urge of the Spirit, and also attract and move men to blessedness. Therefore, since they are composed and made by the inspiration and urge of the Spirit of Christ, they must also be sung as inspired by the same Spirit, if they are to be sung aright and to be of service to men.

Where this is not the case, and one sings only for carnal joy or for the sweet sound or for some such reason, one misuses them, changing them into what is carnal and worldly, and does not sing songs of the Spirit, but of the letter. Likewise also, he who enjoys listening for the music's sake—he hears in the letter and not in the Spirit, so with him also is it without fruit; and because they are not used, sung and heard aright, he that so does sins greatly against God; for he uses his word, which was given for his salvation and as an urge to blessedness, as leading to the lust of the flesh and to sin. Thus, it is changed by him into harm, for though the song in itself is spiritual, yet is it to that man no longer a spiritual song. It is a worldly song, for it is not sung in the Spirit.

He, however, who sings in the Spirit, considers diligently every word, how far and where it goes, why it has been used and how it may serve to his betterment. He who does this sings to the Lord's praise, to the betterment of both himself and others and as an instigation to a godly life. This is to sing well; to sing in any other way is in vain. Thus, we allow it not among us that other than spiritual songs are sung.

6.13   Peter Riedeman, *Account*, 1542, 129-130

CONCERNING COMING TOGETHER

When we come together, we do so with the desire to encourage and awaken our hearts in the grace of God, to walk in the Lord's sight with greater diligence and attention. Therefore, the people are first encouraged to mark diligently and to consider why we have met and come together, that they may prepare their hearts for prayer, so that they may come worthily before the Lord and pray for what concerns the church and all her members.

After this we give thanks to God for all the good that he has given us through Christ, and for accepting us into his grace and revealing to us his truth. This is followed by an earnest prayer that he keep us faithful and devout therein to the end, and supply all our desires and needs, and open our hearts that we may use his word with profit, hear, accept and keep it. When this is done, one proceeds to proclaim the Lord's word faithfully, according to the grace given by God, encouraging the heart to fear the Lord and to remain in his fear. When all this is completed the minister commends the church to God the Lord and lets them depart one from another, each to his place. When, however, we come together to keep the Lord's Memory or Supper the people are encouraged and taught for one, two or three days and told vividly what the Lord's Supper is, what happens there and what one does thereby, and how one should prepare himself worthily to receive the same. Every day, however, has also its thanksgiving and prayer. When all this has taken place, and the Lord's Supper has been kept, a hymn of praise is sung to the Lord. Then the people are admonished to walk in accordance with what they have shown to be in their hearts, and then they are commended to the Lord and allowed to separate.

6.14   Pilgram Marpeck, "Judgment and Decision," 1542, *The Writings*, 338-339

The third: You shall keep the Sabbath holy, that is, the seventh day. This is a ceremonial law, in force until the human coming of Jesus Christ, the Son of God, into the world. He is the Lord of the

Sabbath of God, his heavenly Father, and he completely fulfills it. If, during an entire lifetime, even unto death, a person seeks only work for himself, and thus to find himself only in work, he does not keep the Sabbath of Jesus Christ, the Son of God. Both those who do no work and those who stand idle also break the Sabbath. The Son of God has established, for all flesh and blood, the celebration and the obedience to death, yes, the death on the cross. Whoever seeks to save himself will find death, and whoever loses his life finds life. That is the Sabbath which the children of God observe, and of which they are lords with Christ. For their flesh and blood, with all its lusts and with all its sinful works must in Christ celebrate, even unto death. This is not a reference to physical work necessary for life; otherwise, we could not eat and drink, nor clothe ourselves. Whoever breaks this Sabbath is destroyed from among the people.

However, the literal celebration of the Sabbath can be good, provided it is done in freedom of the Spirit and is not bound by a law to time, state, and person. Otherwise, it is not a celebration for God, nor is it done out of love for the neighbor, which is the true celebration.

Rather, one accepts the tyranny of time. But Jesus Christ has already fulfilled time, and thus, we now should rule over time. If we bind it to the state,[29] we cause the kingdom of earth to rule over man when in fact, with Christ in patience, man is lord of the whole earth. If we bind it to a person, for example, to the deceased saints because of their deeds of merit, we bind life to death, for I cannot be saved by the works of someone else.[30] Only Christ, the Son of God and Son of Man, is the time, state, and person of the true celebration of the Sabbath for God, and for the neighbor, in the gloriously free love of God the Father with his own.

6.15   Dirk Philips, "The Lord's Supper," 1564, Kolb/ Klaassen, *Philips*, 87-89

But to a right observance of the Holy Supper belong the following essentials:

First, there must be a Christian congregation that has assembled in the name of the Lord and that declares and shows the Lord's death with a true faith and confession, that just as Christ Jesus gave and committed to his apostles and all believers the eating of the bread and the drinking of the wine, so he freely gave them his body and blood as a gift for an eternal salvation (1 Cor. 10:16; 11:23).

To the Supper belong admonition, and a sincere remembrance of the suffering and death of the Lord, of the conformity to his suffering and death, of unity of the Spirit and of faith, of love to God and the neighbor. All of these belong especially to the observance of the Lord's Supper (Phil. 3:10).

Second, we believe that this Supper must be taken with those only who are the friends of God, the true Christians, who have accepted the gospel and have amended their lives, and who, upon confession of their faith, have been properly baptized in the name of the Father, and of the Son, and of the Holy Spirit (Mt. 28:19). In this faith they are faithfully concerned to lead a Christian life, and diligently meditate upon conformity to Christ, his suffering and death, his burial and resurrection; in short, to be one body with Christ and all the saints. These, and no others, are, according to the teaching of the gospel, to be renewed by this Supper, admonished and confirmed in the fellowship of Christ and all the saints.

Third, this Supper is to be observed harmoniously by all believers (as many as are gathered together) and not by one alone, as commonly happens. For thus the Lord ordained, and thus he desired it to be observed; all Christians must conform thereto. For if it is not right to despise or alter a legal will made by man, how much more it is improper to despise the testament of Jesus Christ or to break his commandments (Gal. 4:15 [14]).

Moreover the minister is to observe the Supper with the congregation, and the bread is to be broken. What the Lord did, the apostles continued to observe. Hence Paul writes to the Corinthians (1 Cor. 10:16): "The bread which we break," etc. And Luke writes: "And they continued steadfastly in the apostles' teaching and fellowship, and in breaking of bread, and in prayers. And they were together daily in the temple, breaking bread from house to house" (Acts 2:46). This means that the disciples gathered together to break the bread. Therefore the bread must be broken in the Supper, and both parts of the Supper, that is, the bread and the cup, must be

134

given, divided and received by every one. No one is to eat his own bread by himself, which is what is done in the world. Whoever does this, shows that he is eating his own supper, and not the Supper of the Lord.

Fourth, Paul admonishes us that every person should examine himself before he eats of that bread and drinks of that cup (1 Cor. 11:28). For whoever has not true faith in Jesus Christ, is not a member of the body of Christ, will not die and live with Christ, has not genuine love for Christ and his neighbor and is not in one body with Christ and all the saints, can never rightly observe the Supper (which is a sign of divine and brotherly love and unity), not rightly discern the Lord's body. For in the body of Christ two things are especially noted, namely, the Head and the members. The Head, which is Christ, reminds us that from it we all receive grace and life (Eph. 1:23), and that one must cleave to the Head alone. From it also we take an example of love and remember how faithfully the Lord Jesus Christ served us. Then we must take note of the members of the body with whom we are one, and remember how Christ has served us with his gifts and is still serving us. With the gifts which we receive from God—be they spiritual or natural—we likewise serve our members for the perfecting and edifying of the body of Christ, and all this in love. This, then, is what it means to rightly discern the body of Christ.

6.16   Dirk Philips, "Sending of Preachers," 1559, "The Church of God," 1562, Kolb/Klaassen, *Philips*, 179-181, 195, 384-386

Therefore let everyone see to it that he run not of himself before he is called by the Lord or by his church in the prescribed manner. No one is sent by the Lord, however, or rightly chosen by the church, except by the Holy Spirit; he must touch his heart and make him fervent with love to willingly feed, drive and send forth the church of God (Jn. 21:15; 1 Pet. 5:2). It is written of Paul and Barnabas, that they went out, being sent forth by the Holy Spirit (Acts 13:4). Paul says to the elders of the churches: "Take heed therefore to yourselves, and to all the flock, over the which the Holy

Spirit has set you as bishops, to feed the church of God, which he purchased with his own blood" (Acts 20:28).

Now, if the true teachers are moved and sent forth and set over the churches by the Holy Spirit, it is evident, from this alone, how they must be qualified for their service.

. . . .

From this it follows strongly that the ministers of Christ, the teachers and leaders of his churches, must have the Holy Spirit, by whom they must, first and above all things, be well instructed in the word of God. For the common people must err and walk in darkness if the teachers themselves are ignorant. Why? Because Christ calls the teachers a light of the world, a salt of the earth (Mt. 5:14). How can the world see aright when those who should be a light unto the world are themselves in entire darkness? That is, how should the world rightly understand and know the Holy Scripture and the power of God, when those who ought to be the salt of the earth have lost the power of the divine word and do not themselves know what a good Christian ought to know? How should the world not err when those who are expected to be the city that is built on a hill to show the right way to all who err, are themselves those who mislead? Therefore I say again that the teachers themselves must, above all things, be thoroughly informed and instructed in the Word of God. It is written: "The priest's lips should preserve teaching so that one may find the law in his mouth: for he is the messenger of the Lord of hosts" (Mal. 2:7). Paul says: "A bishop must hold fast the teaching of the trustworthy Word, be able to teach it, exhort with power by the saving faith, and to punish those who contradict it" (Tit. 1:9).

Moreover the teachers of God's Word must teach true and unadulterated doctrine, as the evangelist says: "He whom God has sent speaks the words of God" (Jn. 3:34). Paul says: "I may not speak of anything except what things Christ has wrought through me" (Rom. 15:18); and in another place: "We are not as some who counterfeit the Word of God. Rather in purity we speak from God through God in Christ" (2 Cor. 2:19; 4:2). "We are messengers in Christ's stead, for God admonishes through us; we beg you in Christ's stead, let yourselves be reconciled to God" (2 Cor. 5:20).

. . . .

We have now briefly shown which teachers are sent of God; that is, those who are qualified according to scriptural teaching, who teach God's Word aright, who are conformed to the image of Christ and his saints, and that which they yet lack they seek with all zeal at the fount of all grace, Christ Jesus. All such are without doubt sent of God.

· ·

How the ministers are appointed by God and how they must be qualified may be readily observed and understood from the Old Testament figures of Aaron and his sons.

· ·

The figure of Aaron and his sons may properly be understood, according to the Spirit, to mean that the ministers of Christ who preach his Word and proclaim his gospel must be washed with the pure water of the Holy Spirit and sprinkled with the precious blood of the spotless Lamb Jesus Christ who offered himself for us (Heb. 10:22; Jn. 1:29; 1 Pet. 1:26), first on the right ear, that the ears of their understanding may be opened to hear what God speaks to them. Secondly, they must be sprinkled on the thumb of their right hand (Heb. 12:12), that they may lift up clean and holy hands to God (1 Tim. 2:8), and thirdly, on the great toe of their right foot, that they may walk uprightly before the Lord, in the way of righteousness. They must be clothed with sacred garments, that is with Christ Jesus (Rom. 13:14; Gal. 3:27; Eph. 5:5; 6:11), equipped with the girdle of love and of truth, and adorned with the silk of righteousness (Rev. 19:8). The breastplate with Urim and Thummim and with the twelve precious stones must be hung upon them, that is, they must have the treasure of the Word of God in their hearts, for they are ministers of the Lord (Gal. 6:8) over the spiritual Israel, to teach Jacob the law of God, and Israel his judgments (Deut. 33:10). The mitre with the gold crowned frontlet is upon their heads, that is, they have the Word of God with the proper distinction between the Old and New Testaments, between the letter and the Spirit, with a clear understanding of the divine mystery (Mt. 13:52; 1 Tim. 3:9; Eph. 3:19). They have also a living hope of salvation, and the crown of righteousness is preserved for them for that day (2 Tim. 4:8). They enter the sanctuary of the Lord and offer the living sacrifices for the church of the Lord (Rom. 12:1; 1 Pet. 2:5), and their prayers tinkle and are heard by the Most High, so that he remembers his church. The anointing oil is poured out upon them, for they have received the anointing of him who is holy, and by it they are sanctified (1 Jn. 2:27).

Such are the ministers whom Christ has chosen and sent forth to make known his Word, to preach repentance and forgiveness of sins unto all who believe the gospel (Lk. 24:46; Jn. 20:23) and obey it. But faith must be genuine, that is, of such nature and power, and may be recognized in this that all the words of God are believed, all human doctrines are rejected, and that all hope is placed upon the grace of Jesus Christ with the whole heart. All earthly things are despised. He forsakes himself and seeks after heavenly things with all diligence (Deut. 4:2; 12:32; 1 Pet. 1:3; Heb. 11:10; Col. 3:2; Phil. 3:20; 2 Cor. 4:18). Out of pure fear of the Lord he hates sin and loves righteousness (Ps. 44 [45]:8[7]; Heb. 1:9), and thus shows forth the fruits of the Holy Spirit. Where this is the case, there is true faith; but where this is not the case, there is a vain and false boasting of faith.

6.17   Interrogation of Hans Mändl, 1561, Beck, *Geschichtsbücher*, 648

The servants of the Word of God, who are ordained by the congregation for this service, preach the Word of God, and show the sinner his sinful life. They admonish him to abandon it, proclaim repentance to him, and show him that Christ forgives the sins of the sinner who is sorry and repents. However, only those are forgiven who confess their sinful life, who sincerely desire to abandon it, and who desire to live according to the will of God.

Those then who accept it and who agree to live accordingly who sorrow and repent for their sins, and who desire the covenant o. baptism as a sign of their repentance, kneel down. The whole church that has come together kneels with them and prays to God the Lord for the forgiveness of sins. The servant of the Word then baptize them again with pure water in the name of God the Father, God the Son, and God the Holy Spirit.

6.18 Interrogation of Hans Mändl, 1561, Beck, *Geschichtsbücher*, 649

When we observe the Supper, we do it publicly, that all who wish to see or hear the Word may attend. The servants preach the Word of God a day or three before and remind everyone that the Supper is an important, lofty, and holy observance. Then we observe the Supper as Christ commanded it and the apostles taught it. Thus we are sure that it is the true, proper Supper of Christ.

For further reading:

Armour, *Baptism,* 54-56, 94-96, 107-109, 133-134

Alvin J. Beachy, "The Theology and Practice of Anabaptist Worship," *MQR* XL (July 1966), 163-178.

Clasen, *Anabaptism,* 49-86.

Robert Friedmann, "The Oldest Church Discipline of the Anabaptists," *MQR* XXIX (April 1955), 162-166.

——————, "Hutterite Worship and Preaching," *MQR* XL (January 1966), 5-26.

Keeney, *Dutch Anabaptist,* 45-56.

William Klassen, "A Church Order for Members of Christ's Body," *MQR* XXXVIII (October 1964), 354-356, 386.

Paul Peachey, "Anabaptism and Church Organization," *MQR* XXX (July 1956), 213-228.

VII

The Bible

Anabaptists joined Protestants in rejecting the authorities of popes and councils and elevating the Scriptures into the vacancy. But there were considerable differences between Anabaptists and Protestants and, indeed, among Anabaptists themselves, as to the nature and function of the Scriptures.

There is first of all the view expressed by the Swiss Brethren, by writers like Riedeman and Marpeck, and by the Dutch from Hoffman to Philips that the Scriptures are the Christian's final authority. While this sounds very Lutheran—and even particular discussions support this (see 7.17)—closer examination reveals that the Anabaptist understanding of scriptural authority was closer to the humanist view. This view understood the Scriptures to provide models both for Christian teaching as well as for church organization and order. It is this view, precisely, that we find in Anabaptism.

This explains why Anabaptists were more interested in the New Testament than in the Old. For the Old Testament belonged primarily to the Jewish people, while the New Testament contained the "doctrine of Christ and the apostles" as well as instructions for the basic structure and functioning of the church. These Anabaptists did not reject the Old Testament, but they subjected it to the interpretive principle of "the doctrine of Christ and the apostles." Anything that agreed with this principle was also the Word of God for the present (7.8); anything that disagreed was not.

But there was also one other major view on the question of the Scriptures. This view is found in the selections by Hans Denck (7.2),

140

Hans Hut (7.3), and Ulrich Stadler (7.2). This view rejects the simple identification of the Word of God with the Scriptures. These writers reflect the ancient dualism of matter and spirit. The material, while good and used by God in his purposes, can, by its very nature, not be a bearer of spiritual life. Since the Scriptures are material, eternal life cannot be found in them. This view was a protest against the Lutheran identification of Scripture and Word of God and that only through contact with that Word could one have eternal life.

The Scriptures, say these Anabaptists, are not the wine but the sign outside the inn which advertises the wine (7.2). One does not gain eternal life from simply believing the Scriptures, but rather by coming to faith like Abraham and Moses and Paul of whom the Scriptures tell us. And this process of justification happens as God works directly in the hearts of men.

The Scriptures are often referred to as the outer word and the voice of God in the soul as the inner word. Most Anabaptists acknowledged that the outer can lead to the inner. At the same time they made the point that if people could not read, how then could God work in them if the outer word were necessary to salvation (7.1). Thus the written Scriptures were clearly important, but not indispensable.

As time went on Anabaptists as well as others became more and more aware of the problems which arose wherever the Scriptures were regarded as the sole authority. Which of the many possible interpretations was the correct one and by which marks could one identify it? The established churches could simply enforce their interpretations without explaining. Among Anabaptists one could insist that one had the only valid interpretation and, if possible, excommunicate those who disagreed. But some writers were more perceptive and began to identify marks by which interpretations could be checked for accuracy (7.12, 7.7). Bernhard Rothmann (7.7) said quite simply that an interpretation is reliable if it leads to behaviour that conforms to Christ. If such behaviour is not there, Scripture has not been understood.

Their interrogators were frequently astonished at the wealth of biblical knowledge held even by uneducated Anabaptists. The Bible was, in fact, indispensable even for people like Denck and Hut. They were biblical people, but not "fundamentalists." They reflected on the function of the Bible but were not "liberals." They were most concerned, not with the intellectual questions, but with humble obedience to Jesus to whom the Scriptures testify.

One final note. Anabaptists seem to have leaned to the Catholic definition of the biblical canon, for they quote frequently from the Apocrypha without distinguishing them from the rest of Scripture as Luther did. The Zürich Froschauer Bible, which many Anabaptists used, did not separate the Apocrypha from the rest of the Old Testament.[31]

7.1 Hans Denck, "Recantation," 1527, Fellmann, *Denck I*, 106

CONCERNING THE HOLY SCRIPTURE

I value the Holy Scripture above all human treasures but not as high as the Word of God, which is living, powerful and eternal, and which is free and unencumbered by all of the elements of this world. For insofar as it is God himself it is spirit and no letter, written without pen and paper that it may never be expunged. Therefore also salvation cannot be tied to the Scriptures, however important and good they may be with respect to it. The cause is that it is not possible for the Scriptures to improve an evil heart even if it is highly learned. A pious heart, however, that is a heart in which there is a true spark of godly zeal, will be improved through all things.

Thus, the Holy Scriptures serve the believer for good and for salvation, but the unbeliever to damnation as indeed all things do.

Thus, a person, who has been chosen by God, may be saved without preaching and Scriptures, but that if salvation were tied to preaching and Scripture all those who are unlearned would not be able to attain salvation because they cannot read and the consequence would be that many cities and lands would be lost because they had no preacher sent from God.[32]

7.2   Ulrich Stadler, "The Living and Written Word," Müller, *Glaubenszeugnisse*, 212-215

CONCERNING THE LIVING AND THE WRITTEN WORD

All things have been ordered and made by God and are good creatures of God in which his eternal power and deity are known if one can perceive it. This includes the Scriptures and the spoken word. Therefore whoever wishes to use the Scripture with true reverence and not to attribute to it more than it deserves or belongs to it, the same must radically separate the Scriptures and the spoken word from the inner word of the heart.

The outer word is that which Christ commanded his apostles to preach when he said: preach the gospel of all the creatures. Whoever believes and is baptized will be saved. Here preaching, faith, and baptism are all understood and handled externally and are only signs of the living Word, faith and baptism all of which God works through his righteousness. Thus also Paul says that faith comes through hearing the preaching, but hearing through the word of God.

A genuine preacher must receive the true Word of God in the abyss of his soul through much tribulation. That is the Word of God in the abyss of the soul. But the preached word is only the witness or the sign of the true Word. This eternal Word is not written on paper or tablet. Nor is it spoken or preached. God himself assures man of it in the abyss of the soul. It is written into the fleshly heart through the finger of God. This difference is also made by St. John when he says: I do not write you a new commandment but the old commandment which you have had from the beginning. The old commandment is the Word that you have heard. There he shows that whatever one reads in books, that one hears, that one sees men do or that is in the creatures that is not the living Word of God but only a letter or likeness or witness of the inner or eternal or living Word. This living Word is internally witnessed to by the outer word if one pays close attention to it. It is like a sign on an inn which witnesses to the wine in the cellar. But the sign is not the wine.

This is the order of God that something physical always precedes the spiritual. The faith that comes from hearing always precedes justification after which the enduring faith emerges and works powerfully before God and all the creatures. This takes time and does not happen quickly as our scribes say when they persuade the poor people so that they say: believe, believe, yes, yes. That will soon be clearly evident. They say: My dear fellow, everything is possible to God through his omnipotence. I answer: True. God is almighty and *can* do everything, but he *does* not do everything. Rather he orders all things within his omnipotence according to measure, number and weight.[33]

Abraham heard God's Word from God externally and believed. His faith was untested, but was still reckoned to him for righteousness. The external word was sufficient for justification, but in that justification he lost both word and faith. For when Pharaoh took his wife he was completely swallowed up by unbelief. He denied that she was his wife. Before he discovered God's goodness and mercy he abandoned his faith and acted rashly with respect to his wife. Nevertheless God did not forsake him. Faith such as Abraham had at the beginning is overcome by unbelief, even as the apostles and the father of the lunatic boy said to the Lord: I believe; help my unbelief. O how painful it is for man until unbelief is separated from true faith in justification and in the test. No matter how strongly he believes at the beginning, word and faith disappear entirely before he becomes aware of goodness and mercy. In order to be comforted by God he must first experience unrest and forsakenness.[34] For thus speaks God: for a little while I have forsaken you but with great compassion I have had mercy on you.

Thus it happened to Jacob when God said to him: I am the Lord, the God of Abraham your father, and Isaac's God. I will protect you wherever you go; I will not forsake you until I have accomplished everything that I have promised you. O dear God! When he had to go home he was frightened and greatly feared his brother Esau. The word and faith that he had heard was swallowed up by unbelief. He fell down before his brother Esau and prayed for mercy. What had happened to the external word and faith? He should have depended more on the promise of God than on the goodwill of his brother Esau. Wonderful indeed are the works of our God. Therefore no one can boast except in God alone.

David was the chosen king of Israel. Before he came to reign he experienced tribulation in abundance till he was tried to the utmost and justified. For when he was surrounded by Saul and sought among thousands he thought he was forsaken by God and could not believe the words which God spoke to him through the prophet Samuel, but rather said: I have been cast away from your countenance.

Thus it happens to all chosen godly people. The kernel must first die in each one before it becomes fruit. It must first be swallowed up in unbelief before God reveals himself in his mercy. Man must be justified and ground up before he becomes susceptible to the goodness of God. For God works in man with some sharpness according to his order so that man becomes aware of the working of God. To all this the Scripture testifies.

But everyone must have the eternal word in himself. Even if he knows what happened to Abraham, Isaac, and Jacob and all the elect friends of God about whom the Scripture speaks, it will do him no good. It concerns him too; he too must become one of their number and fulfill the work of justification, otherwise he remains like any other worldly person. Even if he knew the whole Bible it would be nothing but miracles and an illusion and no good to him or anyone else. But the man who surrenders himself to God as a sacrifice and renounces the world daily awaits the working of God. Even if he is overcome by unbelief and swallowed up in it God does not forsake him, for unbelief does not suspend God's faith and promise.

Since the word that one hears, believes, and accepts is not justified or tried it remains a witness to or the letter of the living Word. It is the opposite of the true Word like a drawn image for the sake of man. With this word the preachers deceive the poor people and point only to the witness that is preached and heard, and that one reads in books. They convince the people that it is the Word of God but the people remain for ever unsatisfied. It is evident that no improvement of life follows. O the boundless deception! With great irreparable injury the world will experience it.

The true inner Word is the eternal almighty power of God, of the same form in man as in God, which is capable of all things. It is given after perseverance in many tribulations in the discipline of the

Lord. John calls this the new commandment that is true in him and in you. Only Christ under the holy cross teaches this. According to the true order of God this Word is preceded by the outer word. The preacher is to admonish by means of the external word that one should surrender and listen to the internal teacher and not to allow the people to depend upon the outer word. Otherwise preachers, Scriptures, and words become idols. For they are only pictures, signs and instruments. They must disappear so that we are left without the image of the creatures as God also said to Moses.

Then man comes to the point where he confesses that Christ has come in the flesh. But this confession is not like that of the world which also confesses that Christ came in the flesh in Mary. That does no good because it is not enough to say that the Word became flesh and dwelt among us. Christ must also come into our flesh. Now man must confess that Christ has become flesh in him and that his flesh is ruled by the Word through the Holy Spirit. All worldly pleasure is renounced as Paul says: I live, yet not I but Christ lives in me. The world is crucified to me and I to the world. Whoever knows Christ thus may rightly boast that he has the inner Word and can truly testify to the truth. Such preachers we need and will await from God. All the others who come without this confession and who do not get beyond the shouting of the external sound come without Christ. He does not yet live in them as the whole world can see with seeing eyes. They are nothing but thieves and murderers. The whole world is full of such preachers and their associates. May God turn it all into good and may he protect all the miserable folk from them, for they do not preach God but their own belly.

The Old Testament, written as it is in the letter, is no different from the New, for its message comes through the creature in parables like the New. Insofar as it remains a witness, and is heard, read or preached as such it is all the Old Testament, commandment, law or Word, whether it be Moses or the prophets, the evangelists or the apostles, Peter or Paul. As John says: I give you no new commandment but the old one which you have had from the beginning. The old commandment is the Word which you have heard. On the other hand New Testament is that according to which we live, which is planted in our hearts through the spirit of God which is truly with us

146

and with God. It is all called New Testament, the new commandment or the living Word of God, whether Moses or the prophets or
the apostles have written it. It is called the New Testament if it lives
in us and rules us, and if through it we are born again in mind and
speech according to the will of God as God wants and desires it of us,
a new man in Christ Jesus.

7.3 Hans Hut, "A Christian Instruction," 1527, Müller, *Glaubenszeugnisse*, 36

Thus all judgments concerning Scripture and all the discourses
and commands of the Lord must be placed into this threefold
scheme and one part cannot be substituted for another in order to
understand. Thus the whole Scripture must be divided into three
parts[35] and one must always notice which part is being spoken about.
For in one place the Scriptures speak about the creatures which God
has made in whom the power and omnipotence [of God] is shown.
Through the pleasure and love of the creatures man is darkened and
becomes gross. The other two parts which must first be
comprehended must be separated from this.

There is first the Scripture that proclaims the cross and suffering, the means and the righteousness through which one comes to
the third part. That deals with right living according to the command of God. Thus the Scriptures must always be properly judged
and used in the right order of the three parts. If it speaks about the
means, then you must indicate why man suffers, wherein he has become guilty, and conclude by saying what its purpose is. But if the
Scripture speaks about the true godly life then one needs to know
how one arrives at it. This must be said even though there is nothing
about it at that particular place. Those who have the Spirit of God
judge all things.... Thus a truly taught preacher may judge accurately and know what he should preach and teach the people.

7.4 Leonhard Schiemer, "A Letter to the Church at Rattenberg," 1527, Müller, *Glaubenszeugnisse*, 45

Come together often. If you cannot all meet at once, let half
come, or even a quarter. When you read, read mostly in the New

Testament and the Psalms. You must know that God spoke to the Jews through Moses and the prophets in a hidden manner. But when Christ himself came, he and his apostles illuminated all things with a much clearer understanding. Christ said quite openly that the law and all the prophets are summed up in these two commandments: love God with your whole heart, and your neighbor as yourself.... Although it is good to read in the prophets and in the books of the kings and Moses it is not really necessary. One finds everything in the New Testament.

7.5 Melchior Hoffman, "Ordinance of God," 1530, Williams, *Spiritual*, 202-203

Therefore I warn all lovers of truth that they do not give themselves over to lofty arguments which are too hard for them, but that they hold themselves solely to the straightforward words of God in all simplicity. Do not quarrel and struggle much over words and take a piece somewhere out of God's Word and hold fast to it stubbornly and without understanding. Do not excoriate as lies all other words which are against it and thus abuse and make the apostles and the prophets along with the Holy Spirit of God into liars. For all words of God are of equal weight, also just and free, to him who acquires the right understanding of God and the Key of David. The cloven claws and horns [only] the true apostolic heralds can bear, because [to explicate] the Scripture is not a matter for everybody—to unravel all such involved snarls and cables, to untie such knots—but only for those to whom God has given [the power].

Who finds therein a lack, let him pray to God, as the apostle [James 1:5] teaches, and do not hurry or rush him. For to many in this day the Scripture will become a poison and eternal death, which nonetheless is in itself very good, because often it is misused without understanding, and leads the unwary and the willful into damnation and all who are without fear into abiding unbelief and damnation. And this is absolutely not the fault of Scriptures but the willfulness and misapprehension of the interpreters themselves.

7.6 "Conversation with Pfistermeyer," 1531, Haas, *Quellen*, 7, 12

The New Testament is more complete than the Old. The Old has been fulfilled and explained by Christ. What Christ has explained and helped us to understand, I will adhere to, since it is the will of his heavenly Father.

. . . .

I accept the Old Testament wherever it points to Christ. However, Christ came with a more exalted and perfect teaching. He showed his people a new covenant which they would need if their righteousness were to exceed that of the scribes and hypocrites.

7.7 Bernhard Rothmann, "Restitution," 1534, *SBR*, 221-222

The divine, unquestionably Holy Scriptures which are called the Bible alone have the fame that they are needful and sufficient for teaching, reproof, correction, and for instruction in righteousness, for which purpose also almighty God has given them, in order that the man of God be without error and equipped for every good work. Since the apostasy first began through human writing and teaching by means of which the divine Scriptures were darkened, the Almighty has among us provided that all writings both new and old which are not biblical should be destroyed [This is a reference to the destruction of all books in Muenster on March 15, 1534], so that we should cling only to the Holy Scriptures. We are minded, by the grace of God to hold to this, since God's actual will is sufficiently expressed in them. It is God's earnest command that we should not stray from them to the right nor the left in word and action. Christ himself points to the Scriptures that we should search them. Consequently we have nothing to do with what the ancient or modern scholars have written. We are not concerned about them but only with what we find in the same Holy Scriptures which is God's Word and will. To this we surrender ourselves by his grace with all necessary diligence. . . . For he who holds only to the Scriptures needs no other writings. Rather he will have enough to do with the

Scriptures and he will be abundantly taught by them about God as long as he approaches them with the right understanding. Yes, you say, how shall I understand the Scriptures correctly? I must have someone's interpretation, for of myself I cannot grasp it.... Peter says: No prophecy is a matter of one's own interpretation. Each one must be taught, but not through the written interpretation of men in glosses or postils. Rather God and his Spirit must be the master here. It may well be that sometimes I will consider the interpretation of man and grasp the understanding of the interpreter and then be able to speak about it in flowing words. However, since God's kingdom does not consist in words but in power, I will never achieve the power of the knowledge of God unless God's Spirit drives me with power, teaches me, and leads me into the Scriptures. As Christ says in John 16 [13]: When the Spirit of truth comes he will lead you into all truth.... But if you wish to understand the Scriptures correctly, very well, for this we will give you good advice. The content of the whole Scripture is briefly summarized in this: Honour and fear God the almighty in Christ his Son. This is the beginning of all wisdom. And in the same breath, that as Christ was obedient to the Father and fulfilled his will, we too should fulfill his will with trembling and quaking. Whoever understands this and proves it by his deeds is not blind but has understood the whole Scriptures. Now how men should honour and fear God and what his will is is so clearly expressed in the Scriptures that no glosses or interpretations are necessary. The fear of God is truly called the beginning of wisdom, and it is so in truth. For whoever fears God should not resist his words and not be faithless. Whoever believes, comes to the right understanding. He will grasp God's will through faith and carry it out in deed.... Thus God has restored the Scriptures among us. In them his will is abundantly known to us and we will adhere to them alone. And if we, with constant diligence, earnestly do what we understand we will daily be taught further by God. To him be praise, honour, glory, and thanks for it to eternity. Amen.

7.8   "Bern Colloquy" 1538, Haas, *Quellen*, 271-272, 273

Firstly, we acknowledge the law insofar as it agrees with the New Testament and is an announcement, witness, type or sign of

Christ, and that it is useful for the faithful in strengthening their faith. To that extent we grant it validity, for Moses himself witnessed to the prophet whom God would raise up and whom we should hear. It is valid insofar as it illuminates and reveals Christ. We are also satisfied with the way it deals with judicial matters and the punishment of evil and have nothing to criticize. But we do not find that Christ established and commanded the punishment of the body even to death. Instead he instituted the Christian ban....

. . . .

We confess that the Old Testament is a witness to Christ. Further we grant it validity wherever Christ has not suspended it and wherever it agrees with the New. We consider it right and good if it serves faith, love, and a good Christian life.

7.9   Menno Simons, "Foundation," 1539, *CWMS*, 159-160

We certainly hope no one of a rational mind will be so foolish a man as to deny that the whole Scriptures, both the Old and New Testament, were written for our instruction, admonition, and correction, and that they are the true scepter and rule by which the Lord's kingdom, house, church, and congregation must be ruled and governed. Everything contrary to Scripture, therefore, whether it be in doctrines, beliefs, sacraments, worship, or life, should be measured by this infallible rule and demolished by this just and divine scepter, and destroyed without any respect of persons.

7.10   Menno Simons, "Foundation," 1539, *CWMS*, 214

You say, we are inexpert, unlearned, and know not the Scriptures. I reply: The Word is plain and needs no interpretation: namely, Thou shalt love the Lord thy God with all thy heart, and with all thy soul, and with all thy strength, and thy neighbor as thyself. Mt. 22:37, 39. Again, You shall give bread to the hungry and entertain the needy. Is. 58:7. If you live according to the flesh you shall die, for to be carnally minded is death. The avaricious, drunkards, and the proud shall not inherit the kingdom of God. God will condemn adulterers and fornicators. Rom. 8; 1 Cor. 6, and many like passages. All who do not understand such passages are more like irrational creatures than men, more like clods than Christians.

7.11   Menno Simons, "Spiritual Resurrection," ca. 1536, *CWMS*, 57-58

As said above, every creature has the nature and disposition of that of which it is born, and is disposed in the same way as is the seed from which it comes. Therefore we will speak a few words concerning the nature, properties, and effects of the seed of the divine Word whereby we are begotten by God from his bride the Holy church, like unto his image, nature, and being, for where this seed is sown upon good ground into the heart of man, there it grows and produces its like in nature and property. It changes and renews the whole man, that is, from the carnal to the spiritual, the earthly into the heavenly; it transforms from death unto life, from unbelief to belief and makes men happy. For through this seed all nations upon the earth are blessed. Therefore, says James, Lay aside all filthiness and superfluity of naughtiness, and receive with meekness the ingrafted Word which is able to save your souls. It is also the pure, unadulterated milk whereby the young and newborn children of God are nurtured until they attain to a perfect man, unto the measure of the stature of the fullness of Christ. It is also strong food for the perfect and adult in Christ Jesus. In short, this seed of the divine Word is spiritual food whereby the whole man is nourished inwardly lest he perish and faint in the wild desert of this waste world, as all must do who do not gather daily the bread of the divine Word to satisfy their starving souls. For man shall not live by bread alone, but by every word that proceedeth out of the mouth of God. Therefore is he blessed who hungers after this heavenly bread and receives the ingrafted Word, for it will bring forth after its nature, in due time, an hundredfold. For, says the Lord, As the rain cometh down, and the snow from heaven, and returneth not thither, but watereth the earth, and maketh it bring forth and bud, that it may give seed to the sower and bread to the eater, so shall my Word be that goeth forth out of my mouth; it shall not return unto me void, but it shall accomplish that which I please.

Behold this is the nature, property, and effect of the seed of the Word of God. By it man is renewed, regenerated, sanctified, and saved through this incorruptible seed, namely, the living Word of God which abides eternally. He is clothed with the same power from above, baptized with the Holy Ghost, and so united and mingled with God that he becomes a partaker of the divine nature and is made conformable to the image of his Son, who is the first of the born again and of those who rose with him from the sleep and death of sin, henceforth to serve him, not in the oldness of the letter, but in the newness of the Spirit.

7.12   Pilgram Marpeck, "Judgment and Decision," 1542, *The Writings*, 357-359

I find that Christ, Moses, the prophets, and apostles used divine and biblical Scriptures in three ways. First, for teaching. What is used when one knows nothing of the witness of God and his Word is called teaching by all. The letter to the Hebrews mentions not repeating again those matters belonging to the beginnings of Christian life. If one is ignorant of something, the Scripture serves as guide and teacher.

Second, Scripture is used for admonition and warning to him who is already taught. This is the second function of Scripture, and it is especially important where an evil appearance, the leaves or blossoms which precede the fruit, leads to care or fear that there may in time not be good fruit. But from that no certain judgment of good or evil is possible. That function of Scripture, which is warning and admonition belongs here. The fifth book of Moses is almost all of this kind. That is why it is called the book of repetition or in Latin Deuteronomium. The same is true of the admonition and warning of the apostles to the churches throughout the New Testament.

Third, there are commandments and prohibitions. All the writings that announce punishment, wrath of God, and eternal damnation are directed at the transgression of commandments and prohibitions. Such punitive writings are at times used in the hope of repentance. In such punishment comfort is also offered in order that one does not sink into too much sorrow. But in case of apostasy and denial, they even deliver the sinner to the devil, denying him eternal life, as Paul did when he delivered several to the devil in body and soul.

Whoever does not use Holy Scripture with these three differences in mind cannot, with any certainty, handle Holy Scripture. And especially where the Holy Spirit, the true teacher, does not precede in all knowledge of Christ, everything will be misused and wrong when one tries to admonish, where one has not yet learned, or to punish, where there is no certainty of sin, or make sin, where there is no commandment. All that brings error.

7.13   Peter Riedeman, *Account*, 1542, 65-66

CONCERNING THE LAW

The law is the testimony or word which bears witness to the old covenant, that is the covenant of bondage, and is therefore called a yoke of bondage, doing nothing but driving, commanding and demanding, and yet on account of its weakness not able to give but only to demand and to require. For where the Spirit does not accompany the word, it is impossible to attain the righteousness that stands before God.

Nevertheless, it shows, points out and makes men conscious of sin; strikes, breaks and terrifies the conscience, that by so doing men might be moved to seek and ask for something better. Wherefore is the law our schoolmaster until we are in Christ, through whom the promise of the Father is poured out on all who believe in his name, which promise is the Spirit of grace through whom, if we suffer him to rule and lead us, we are set free from the law, as Paul says, "If ye walk in the Spirit, ye are no more under the law." Thus is Christ the end of the law; whoever believes in him is righteous.

Christ is not the end of the law, however, in that sense that God's law is done with and ceases, for Paul says, "Do we then make void the law through faith? God forbid, yea, we establish the law." Therefore the law, in so far as it is spiritual, is not made void, but its true spiritual nature is established and ordained and it is led to true

154

ulfillment and perfection in accordance with God's will by the Spirit
of Christ. Therefore it is only the law in so far as it is summed up in
writing, in the letter, which is done away with by Christ, because the
letter kills, for Christ has given us his Spirit, who performs within us
all that God wills with joy, and not from the coercion and force of the
commandment. Thus we are no more under the law, and yet we are
not without God's law. Now all that is expressed in words, in so far as
it is of the letter, whether it was written by Paul, Peter or any other
from among the apostles, we call law and command, for so it is. For
that letter, likewise, does nothing but kill, like the letter of the law of
Moses. In so far as it is spiritual, however, and treated and accepted
spiritually, it is a word of grace, even though written by Moses.
Therefore those who have not the Spirit of Christ cannot be servants
of the gospel, but only of the letter of the law.

7.14   Peter Riedeman, *Account*, 1542, 63-65

CONCERNING GOD'S COVENANT

God's covenant is an eternal covenant, which is from the beginning, continues in eternity and ceases not. It implies that it is his will
to be our God and Father, and that we should be his people and
loved children, and that he desires through Christ to fill us at all
times with every divine blessing and with all that is good.

That such a covenant of God was from the beginning is shown
in God's creating man in his own likeness, so that all was well with
him and there was none of the poison of destruction in him. Even
when man was deceived and robbed of this likeness by the counsel of
the serpent, the purpose of God endured none the less, and the
covenant which he had previously made—that he should be our God
and that we should be his people—expresses this clearly with a
promise, in that it threatens to take away the devil's power through
the woman's seed. From this it can well be seen and known that it
was God's intention to redeem us from this power and restore us and
accept us as his children.

Thus God has made his covenant firstly with Adam and then
also with Abraham and his seed, the latter with more definite words

155

than the former; and now he has made it with us through Christ and established and confirmed it through his death. For as a testament is not valid except through the death of him who makes it, even so did God give his Son in death, that we, redeemed from death through him, might be the children of his covenant and that the same might be ours eternally.

CONCERNING THE OLD COVENANT

The old covenant, in so far as it is called old, is that which was given to Israel without the pouring out of the Spirit of grace, for which reason also their obstinate heart was not circumcised and sin not taken from them as the apostle shows, "It is not possible that the blood of bulls and goats should take away sins." With this Esdras also agrees saying, "When you led the seed of Israel out of Egypt, you brought them up to the Mount Sinai, and bowing the heavens, you did set fast the earth, and made the earth to quake and the depth to tremble, and terrified the men of that age. And your glory went through four gates, of fire, of earthquake, of wind and of cold; that you might give the law unto the seed of Jacob and diligence to the generation of Israel. And yet you did not take away from them a wicked heart, that your law might bring forth fruit in them."

Now because the heart was not changed by all this, and the people remained the same old people, it was no testament of sonship, but one of servitude, as indeed Paul terms it, when he speaks of the two covenants in the terms of two women saying, The covenant from the Mount Sinai genders to bondage and is in bondage with her children.

Although it genders to bondage, yet is it the bringing in of something better and more perfect. Now, because something better is come, that is, the covenant of God is more clearly and perfectly revealed and come fully to the light, that which is dark and imperfect must cease and come to an end.

"Wherefore also Moses," says Paul, "put a veil over his face so that the children of Israel could not look to the end of that which ceases."

But that it ceases is testified by the apostle in that he says, "In that God promises a new covenant, he makes the first old. Now that which decays and waxes old is near its end." Not that God's covenant is finished and done with, but the imperfect revelation and darkness of the same is ended and ceases that the covenant itself might be revealed in its strength and clarity and brought to light, as has been done in Christ. Thus the apostle names the new better, because of the overflowing clarity of its revelation. Of which more later.

7.15　Peter Riedeman, *Account*, 1542, 67-68

CONCERNING THE NEW COVENANT

Since the old covenant comes to an end on account of its darkness and imperfection, God has established, revealed and brought to light a covenant that is perfect, that abides unchanged throughout eternity, as he has promised aforetime, "Behold, the days come, says the Lord, that I will make a new covenant with the house of Israel, but not according to the covenant I made with their fathers in the day that I took them by the hand to bring them out of the land of Egypt, because they continued not therein."

This covenant is a covenant of the grace, the revelation and the knowledge of God, as the Word signifies, "They shall all know me, from the least unto the greatest." This knowledge, however, comes alone from the receiving of the Holy Spirit. Thus the covenant of God is confirmed by Christ, sealed and established by the Holy Spirit, as is promised, "And it shall come to pass in the last days, saith the Lord, that I will pour out my Spirit upon all flesh; and your sons and your daughters shall prophesy, and upon my servants and upon my handmaids in those days I will pour out my Spirit."

This is the covenant of childlike freedom; of which we also are the children if we let ourselves be sealed by this covenant and submit and surrender ourselves to its working. As Paul also saith, "The law of the Spirit hath made me free from the law of sin and death." Now whom Christ thus makes free, is free indeed. Therefore Paul says, "Stand fast therefore in the liberty wherewith Christ hath made us free, and let not yourselves be entangled again with the yoke of bondage." For if you again let yourselves be led into the yoke of bondage, then you are led from the Spirit to the letter and Christ profits you nothing. For which reason those who have not the Spirit are not the children of this covenant.

7.16 Dirk Philips, "Spiritual Restitution," 1560; "The Church of God," 1562; Kolb/Klaassen, *Philips*, 325-326, 377-379

Christ Jesus is the spirit and the truth of all the figures that have passed away, the end and fulfillment of the law of figures, but the beginning of the true substance and completeness eternally (Jn. 6:63; 14:6; Rom. 10:4). In Christ Jesus, says the apostle, is genuine substance (Eph. 4:21). In him are hid all the treasures of the wisdom and knowledge of God (Col. 2:3). Indeed, in him dwells the fulness of the Godhead bodily, and all shadows and figures are fulfilled in him. He is the clear morning star (Rev. 22:16), the Sun of Righteousness (Wisd. of Sol. 5:6) that illuminates everything. The brightness of Moses' face (which glory was to be done away, and signified the law) (2 Cor. 3:7) is no glory at all beside the glory of Jesus Christ and his holy gospel. The veil that hid the face of Moses, and which still hangs over the eyes and covers the hearts of the Jews so that they cannot understand Moses and the prophets, is taken away by Christ, as Paul says (2 Cor. 3:16). Therefore all things are changed in Christ and are transfigured and made new by him, that is, changed from the letter to the Spirit, from the carnal to the real, from the old to the new, from the figure into the true abiding truth, and from the transitory to the eternal and heavenly. It is necessary to know this, in order that we may seek all truth, righteousness, holiness, salvation, yea all divine wisdom, gifts, virtues, powers and activity in Christ Jesus alone, and not from any other source (1 Cor. 1:21[24]; Jer. 23:5[6]; Eph. 1:8; Col. 2:3). All those will be made ashamed who in these last perilous times have so presumptuously and impudently set themselves up in great pride as though they were about to take possession of the kingdom and restore all things to order. This can never be done by any one but by the Lord Jesus Christ, who is the fullness of all wisdom, truth and righteousness. He has a name which is above every name (Phil. 2:9) that can be named in this world or in

158

the world to come, who is the Head of all principalities and powers. Briefly, by him all things are made and upheld, who with God does all things, and without whom nothing divine is performed.

· ·

Moreover the Word of God is known in two ways, the law and the gospel. The law is the word of command, given by God through Moses on Mount Sinai with such terrible voices and storms, thunder and lightning (Ex. 19:16-18) that the children of Israel could not bear it, but said to Moses: "You speak with the Lord, but let not the Lord speak with us, lest we die" (Ex. 20:19). Even Moses himself was afraid and trembled (Heb. 12:19). This shows the sternness of the law, for it reminds us of sin and condemnation, because it demands from everyone perfect righteousness in the inner man (Rom. 4:13-15; Deut. 4:1-6; 6:1-3; Mt. 19:17-21), the holiness of perfect human nature, exalted understanding full of the true knowledge of God, as well as a holy, pure heart that is fervent in love to God.

Moreover the law condemns the internal uncleanness, that is, the destruction and loss of the natural wisdom and knowledge of God and the righteousness and holiness which has been implanted in the heart (Ps. 51:12; Eph. 2:1). It condemns the wicked desires and tendencies that are contrary to the law of God. Whoever reads the law with unveiled face must be terrified and humbled at God's wrath (Rom. 3:20; 7:7; 2 Cor. 3:16; Ex. 20:19; Heb. 12:10) just as was Israel and even Moses himself, who are given to us as examples.

The law of God is given, not that it might bring to man perfect righteousness, salvation and eternal life (for by the deeds of the law shall no flesh be justified) (Rom. 3:20; Gal. 2:17[16]), but that, by revealing sin it might teach man to fear God, to know and humble himself under the mighty hand of God, and thus be prepared with penitent heart to accept Jesus Christ the only Saviour and to seek for and hope for salvation by his grace and merit alone (1 Pet. 5:6; 1 Tim. 2:6; Eph. 2:13; Acts 14:14, 15:3).

The law teaches the knowledge of sin and such knowledge brings the fear of the Lord, which is the beginning of all wisdom (Rom. 7:7; Ecclus 1:16; [Prov. 1:7]), and without which no man may be justified. The fear of the Lord produces a broken and contrite and humbled heart, which is acceptable to God (Ps. 51:19[17]).

Therefore the law contributes to the new birth, in view of the fact that no one can be born again or made spiritually alive, nor can anyone believe the gospel, except he first sincerely repents, as the Lord Jesus Christ himself testifies. For he first taught the people repentance, and then faith, and so he also commanded his apostles to do (Mt. 3:2; Lk. 24:46[47]).

The gospel is the word of grace. It is the joyful message of Jesus Christ the only begotten Son of God, the only Redeemer and Saviour (1 Tim. 2:5; Tit. 1:15 [2:14]), who gave himself for us that we might be ransomed from the power of Satan, sin, and eternal death. He has made us children and heirs of our heavenly Father, to be a royal priesthood (Gal. 1:4; Heb. 2:15; Rom. 8:14; Eph. 1:5), a holy nation, a chosen people, and a possession of God in the Spirit (1 Pet. 2:9). . . .

This is the true gospel, the pure teaching of our God, full of grace and mercy, full of comfort, salvation and eternal life. It is given to us by God's grace without any merits of our own or the works of the law, for the sake of our only and precious Saviour Jesus Christ. He became subject to the law for our sakes, and became the fulfillment of the law to eternal salvation for all believers, if we accept it in true faith.

For further reading:

"The Anabaptist Interpretation of the Scriptures," *MQR*, Apr. 1966 issue.
Beachy, *Grace*, 140-142.
Estep, *Anabaptist Story*, 140-145.
Keeney, *Dutch Anabaptist*, 31-42.
Klaassen, *Anabaptism*, 37-47.
Klassen, *Covenant and Community*, 57-148.
Ozment, *Mysticism*, 103-115, 125-132.
Henry Poettcker, "Menno Simons' View of the Bible as Authority," Dyck *Legacy*, 31-54.
John C. Wenger, "The Biblicism of the Anabaptists," Hershberger *Anabaptist Vision*, 167-179.
_____, "An Early Anabaptist Tract on Hermeneutics," *MQR* XLI (January 1968), 26-44.
_____, *Even Unto Death*, 57-78.

Wilhelm Wiswedel, "The Inner and the Outer Word: A Study in the Anabaptist Doctrine of Scripture," *MQR* XXVI (July 1952), 171-191.

John H. Yoder, "The Hermeneutics of the Anabaptists," *MQR* XLI (October 1967), 291-308.

VIII

Baptism

Not surprisingly this is one of the longest chapters. For the whole matter of the beginning of the Christian life as well as its nature focused on baptism. Moreover, baptism was the external act by which Anabaptists expressed their rejection of the sacramental church of Rome and the territorial churches of Protestantism. Their view of baptism also touched on questions of original sin, predestination and free will, and eschatology.

At the most fundamental level baptism was viewed as a sign that the old life of sin had been abandoned and a new life of following Christ begun. This was done voluntarily and after careful consideration. It was assumed by all that man had the capacity to respond to God's call. Also universal was the view that baptism was the rite by which one entered the church. Most Anabaptists regarded the Christian life as communal life; all Christians were members of one body. Therefore baptism also involved the acceptance of the process of discipline, of mutual aid both spiritually and materially. Commitment to the "rule of Christ" (Mt. 18:15-18) was necessary since the reality of sin even in the church was taken for granted.

In addition to this baptism was also the sign of belonging to God's elect in the Hut and Melchiorite traditions. They believed themselves to be chosen by God to carry out his vengeance upon the godless at the time of the end.

In several selections (8.4, 8.9) we encounter the teaching about the threefold baptism, the inner baptism of the Spirit, water baptism, and the baptism of blood. The baptism of blood was the experience of tribulation and suffering. For Hubmaier and most Anabaptists

162

this meant persecution. For Hut, however, it meant also, and more importantly, the experience of desolation and tribulation that each person encounters as he is liberated from dependence on all external things. It is a baptism, says Hut, that all the righteous from the beginning of the world have experienced. This view is part of the tradition of the German mystics which came to Hut through Thomas Müntzer.

A number of the selections contain discussions of original sin. Its reality in terms of total depravity is rejected by all. Most writers, however, recognize a tendency to sin which merely awaits the dawn of the knowledge of good and evil to begin its destructive work. At that point repentance and faith become necessary. Before that children are saved without repentance and without baptism by the grace of God. Ulrich Stadler sounds the old note that sin is transmitted from parents to children in the act of procreation (8.13).

Melchior Hoffman's statement in 8.12 about the necessity of administering baptism only to adults deserves special attention. Baptism "is the sign of the covenant of God, instituted solely for the old, the mature, and the rational, who can receive, assimilate, and understand the teaching and preaching of the Lord." Few statements by Anabaptists put such a strong emphasis on knowing, reasoning, and understanding as conditions for becoming a Christian.

It is also in connection with the discussions of baptism that we get forays into early church history to explain that infant baptism did not belong to the apostolic era but was an invention of later years (8.1, 8.2, 8.16). Anabaptists tried to establish their case for rejecting infant baptism not only on scriptural evidence which pointed to the baptism of adults, but also by appealing to history. It may be that this appeal became necessary because the New Testament does not explicitly forbid infant baptism, an argument used against them frequently. If it could be shown that it was a development of later centuries, their case was made, and the scriptural silence explained.

In the sixteenth century adult baptism, as the Anabaptists practiced it, was viewed as an act of schism and even sedition. Anabaptists were often compared to Donatists. The old imperial Roman law providing the death penalty for rebaptism was invoked against them, and became the legal basis for prosecuting them.

8.1   Conrad Grebel, "Letter to Müntzer," 1524, Williams, *Spiritual*, 80-81

On the matter of baptism thy book pleases us well, and we desire to be further instructed by thee. We understand that even an adult is not to be baptized without Christ's rule of binding and loosing. The Scripture describes baptism for us thus, that it signifies that, by faith and the blood of Christ, sins have been washed away for him who is baptized, changes his mind, and believes before and after; that it signifies that a man is dead and ought to be dead to sin and walks in newness of life and spirit, and that he shall certainly be saved if, according to this meaning, by inner baptism he lives his faith; so that the water does not confirm or increase faith, as the scholars at Wittenberg say, and [does not] give very great comfort [nor] is it the final refuge on the deathbed. Also baptism does not save, as Augustine, Tertullian, Theophylact,[36] and Cyprian have taught, dishonoring faith and the suffering of Christ in the case of the old and adult, and dishonoring the suffering of Christ in the case of the unbaptized infants. We hold (according to the following passages: Gen. 8:21; Deut. 1:39; 30:6; 31:13; and 1 Cor. 14:20; Wisd. of Sol. 12:19; 1 Pet. 2:2; Rom., chs. 1; 2; 7; 10 [allusions uncertain]; Mt. 18:1-6; 19:13-15; Mk. 9:33-47; 10:13-17; Lk. 18:15-17; etc.) that all children who have not yet come to the discernment of the knowledge of good and evil, and have not yet eaten of the tree of knowledge, that they are surely saved by the suffering of Christ, the new Adam, who has restored their vitiated life, because they would have been subject to death and condemnation only if Christ had not suffered; but they're not yet grown up to the infirmity of our broken nature—unless, indeed, it can be proved that Christ did not suffer for children. But as to the objection that faith is demanded of all who are to be saved, we exclude children from this and hold that they are saved without faith, and we do not believe from the above passages [that children must be baptized], and we conclude from the description of baptism and from the accounts of it (according to which no child was baptized), also from the above passages (which alone apply to the question of children, and all other Scriptures do not refer to children), that infant baptism is a senseless blasphemous abomination, contrary to all Scripture, contrary even to the papacy; since we

164

find, from Cyprian and Augustine, that for many years after apostolic times believers and unbelievers were baptized together for six hundred years, etc.

8.2 "Confession of Wolfgang Ulimann," 1525, Fast, *Quellen*, 379

He believes concerning baptism what his heavenly Father taught him. Christ, after he had fulfilled the will of his Father, commanded his disciples to teach, believe, and baptize. That was obeyed about two hundred and a few years to the times of Cyprian and Tertullian. These men admitted small sick children and those who could say the "Our Father" to baptism, and baptized them at the time of Easter and Pentecost. After that followed Augustine and Theophylactus, and baptism was administered more and more according to human wisdom and not according to Scripture. The marks of those who are baptized are death to sin, and living in Christ, in constant obedience to him.

8.3 Balthasar Hubmaier, "The Sum of a Christian Life," 1525, Westin, *Quellen*, 111-112

Third: After man has inwardly and in faith surrendered himself to the new life he confesses it openly and externally before the Christian church into which he allows himself to be inscribed according to the order and establishment of Christ. In doing so, he indicates to the Christian church, that is to all the sisters and brothers who live in the faith in Christ, that he has been so taught inwardly in the Word of Christ and that he is so minded, that he has already surrendered himself according to the Word, will, and rule of Christ to live henceforth for him, to regulate all his actions according to him, to fight under his flag unto death, and to allow himself to be baptized with external water in which he publicly confesses his faith and intention: namely, that he believes that he has a gracious, good and merciful God and Father in heaven through Jesus Christ, and that in this he is well satisfied. He has also decided and already inwardly given his intention that from this time on he will change and improve his life, and that he confess this openly in the reception of the water. Also [he agrees] that he will henceforth not besmirch the name of Christ with open and scandalous sins and that he commits himself and surrenders himself in brotherly admonition according to the order of Christ. Mt. 18.

Fourth: Since however a man knows and confesses that by nature he is a bad and poisonous tree and that in himself he cannot produce any good fruit, this commitment, consent and open witness does not take place in human power or ability, for that would be human presumption, but in the name of God, Father, Son, and Holy Spirit, or in the name of Our Lord Jesus Christ, that is in the grace and power of God. From all of this follows that the external baptism of Christ is nothing other than an open witness of the inward commitment with which man publicly testifies before everyone that he is a sinner and that he regards himself as guilty. But he also believes fully that Christ has forgiven him his sin through his death and that through his resurrection he has made him just before the face of God, our heavenly Father. Therefore he has also become willing from now on openly to confess faith in the name of Jesus Christ before everyone and has committed himself and decided to live from now on according to the word and commandment of Christ, not from human ability in order that he be not like Peter, for without me you can do nothing, says Christ, but in the power of God, the Father and Son and Holy Spirit. Now man breaks out in word and deed, announces and magnifies the name and praise of Christ in order that others through us may become holy and blessed as indeed we through others who preached Christ to us also have come to faith in order that the kingdom of Christ may be increased.

8.4   Balthasar Hubmaier, "A Short Justification," 1526, *Armour*, 53

I confess three types of baptism:[37] that of the Spirit given internally in faith; that of water given externally through the oral confession of faith before the church; and that of blood in martyrdom or on the deathbed. Christ spoke of the latter in Luke

166

12[:50-53], and he also told of the spiritual wine and oil which the Samaritan poured into the wounds of the injured man (Lk. 10[:34]). John names these three baptisms with which all Christians must be baptized "the three witnesses on earth" ([1] Jn. 5[:8]). Whoever will cry to God with Christ, "Abba Father, dear Father," must do so in faith and must also be baptized with Christ in water and suffer with him in blood. Then he will be a son and heir of God, a coheir with Christ, and will be glorified with Christ (Rom. 8[15-17]). Thus, no one should be surprised at persecution or suffering, for Christ had to suffer to enter into his glory (Lk. 24[:46]). And Paul writes that all who want to live godly lives in Christ Jesus will suffer persecution (2 Tim. 3[:12]). This is the third or last baptism in which one is to be anointed with the oil of the holy and comforting gospel by which we are made pliable and ready for suffering. Thus is our sickness healed and we receive forgiveness of sins (Jas. 5[:13-15]).

8.5   Balthasar Hubmaier, "A Christian Instruction," 1526-1527, Davidson/Klaassen, *Hubmaier*, 281-283

Leon: What do you desire subsequent to faith? *Hans:* Baptism in water. *Leon:* How many kinds of baptism are there? *Hans:* Three. *Leon:* Which? *Hans:* The baptism of the spirit; the baptism in water; a baptism in blood. *Leon:* What is the baptism of the spirit? *Hans:* It is an inward enlightenment of our hearts, caused by the Holy Spirit through the living Word of God. *Leon:* What is water baptism? *Hans:* It is an outward and public testimony to the inward baptism of the spirit. A man makes it by receiving the water, when in the sight of all he acknowledges his sins. He also testifies hereby that he believes in the pardon of those sins through the death and resurrection of our Lord Jesus Christ. He then allows himself to be outwardly marked, enrolled, and incorporated into the community of the church by baptism. This is in accordance with the behests of Christ. Thus man publicly and orally makes his pledge to God before the church in the strength of God the Father and the Son and the Holy Spirit, that henceforth he will believe and live according to the divine Word.

And if he should err therein he will submit to fraternal punishment according to the order of Christ (Mt. 18). That is the proper baptismal vow which was lost for the space of a thousand years. In the meantime Satan with his monastic vows and priests' oaths has pressed in and taken his seat in the holy place. *Leon:* What is the baptism of blood? *Hans:* It is the daily mortification of the flesh even unto death.

8.6   Balthasar Hubmaier, "A Form for Baptism," 1526-1527, *Armour*, 43

In receiving water baptism, the baptizand confesses publicly that he has yielded himself to live henceforth according to the rule of Christ. In the power of his confession he has submitted himself to the sisters, the brethren, and the church, so that they now have the authority to admonish him if he errs, to discipline, to ban, and to readmit him.... Whence comes this authority if not from the baptismal vow?

8.7   Michael Sattler, Schleitheim Confession, 1527, *Legacy*, 36

I. Notice concerning baptism. Baptism shall be given to all those who have been taught repentance and the amendment of life and [who] believe truly that their sins are taken away through Christ, and to all those who desire to walk in the resurrection of Jesus Christ and be buried with him in death, so that they might rise with him; to all those who with such an understanding themselves desire and request it from us; hereby is excluded all infant baptism, the greatest and first abomination of the Pope. For this you have the reasons and the testimony of the writings and the practice of the apostles. We wish simply yet resolutely and with assurance to hold to the same.

8.8   Hans Denck, "Recantation," 1527, Fellmann, *Denck I*, 109

Baptism is the enrollment in the fellowship of believers. This does not mean that all who are baptized believe in God, but that they are all regarded as believers in so far as it is possible to recognize this. Thus infant baptism is contrary to the command of Christ for in the infants it is not possible to tell which one is a Jacob and which one is an Esau, a matter which a servant of Christ should primarily test according to his ability to know such things.

Infant baptism is a command of men and free to the Christian. It does no harm to any believer if he has been baptized in infancy and God does not demand any other baptism as long as that order is maintained which is proper for a Christian congregation. If that is not the case, I do not know what God will do. Whoever now is baptized again let him see to it that he does not serve before he has been employed. For whoever has not been called and sent to teach he undertakes in vain to baptize. For this reason I, God willing, will cease forever to baptize until such time as another call comes to me from God.

What I have done has been done; what I desire to do will not harm anyone. The zeal for the house of God has sent me out and has called my understanding back home again. To do right in the house of God is always good, but not everyone is commanded to preach to and persuade others.

8.9   Hans Hut; 1527, Schornbaum, *Quellen*, 43

Baptism has three parts,[38] that is Spirit, water, and blood. These three are one and witness upon the earth. Firstly, the Spirit is the assurance in and surrender to the divine Word that a man will live according to what the Word proclaims. This is the covenant of God which God makes with them through his Spirit in their hearts. Secondly, beyond that God has given them the water as a sign of the covenant. In this one indicates and confesses that he wishes to live in true obedience towards God and Christians and to live a blameless life. And whoever transgresses and does not live right and acts against God and love, he is to be chastised by the others with words. That is the ban about which God speaks. It is to be a witness before the church. The third is blood which is the true baptism which Christ shows his disciples when he says that they are to be baptized with the baptism which witnesses to the whole world when a disciple's blood is spilt. This is what he holds concerning baptism since he has understood it.

8.10   Hans Hut, "The Mystery of Baptism," *Armour*, 83-84

The [outer] baptism which follows preaching and faith is not the true reality *(wesen)* by which man is made righteous, but is only a sign, a covenant, a likeness, and a memorial of one's dedication, which [sign] reminds one daily to expect the true baptism, called by Christ "the water of all tribulation." It is through this baptism that the Lord makes one clean, washing and justifying him of all fleshly lusts, sins, and impure works and life.

Man knows that no creature can justify *(rechtfertigen)* itself and achieve its final nature *(wesen)* without man to whom it is subject. In the same way, no man can justify himself and reach his end *(end)*, i.e., come to salvation, except through the work of God in the baptism of all tribulation. . . .

Thus the water of all tribulation is the true essence and power of baptism, whereby one sinks into the death of Christ. Nor was this [true] baptism first instituted at the time of Christ. It has been since the beginning, and every elect friend of God from Adam on has been baptized in it, as Paul says.

Christ also accepted this covenant from God at the Jordan and testified thereby that, obedient to the Father, he would manifest love toward all men for an example, even unto death. Thereafter, he found the baptism of all tribulation poured over him by the Father in great profusion.

Therefore, the sign and the essence *(wesen)* of baptism must be sharply distinguished. The Christian church gives and administers the sign or the covenant of baptism through a true minister, as Christ received it from John. Thereafter follows the true baptism which God gives, first through the water of all tribulation, and second in the comfort of the Holy Spirit. God lets no one be swallowed up in this baptism. As it is written, He leads into hell and out again, He kills and makes alive again. Since even the Lord had to be baptized with this baptism, whoever wants to be His disciple must be baptized in the same way.

8.11   Hans Schlaffer, "A Short and Simple Admonition," ca. 1527, Müller, *Glaubenszeugnisse*, 100-101

You child baptizers say that when a child dies without baptism it is lost and will never see God. Show me, I ask you, one single letter of proof for this in the Holy Scriptures.

Christ says about the children that the kingdom of heaven is theirs or of such, and that whoever receives one of them receives him. They belong to him. Whatever you do to the least of these my own, says the Lord, you have done it to me. Now if they are his, the dear little children are not lost. Never!

Secondly, you exorcise and cast the devil out of the children before you baptize them. Eternal God! How do you know that the child only just born in all innocence is possessed by the devil? Let me advise you that it is of the utmost urgency that you cast the devil out from yourselves. He has knocked your bottoms out so that no one can ever fill you. Then things would soon be better and the strife[39] could easily be settled. Take note that the Lord says concerning the children that their angels always see the face of their Father in heaven. Now if the children have angels that always see the face of God, it is impossible that they have a devil who is excluded from the face of God. That is why they are called children of their Father in heaven. God will not tolerate that his children should be possessed of the devil.

Thirdly, you charge us Anabaptists as you call us that we attribute too much to baptism and that we believe that no one may be saved without baptism. To this we say no. If someone believes it or says so it is contrary to the words of Christ. Listen to a simple brother, dear lords and child baptizers, and let me ask you a question. Tell me, which is more important, faith or baptism? You will doubtless answer, faith is more important. Further, may one be saved by faith without baptism? I guess you would say yes to that

171

too. After all, Christ says: whoever does not believe is condemned. He says nothing about water baptism, and the reason is that it is an external thing to which salvation or the kingdom of God is not bound.

I ask further: will baptism without faith save? Clearly your answer will be no. But just a moment. You say that baptism takes away original sin in which the child is conceived in its mother's womb and born.

Again, they say that the child will be saved because of someone else's faith. God knows what your faith or someone else's faith is in which the child is baptized. To which I say, or rather not I but Christ: your faith has made you whole. It is your own and not someone else's faith. Whoever believes and is baptized, it says. That is, whoever believes for himself, he shall be baptized. For baptizing on someone else's faith is as if Abraham believed and was therefore a Christian, whereas Isaac his son was baptized as an heathen and remained a heathen.

Show me with witness of the Scriptures that baptism is necessary because of original sin. Whenever there is talk of original sin and that original sin condemns children because they are children, you quote to me the passage: behold, in sin was I conceived and in evil did my mother conceive me, etc.

But examine the words closely: he says I was conceived in sin not which I did, but which my mother did. He speaks only about conception at which stage the child is not yet a child but only the seed which cannot sin.

8.12   Melchior Hoffman, "Ordinance of God," 1530, Williams, *Spiritual*, 186-188; 192-193

And it is further the order and command or law of the Lord for his apostolic emissaries, according to which they have also in fact instructed, called, and admonished the people, requiring and urging through the gospel and the Word of God that they also who have surrendered themselves to the Lord should lead themselves out of the realm of Satan and from the kingdom of darkness and from this

172

world and that they should purify themselves and lead themselves
into the spiritual wilderness and also wed and bind themselves to the
Lord Jesus Christ, publicly, through that true sign of the Covenant,
the water bath and baptism. This to the end that ever thereafter they
should remain obedient to, and follow the will and pleasure of, the
Father, the Son, and the Holy Spirit and that their own will, life,
desire, spirit, and passion be wholly slain, allowed to be quiescent,
and allowed to die out, and that henceforth they live solely in the
Spirit, and the mind, and the will and from the wisdom of God and
the eternal Word of life, as a true bride, obedient to her dear spouse
in all things, yea, [mindful of] his will and pleasure without any
transgression or vacillation. In like manner also baptism and dying
[to this world] were alluded to or portrayed in the Red Sea through
which the Children of Israel were baptized and deadened [to this
world] and covenanted with the divine Majesty under the semblance
of a pillar of cloud, as also the holy apostle [1 Cor. 10:2] clearly indicates.

And all of this was well acknowledged in the words of the Lord
Jesus Christ [Mt. 28:19] as being a reference to the right ordinance of
God and of his faithful following. And they have also taught and
been taught and received all knowledge of Jesus Christ and wish to
have him for Lord, King, and Bridegroom, and bind themselves also
publicly to him, and in truth submit themselves to him and betroth
themselves to him through the covenant of baptism and also give
themselves over to him dead and crucified and hence are at all times
subject, in utter zeal, to his will and pleasure. That is then such a true
and certain covenant as takes place when a bride with complete,
voluntary, and loving surrender and with a truly free, well-
considered betrothal, yields herself in abandon and presents herself
as a freewill offering to her lord and bridegroom.

Such a bride will no longer live unto herself, neither in darkness
nor in the old Adam; again, neither of what is of the world nor what
might be called of the world, but rather solely of the Lord Jesus
Christ. In this manner also Saint Paul cries [Gal. 2:20]: I live, yet not
I, but Christ liveth in me. They are the true "dead" who have the
true salvation and liberation from sin, who are purified of all
misdeeds through the blood of Jesus Christ, who have their life in

173

Christ Jesus—all who are dead to themselves in the Lord, having routed out and laid aside the old Adam and having, through baptism, taken and put on the new Adam Christ Jesus; [all who] having crucified the old Adam with the urges and desires (who is not at leisure and rests from all sins and who must rest from all his works). And that sinful seed, being dead, cannot make unrighteousness fruitful, for he who has been born of God has the upper hand and victory, and therefore no sin can issue.

They therefore who have now in truth put on Christ Jesus through faith and in baptism in such a way that they are in Christ Jesus and Christ Jesus in them—in them there is nothing more to be condemned. The law has no sovereignty over them any more, because they live unto righteousness and no longer unto sin. Therefore the law cannot make them guilty, nor like a mirror show up blemishes and spots, because they are pure and live no more according to the flesh but according to the Spirit and have been found unpunishable before the judgment seat of God.

. . . .

Such aforesaid promises, such an ordinance—this is the content of that high covenant of God and of the Lord Jesus Christ. It is the sign of the covenant of God, instituted solely for the old, the mature, and the rational, who can receive, assimilate, and understand the teaching and the preaching of the Lord, and not for the immature, uncomprehending, and unreasonable, who cannot receive, learn, or understand the teaching of the apostolic emissaries: such are immature children; such also are bells which toll for the dead, and churches, and altars and all other such abominations. For nowhere is there even a letter in the Old or the New Testament in reference to children. And there is absolutely no order enacted by the apostles or Jesus Christ nor have they taught or written a single syllable about it. And also it has not been discovered that they ever baptized any child, nor will any such instance be found in all eternity!

For that alone was enjoined upon them by Christ Jesus their Lord, namely, to baptize the nations who accept their word and preachment of the crucified Christ Jesus and give themselves over to him of their own free will. To such as these belongs the covenant and baptism. Thereafter, only that should be taught by our apostles

174

which the Lord has commanded them and otherwise nothing. It is for this that Saint Paul also says [Rom. 15:18]: I dare say nothing unless Christ hath wrought the same by me. Thus now let every teacher and servant of the Lord hold to him and teach nothing more than he was taught by God and proceed according to this rule. Then it will go very well with him, and thus many countless souls will not be done to death by these blind leaders, who so very brazenly, without any fear, spit in the face of God Almighty, crucify the Son of God, and then tread upon him with their feet. O how heavily will such a one be visited by God with stern wrath and be tormented and made to pay with the eternal unending zeal of the Fire of the Almighty!

Accordingly, all human notions are sternly forbidden by the Lord, and pedobaptism is absolutely not from God but rather is practiced, out of willfulness, by anti-Christians and the satanic crowd, in opposition to God and all his commandment, will, and desire. Verily, it is an eternal abomination to him. Woe, woe to all such blind leaders who willfully publish lies for the truth and ascribe to God that which he has not commanded and will never in eternity command. How serious a thing it is to fall into the hands of God and willfully to mock and desecrate the Prize of God the Highest! Yea, all who do this will be stricken with heavy, great, and eternal blindness, and they will inherit the eternal wrath of God. For God is the enemy of all liars, and none of these inherits or has a part in his kingdom. Their inheritance and portion is rather eternal damnation.

8.13   Ulrich Stadler, "Several Pleasant, Comforting Epistles," "Müller, *Glaubenszeugnisse*, 228-229

Original sin is that all of us, Adam's children, are by nature children of wrath, made in vice, conceived in sin. What is born of the flesh is flesh. As someone says: we are assailed by what is in us, that is the lust of the flesh out of which we were born in lust.

If man had remained pure and good as he was created by God, impregnation would have occurred without lust and evil concupiscence. That is not the way it is now. But now God winks at our ruined bodies in the nuptial act for the sake of the children and does not charge those who do it in fear and discipline with the act. God's spirit groans in all the children of God that man is so ruined, and that this act, which is not advisable for everyone (for it is not given to everyone), cannot be carried out purely as the blessing of God, to be fruitful and multiply, without evil lust. To put it briefly: original sin is the defect which all flesh, born of Adam, has inherited. That is, that all the imagination and the thinking of the human heart is only evil from youth onwards. The Lord himself testifies to it and our own experience bears it out that our flesh is evil, malignant and lustful, destroyed and ruined by lust. By itself it is capable only of sinning against God in disobedience according to its will and lust. For this reason also death rules over all flesh born of Adam, and is its recompense.

8.14   Pilgram Marpeck, "Confession," 1532, *The Writings*, 129-130

In the New [Covenant], the children are pronounced holy without baptism, without sacrifice, without faith or unfaith; they are simply received by Christ, although Paul says: "Without faith no man can please God." Children and the retarded are not required to believe or disbelieve these words, but those who are born from the knowledge of good and evil into the innocence and simplicity of faith are required to believe. The witness of God and Christ belongs to the process of becoming like children; but human understanding, all fleshly pretension, deceit, and desires are to be crucified with Christ and, through baptism and confidence in the future life, they are buried into the death of Christ. Here reason is again included in faith in the true sonship of Christ. Christ has accepted the children without sacrifice, without circumcision, without faith, without knowledge, without baptism; he has accepted them solely in virtue of the Word: "To such belongs the kingdom of heaven." That is the difference between the children and understanding. And even if the children were referred to here, it would not follow that they should

176

be baptized, or that they should be sacrificed in baptism, but that they should be left in the order into which Christ put them.

8.15   Bernhard Rothmann, "Confession of Faith," 1533, *SBR*, 149-150

We have already said what it means to baptize, namely to dunk in water. That is the natural understanding. Now we want to examine what Christian baptism is, for not all dunking in water is the baptism of Christ. For although this natural baptism may be called baptism, it is not the Christian understanding that whatever is dunked in water is baptized. A Christian baptism is that which takes place according to the commandment and order of Christ. Thus if we want to discover what Christian baptism is we have to discuss why Christ commanded it and in what way it is to be used. For it is not the work itself but the understanding and meaning of the work that is valid. It is a small thing to be put in the water, indeed it is of no value to the soul that the dirt of the flesh is washed away. For the certain knowledge of a good conscience, the putting off of the old man, sin, and lust, and the determination to live henceforth in obedience to God are necessary to salvation. This is what is promoted in baptism. . . .

Baptism, as the apostles write about it and had already used it is to take place with this intention. Those who are baptized shall confess their faith in it. In the power of this faith they are to put off the whole old man and to be inclined henceforth to live a new life. Thereupon everyone to be baptized shall receive baptism, that with a certain knowledge of a good conscience he is renewed and born again through the Holy Ghost, and to forsake and die to all unrighteousness and all the works of darkness. According to this, baptism is the burial of the old man and the resurrection of the new, a gate and entry into the holy church and a putting on of Jesus Christ. Whenever the believer (and no one else can do it) in baptism sincerely forsakes the old sinful life and accepts the new in Christ Jesus, baptism is like a betrothal of the believer to Christ. It means that, cleansed from all sin, he surrenders himself to Christ and pledges to live and to die according to his will.

8.16   Confession of Endres Keller, 1536, *Quellen: Bayern* II, 198-200

Just look at the wretched situation of the present time. The child, which cannot yet pray, is said to blaspheme God, and that God will not leave that blasphemy unavenged. I very much fear that the end is approaching. This is what Daniel referred to when he prophesied (9.26) concerning the desolate abomination which will usurp the holy place. Christ himself tells us about it (Mt. 24:[15]), as well as Paul, Peter and John. All of them warn us against mere human teaching, especially Paul in Colossians 2[8], Thessalonians 2 (2 Thess. 2:3), Timothy chapter 6 (1 Tim. 6:3), and Peter chapter 2 (2 Pet. 2:1). They depict this time so vividly that one cannot fail to recognize it; the problem is we don't want to.

You will have to admit that the popes are responsible for this wretched situation. One can plainly see it, and no one can deny that there was no infant baptism in the time of the apostles, and that they baptized no children. Had they baptized children, it would be so recorded in Scripture. Infant baptism cannot be defended from Scripture even if Luther and the pope say so. . . .

Now it follows that if the pope's command to baptize children is legitimate, God is a liar. Moreoever it implies that God did not tell us all we needed to know. It can never be true that God is a liar. You yourselves will no doubt agree that it is much better that all men be liars, but that God remain true. For he remains eternally just and truthful.

If the pope's command is legitimate, it follows further that all the children who lived from the death of the apostles to the time of the popes Eugenius[40] and Nicholas[41] would be condemned, since it was Nicholas who confirmed infant baptism. God opens the eyes of the heart, and such a one confesses the truth. Now tell me, if the apostles baptized children, why would one pope establish infant baptism and another confirm it? Rather the first would have confirmed it instead of establishing it. Anything that one establishes did not exist earlier. Consider carefully, and you will have to agree. . . . Thus it must follow that no apostle baptized a child, regardless of whether Luther and all other teachers say it. It would also follow that the Holy Spirit was a liar, that he did not tell the apostles about baptizing infants, but rather first told the pope.

The Holy Spirit chides the popes for claiming to be a god on earth and for accepting divine homage. Such claims are contrary to all Scripture and a great evil. I believe it is the pope about whom Paul writes to the Thessalonians (2 Thess. 2:4) that he will take his seat in the temple of God and claim to be God. It is all described there so clearly, it is as though one saw it. Tell me, which pope did not add to his empire while he was pope? How many popes kept faith with the pious emperors? Certainly, if you are able to see the matter correctly you will not be able to continue your evil deeds against me. Of a hundred popes not one really kept faith with the emperor, as you can read in many books.

Tell me, where did the first pope come from? You will say: from Peter. I don't believe that Peter ever saw Rome. But if Peter had been involved in such affairs, he would be like Annas and Caiaphas and worse, for he would be teaching contrary to the gospel. However, one cannot believe it. Was not Sylvester the first pope to receive jurisdiction over Rome? I am not quite sure of myself here, but judge approximately. Of course, you must not base your judgment on the chronicles which were produced by the popes themselves. That would be like allowing my opponent in a court action to speak the sentence. You will need to go to a reliable book.[42] There you will find that the pious emperor Constantine first gave Rome to Sylvester. However, he lived long after the time of the apostles; I estimate over 300 years later.

8.17   "Bern Colloquy,"1538, Haas, *Quellen*, 351

Paul writes in Col. 2: you are circumcised with the circumcision made without hands. That is not the circumcision of the heart as Moses says. Paul also calls the circumcision of the heart the circumcision of the sinful life. It is therefore not proved that circumcision is a figure of baptism. Rather it points to the putting off of the sinful life of the flesh. I say the same thing about the sign and seal of the covenants. In the old covenant the circumcision of the flesh was a seal and sign of the covenant of promise as God said: every male not circumcised on the eighth day shall be exterminated from among the

179

people. Similarly with the seal of baptism in the new covenant. Here no eight-day limit is set but whoever believes and is baptized shall be saved. Therefore whoever has remorse and sorrow for his sins and repents, he shall be baptized for the forgiveness of his sins. . . .

8.18   Peter Riedeman, *Account*, 1542, 56-57

CONCERNING ORIGINAL SIN

Just here often arises very much quarreling and strife, for the one wants this and the other that; from which strife comes more destruction than betterment, for since God is not a God of quarreling but a God of peace and of love, he has no pleasure in strife, neither has he anything to do with the same, hence there is nothing therein save destruction.

Now, therefore, we confess and teach that all men save Christ only have a sinful nature which they inherit from Adam, as it is written, "The imagination and desire of man's heart is evil from his youth." David says likewise, "Behold I was shapen in iniquity; and in sin did my mother conceive me." Paul speaks clearly, and says, "By one man sin entered into the world and passed upon all men." Because then it has come upon us all from him, it is thereby clear that we have inherited it from him.

WHAT ORIGINAL SIN IS

But the inheritance that we all have from our father, Adam, is the inclination to sin: that all of us have by nature a tendency toward evil and to have pleasure in sin. This inheritance manifests and shows itself in all the children of Adam—all who are born after and according to Adam—and removes, devours and consumes all that is good and of God in man; so that none may attain it again except he be born again.

This inheritance Paul names the messenger of Satan, who strikes him on the head or buffets him with fists, and speaks thereby of the movement of the sinful inclination which stirs in him, as in all men. Therefore John also says, "He who says he has no sin, deceives himself, and the truth is not in him," and speaks thereby of the

180

inheritance which we all have from Adam, which he calls sin; as also David says in the Book of Psalms: "In sin was I conceived and born." Thus through Adam we have all become sinful and must be justified once more through Christ, if we would have life with him.

8.19   Peter Riedeman, *Account*, 1542, 77-78

CONCERNING THE BAPTISM OF CHRIST AND OF HIS CHURCH

Now because it is a testament of the recognition, knowledge and grace of God, baptism is also, according to the words of Peter, the bond of a good conscience with God, that is, of those who have recognized God. The recognition of God, however, comes, as has been said, from hearing the word of the gospel. Therefore we teach that those who have heard the word, believed the same, and have recognized God, should be baptized—and not children.

For since all who are born in the human way inherit from Adam his nature and partake of his fellowship, that is, of sin, therefore Christ, who was to take away sin and destroy its strength and power, had a quite different beginning of his birth, as is said above. Thus, those who are to inherit his nature, share his fellowship and become members of his body must also be born of him, not in the human way but in the Christian way, which birth comes about through the Word, faith and the Holy Spirit. For whosoever receives the Word in faith, becomes God's child, as also John declares, "As many as received him, to them gave he power to become the sons of God, even to them that believe on his name; which are born, not of blood, nor of the will of the flesh, nor of the will of man, but of God." Therefore, also, Paul says, "They are not the children of God who are children according to the flesh, but the children of the promise are counted for seed."

Since then we must be born of God, and are children of Christ and not of Adam, we must consider carefully how the birth of Christ came to pass, which, as we have said above, took place in faith through the working of the Holy Spirit. Now, whosoever is to be born of his nature and character must also be born of God that he

181

may be his child, together with Christ, as also Peter says, "Being born again, not of corruptible, but of incorruptible seed, namely of the word of truth."

This birth, however, takes place in this wise. If the Word is heard and the same believed, then faith is sealed with the power of God, the Holy Spirit, who immediately renews the man and makes him live (after he had been dead in sin) in the righteousness that stands before God, so that the man is formed a new creature, a new man after God's likeness, or is renewed therein. Thus, whosoever is born in this wise, to him belongs baptism as a bath of re-birth, signifying that he has entered into the covenant of the grace and knowledge of God.

Therefore we teach that as Abraham was commanded to circumcise in his house, even so was Christ to baptize in his house, as the words that he spoke to John indicate, "Suffer it to be so, for thus it becomes us to fulfill all God's righteousness." Now, just as Abraham could not circumcise in his house before the child was born to him, now all his seed after him, neither can anyone be baptized in the house of Christ unless he be first born of Christ through the Word and faith. But he who is born in this manner, is baptized after he has confessed his faith. History has proved, likewise, that all the apostles also did this, and we follow them.

8.20   Pilgram Marpeck, "Admonition," 1542, *The Writings*, 197-198

Baptism is an immersion or sprinkling with water desired by the one who is being baptized. Baptism is received and accepted as a sign and co-witness that he has died to his sins and has been buried with Christ; henceforth, he may arise into a new life, to walk, not according to the lusts of the flesh, but obediently, according to the will of God. Those who are thus minded, and confess this intent, should be baptized. When that is done, they are correctly baptized. Then, in their baptism, they will certainly attain forgiveness of sins and thereby, having put on Jesus Christ, they will be accepted into the communion of Christ. The one who is thus baptized experiences this communion, not through the power of baptism, nor through the

182

word that is spoken there, and certainly not through the faith of the godfathers, the sponsors; as his fleshly lusts depart and he puts on Christ, he experiences it through his own knowledge of Christ, through his own faith, through his voluntary choice and good intentions, through the Holy Spirit.

8.21   Pilgram Marpeck, "Defence," Loserth, *Marbeck*, 192

God has created man to be indestructible and according to his image. Death, however, has come into the world through envy and the spite of the devil (Wisd. 2:[24]). To sum up the Scriptures say: I have found that when God made man he made him upright (Eccles. 7:[29]).

Therefore flesh and blood in and of itself cannot be sin. Rather it is a good creation of God and became a dwelling of sin only after or through the sin of Adam as Paul indicates when he says that no good thing dwells in his flesh (Rom. 7:[18]). He means not that flesh and blood are sin but that they are the dwelling of sin which came in, was born and became rooted in the flesh in the fall of Adam and Eve through the serpent the devil. Even as today the mind of the true believer may be moved from the simplicity of faith in Christ through the serpent, so the serpent with his instant cunning seduced Eve to eat from the forbidden fruit. Adam followed and thus the mind of both was moved from its created innocence. . . . Thus their human flesh was ruined and became a dwelling of sin by the entry of sinful lusts and appetites. . . .

Were flesh and blood in and of itself sin, the flesh and blood of the blessed virgin Mary, the mother of the Lord Jesus, indeed the flesh and blood of Christ himself . . . yes and the flesh of John the Baptist, the prophets, apostles, and all the saints would also be sin. How then could they be saved? Indeed, how could any single man today or in all eternity be saved if flesh and blood were sin? And how could a man get rid of his sin or separate it from his flesh or cleanse his flesh from sin if it were sin itself, the wages of which is eternal death which follows? Then also the error would follow that in the resurrection the godly would be clothed with another flesh to their eternal joy and not the flesh with which they have been clothed in this time.

8.22 Dirk Philips, "Christian Baptism," 1564, Kolb/ Klaassen, *Philips*, 22-24

From all this it is now evident that the apostles first taught the people and preached the gospel. Those who amended their life and believed the gospel (Mk. 16:15) were, upon confession of their faith, baptized by them. Hence it is incontrovertible, both according to the ordinance and institution of the Lord, and the custom of the apostles, that teaching the gospel must precede baptism. From the teaching come repentance and faith. The true, penitent faith must be confessed, proved, and sealed, so to speak, in Christian baptism. Moreover after Christian baptism must follow a consistent, good, and pious Christian life. This is the true order of the Lord Jesus Christ and the custom of the apostles.

[He quotes Romans 6:3-7]

With these words the apostle makes known what Christian baptism signifies to believers, namely, the dying of the flesh, or the putting to death of the old Adam, the burial of sin (Col. 2:11), the putting away of the body of sin, and resurrection into a new life. Christ died and was buried for our sins, and was raised again from the dead for our justification (Rom. 4:25). We are, in the first place, made members of the body of Christ by faith and therefore become partakers of his death, his righteousness, and his holiness, indeed, of all that is his. We have also been established in this fellowship with him by baptism, called into it by the grace of God. We must therefore also for his sake die to sin, bury the same, and live in righteousness in the Spirit, that we may be his true members.

. . . .

Inasmuch as infants know, understand and possess nothing of all that baptism signifies or that belongs to it, baptism is not for them, nor is it necessary for them, because faith, a right understanding, and essence of the sacrament are lacking. Therefore the sign does not follow. Those who are marked by this sign confess that one

184

is baptized in Christ Jesus and into his death in order to be buried, and rise to a new life with him. Where this does not take place in and through baptism, and following that there is no life in true power, baptism has not been rightly received, although the outward sign is there.

8.23 Dirk Philips, "Christian Baptism," 1564, Kolb/ Klaassen, *Philips*, 43-45

That the kingdom of heaven belongs to the children we believe without a doubt, as we have already declared. But that the salvation of children lies in their baptism and is bound to it we do not believe and cannot concede. For Christ accepted the children, and promised them the kingdom of heaven through grace and mercy, and not because of baptism. He neither baptized them nor commanded them to be baptized but laid his hands on them and blessed them.

Christ also makes it sufficiently plain to us why children are acceptable to God, inasmuch as he sets forth the children as an example to us, and moreover admonishes us that we should become like them. For he speaks thus to his disciples: "Truly, I say to you, unless you turn around and become as the children, you will not enter the kingdom of heaven. Whoever now humbles himself as this child, he is the greatest in the kingdom of the heavens." (Mt. 3:4; 19:14).

Since therefore Christ sets the children before us as an example and says that we should become like children, and humble ourselves, it follows without contradiction: first, that children (so long as they are in their simplicity) are innocent and judged by God to be without sin; second, that there is still something good in children (although they have become partakers of the transgression and sinful nature of Adam), namely, a simple, unassuming, and humble bearing, which makes them pleasing to God (yet purely by grace through Jesus Christ) so long as they remain in it. For this reason also Christ sets children before us as an example that we should in these respects become like them.

But many presumptuous people dispute about the salvation of children, and by such disputation make themselves fools in the sight

185

of the Lord, no matter how wise and intelligent they may be considered by the world. They dispute and babble much about the salvation of infants, but they give no thought to what concerns themselves and is most necessary, namely, to learn simplicity and humility from the children as Christ admonishes us.

Since therefore children are saved, are in God's hand, and are included in his grace, the kingdom of heaven is theirs (Mt. 19:14). It is therefore a great folly to baptize infants that they may thereby be preserved and saved, and to damn those infants who die unbaptized. This is openly belittling and slandering the grace of God and the merits of Jesus Christ. For since through Jesus Christ the sin of Adam, indeed of the whole world, is atoned for and taken away (Jn. 1:29), how can infants be damned on account of the sin of Adam, since no sin can be imputed to them except that which comes from Adam? Indeed, who will charge it to the children, for whom Jesus Christ shed his precious blood? Who would condemn the children to whom the Lord in his unfathomable grace and mercy has promised the kingdom? (Mt. 19:14). Who can repudiate the Holy Scripture which so explicitly declares that the sin of Adam (Rom. 5:18) and of the whole world is taken away? The handwriting which was against us has been blotted out and nailed on the cross (Col. 2:14), so that grace triumphed over sin, and life has conquered death through Jesus Christ, our Lord and Saviour. Therefore no one may blame or condemn children because of original sin, without betraying the death, blood, and merit of Jesus Christ. If the infants must be condemned because of Adam or on account of his transgression (Rom. 5:19[18]), then Jesus Christ died in vain for them, and the guilt which came upon us from Adam is not paid by Jesus Christ. Moreover, grace has not triumphed over sin, and life has not overcome death through Jesus Christ. That cannot be! The Scripture stands firm and immovable, and may never be broken (Rom. 5:19; Tit. 2:11; 1 Tim. 2:6), since it witnesses so definitely of the great and saving grace of God, which he has so richly and abundantly shown to mankind through Jesus Christ. The apostles are faithful and true witnesses of God who testify so clearly that all of the curses of men, and the sin of the whole world has been taken away by Jesus Christ (Rom. 8:1; Gal. 3:13).

Hence we conclude with the apostles and the entire Holy Scripture, that original sin has been paid for and taken away by Jesus Christ to the degree the children may not be judged and condemned on account of Adam's trangression (Gen. 6:5; 8:21). We conclude that the tendency of the nature of children is toward evil; but that does not damn them. By the grace of God it is not accounted as sin to them. As long as they are simple and without the knowledge of good and evil, they are pleasing and acceptable to God through Jesus Christ. But why should many words be necessary? It is true and indubitable that children as well as adults—the children by their simplicity, the adults by their faith—are saved by the grace of our Lord Jesus Christ (Acts 15:11).

8.24   Menno Simons, "Foundation," 1539, *CWMS*, 124-125

Dear sirs, friends, and brethren, awake and do not linger. Render to the Most High the praise and honor due him and give ear to his holy Word, for those who maintain that the baptism of irrational children is a washing of regeneration do violence to the Word of God, resist the Holy Ghost, make Christ a liar and his holy apostles false witnesses. For Christ and his apostles teach that regeneration, as well as faith, comes from God and his Word, which Word is not to be taught to those who are unable to hear or understand, but to those who have the ability both to hear and to understand. This is incontrovertible.

The holy apostle Peter also declares the same and says that even baptism doth also now save us, not the putting away of the filth of the flesh, but the covenant of a good conscience with God by the resurrection of Jesus Christ.

Here Peter teaches us how the inward baptism saves us, by which the inner man is washed, and not the outward baptism by which the flesh is washed. For only this inward baptism, as already stated, is of value in the sight of God, while outward baptism follows as an evidence of obedience which is of faith. For if outward baptism could save without the inward, then the whole Scriptures which speak of the new man would be spoken to no purpose. The kingdom of heaven would be bound to ordinary water; the blood of Christ would be shed in vain, and no baptized person could be lost. Oh, no, outward baptism avails nothing so long as we are not inwardly renewed, regenerated, and baptized with the heavenly fire and the Holy Ghost of God. But when we are the recipients of this baptism from above, then we are constrained through the Spirit and Word of God by a good conscience which we obtain thereby, because we believe sincerely in the merits of the death of the Lord and in the power and fruits of his resurrection, and because we are inwardly cleansed by faith. In the spiritual strength which we have received, we henceforth bind ourselves by the outward sign of the covenant in water which is enjoined on all believers by Christ, even as the Lord has bound himself with us in his grace, through his Word, namely, that we will no longer live according to the evil, unclean lusts of the flesh, but walk according to the witness of a good conscience before him.

8.25   Menno Simons, "Reply to Gellius Faber," 1554, *CWMS*, 684-685

The Scriptures clearly testify that God promised Abraham the multiplying of his seed, and the land of Canaan as an eternal inheritance, and in this way it was commanded him that he should circumcise himself, his son Ishmael, etc., also all male children of eight days; for it was a covenant in the flesh. And similarly the blood-sign of the circumcision of the foreskin, on the eighth day of their age, of all the male children and not the female children, etc., was commanded to believing Abraham at the promise of the multiplication of his seed and the possession of the land of Canaan. But to us the blood-sign of circumcision is not commanded, but baptism in the water. Note the first difference: not on the eighth day, but when we, through the service of the Spirit, in faith, are born of God, and have become followers of Abraham. Observe the second change: not only the males, but both males and females; they who through the preaching of the holy Word bury the old life of sin and with Christ arise in newness of life; they who are pricked in their hearts; they who circumcise their minds and hearts; they who put on Christ, and who have the testimony of a clear conscience before God. Observe the third change: not to possess a literal kingdom and land, and to become a great people upon the earth, as was promised to Abraham and his seed. Rather, for the sake of the Word and its witness to bear all manner of anxiety, distress, and misery upon earth; to turn the heart away from all visible and perishable things; to die unto pomp, pride, the world, flesh and blood, and thus to walk in our weakness as Christ has walked in his perfection.

For further reading:

Armour, *Baptism.*
Beachy, *Grace*, 100-116.
Clasen, *Anabaptism*, 95-105.
Estep, *Anabaptist Story*, 150-175.
Vincent G. Harding, "Menno Simons and the Role of Baptism in the Christian Life," *MQR* XXXIII (October 1959), 323-334.
Keeney, *Dutch Anabaptist*, 74-88.
Littell, *Church*, 83-86.
Gerhard J. Neumann, "The Anabaptist Position on Baptism and the Lord's Supper," *MQR* XXXV (April 1961), 140-148.
Oyer, *Lutheran Reformers*, 78-83.
Hillel Schwartz, "Early Anabaptist Ideas About the Nature of Children," *MQR* XLVII (April 1973), 102-114.
Wenger, *Even Unto Death*, 71-75.

IX

The Lord's Supper

Anabaptists rejected the complex of doctrine and drama which characterized the Roman Mass as a sacrament. Because the Mass was at the very heart of Roman Christianity, this rejection was sufficient to brand Anabaptists as heretics. In Roman eyes it was tantamount to denying Christ and therefore Christian faith. Anabaptists indignantly refused to acknowledge as Christian what they considered a manipulation of Christ and his sacrifice, often for human gain.

Anabaptists equally rejected the Protestant discussion about the nature of the presence of Christ in the bread and wine. They regarded such a discussion as totally beside the point, and switched the discussion to a consideration of the presence of Christ in the "body" of believers, for which there was clear scriptural warrant. The presence of Christ was viewed, not as sacramental, but expressing itself in the exercising of the "rule of Christ" and in ethical and moral terms.

All strands of Anabaptism give evidence of a twofold interpretation of the Supper. It was, on the one hand, a remembrance of the love of Christ which expressed itself in dying for his own. Jesus and his sacrifice were the foundation of Christian life and of the church.

On the other hand, the Supper was seen as a celebration of the oneness and unity of the church brought about by Christ's death. The body of Christ, understood by Anabaptists in a very literal sense as the visible community of believers, was the presence of God in the world. The new peaceful, reconciling community was reality. The Supper was a joyous recognition of that fact. Both Riedeman (9.13) and Philips (9.14) repeat the parable from the Didache (9) about the wheat and the grapes scattered far and wide, coming together into

190

one loaf and one cup.[43] The bread and wine were therefore signs of unity as well as signs of sacrifice. The themes of sacrifice and unity[44] were also combined. Even as Christ had given himself for them without reservation, so participation in the Supper signified a readiness on the part of all to give spiritual and material aid without grudging, and even life itself, for the sisters and brothers.

The dependence of some Anabaptists on concepts borrowed from German mysticism has been alluded to frequently. Here it is interesting to note the kinship of Hoffman's allegory-like discussion of the Supper with the Latin mysticism of figures like Bernard of Clairvaux.

9.1 Conrad Grebel, "Letter to Muntzer," 1524, Williams, *Spiritual*, 76-77

The Supper of fellowship Christ *did* institute and plant. The words found in Matthew, ch. 26, Mark, ch. 14, Luke, ch. 22, and 1 Corinthians, ch. 11, alone are to be used, no more, no less. The server from out of the congregation should pronounce them from one of the Evangelists or from Paul. They are the words of the instituted meal of fellowship, not words of consecration. Ordinary bread ought to be used, without idols and additions. For [the latter] creates an external reverence and veneration of the bread, and a turning away from the inward. An ordinary drinking vessel too ought to be used. This would do away with the adoration and bring true understanding and appreciation of the Supper, since the bread is nought but bread. In faith, it is the body of Christ and the incorporation with Christ and the brethren. But one must eat and drink in the Spirit and love, as John shows in ch. 6 and the other passages, Paul in 1 Corinthians, chs. 10 and 11, and as is clearly learned in Acts, ch. 2. Although it is simply bread, yet if faith and brotherly love precede it, it is to be received with joy, since, when it is used in the church, it is to show us that we are truly one bread and one body, and that we are and wish to be true brethren with one another, etc. But if one is found who will not live the brotherly life, he eats unto condemnation, since he eats it without discerning, like any other meal, and dishonours love, which is the inner bond, and the bread, which is the outer bond. For also it does not call to his mind Christ's body and blood, the covenant of the cross, nor that he should be willing to live and suffer for the sake of Christ and the brethren, of the Head and the members. Also it ought not to be administered by thee.[45] That was the beginning of the Mass that only a few would partake, for the Supper is an expression of fellowship, not a Mass and sacrament. Therefore none is to receive it alone, neither on his deathbed nor otherwise. Neither is the bread to be locked away, etc., for the use of a single person, since no one should take for himself alone the bread of those in unity, unless he is not one with himself—which no one is, etc. Neither is it to be used in "temples" according to all Scripture and example, since that creates a false reverence. It should be used much and often. It should not be used without the rule of Christ in Matthew 18:15-18, otherwise it is not the Lord's Supper, for without that rule every man will run after the externals. The inner matter, love, is passed by, if brethren and false brethren approach or eat it [together]. If ever thou desirest to serve it, we should wish that it would be done without priestly garment and vestment of the Mass, without singing, without addition. As for the time, we know that Christ gave it to the apostles at supper and that the Corinthians had the same usage. We fix no definite time with us, etc.

9.2   Balthasar Hubmaier, "The Sum of Christian Life," 1525, Westin, *Quellen,* 113-114

Fifth: After we have clearly known the unspeakable goodness of God in faith out of the Word of God we should be thankful to God for it that he has so fervently loved the world, that he has not spared his only Son, but has given him for us all into death. Yes, the death of the most shameful cross in order that we could be saved. Thus Christ Jesus, our Saviour, has ordered and instituted a beautiful remembrance in his Last Supper in order that we should not forget him. For when he and his disciples were eating one with another he took bread and gave thanks and said: "Take and eat, that is my body which is given for you. This do in remembrance of me." In the same manner also he took the cup and gave them all to drink and said: "Take and drink. This is my blood, which is poured out for you for the forgiveness of sins. Do this in remembrance of me." Here you must see clearly that the bread is bread and the wine wine as other bread and wine, but nevertheless thus instituted by Christ to an admonition and a remembrance that as often as we break the bread with another, distribute it and eat it, that we remember in faith his broken body given for us on the cross. Thus one can see clearly that the bread is not the body of Christ, but only a remembrance of the same. Similarly, the wine is not the blood of Christ, but also a remembrance that he has shed his blood on the cross for the cleansing from sin for all those who have faith even as the sign before the inn is not the wine, but a sign of the same. For it behooves us to remember what Christ has done for us, to announce it loudly and to be eternally thankful for it. Thus Paul earnestly admonishes us when he writes to the Corinthians, 1 Corinthians ch. 11: As often as you eat bread (notice: he calls it bread and it is bread) and you drink the cup, that is the wine (notice: it is wine that men drink), you should announce the Lord's death until he comes. Notice, he says: Until he comes. Thus we hear that he is not here, but that he will come at the hour of the last judgment in his great majesty and glory openly as the lightning flashes from east to west.

From this follows and we clearly learn that the Last Supper is nothing else than a remembrance of the suffering of Christ, who has given his body for our sake and shed his red blood on the cross for the cleansing of our sins. And out of this Supper we have until now made a bear's mass,[46] decorated it with mumbling and bumbling and sold it for a great deal of money and still continue to do so, alas. Whoever now observes the Supper of Christ in the fashion described and regards the suffering of Christ in firm faith, the same will also thank God for this grace and goodness and will surrender himself to the will of Christ, which is what he has done for us. We also now should make our life, body, material goods and blood available to the neighbour. That is the will of Christ.

9.3 Balthasar Hubmaier, "A Christian Instruction," 1526-1527, Davidson/Klaassen, *Hubmaier*, 295-297

Leon: What is the Lord's Supper? *Hans:* It is a public token and testimony of love, in which one brother pledges himself to another before the church. Just as they are now breaking bread and eating with one another, and sharing the cup, so each will offer up body and blood for the other, relying on the power of our Lord Jesus Christ. They are mindful of his sufferings, when they break the bread and share the cup and the Supper, and show forth his death till he come. That is the loving duty of the Supper of Christ which one Christian fulfills toward another so that every brother may know what good he can expect from the other. *Leon:* Is not the bread the body of Christ and the wine his rose-coloured blood as the sayers of the Mass have told us hitherto? *Hans:* By no means. Bread and wine are only memorial signs of the suffering and death of Christ for the pardon of our sins through the institution of Christ on Maundy Thursday. On that day he had determined to go forth and show the greatest of all the signs of love, the sacrifice of his flesh and blood for our sakes, even unto death on the next day. This was by our forefathers called Good Friday (a caritate) that is, from love. Let me say at once: the Supper is a sign of brotherly love to which we are obliged, just as baptism is a vow and token of faith. The water concerns God; the Supper concerns our neighbour. Thereon hang all the law and the prophets. No other rites has Christ enjoined upon us and left behind him on earth. He who teaches these two signs aright, teaches faith and love aright.

9.4 Michael Sattler, "Trial," 1527, Williams, *Spiritual*, 140

Secondly, that the real body of Christ the Lord is not present in the sacrament, we admit. For the Scripture says: Christ ascended into heaven and sitteth on the right hand of his heavenly Father, whence he shall come to judge the quick and the dead, from which it follows that, if he is in heaven and not in the bread, he may not be eaten bodily.

9.5 Michael Sattler, Schleitheim Confession, 1527, *Legacy*, 37

III. Concerning the breaking of bread, we have become one and agree thus: all those who desire to break the one bread in remembrance of the broken body of Christ and all those who wish to drink of one drink in remembrance of the shed blood of Christ, they must beforehand be united in the one body of Christ, that is the congregation of God, whose head is Christ, and that by baptism. For as Paul indicates, we cannot be partakers at the same time of the table of the Lord and the table of devils. Nor can we at the same time partake and drink of the cup of the Lord and the cup of devils. That is: all those who have fellowship with the dead works of darkness have no part in the light. Thus all who follow the devil and the world, have no part with those who have been called out of the world unto God. All those who lie in evil have no part in the good.

So it shall and must be, that whoever does not share the calling of the one God to one faith, to one baptism, to one spirit, to one body together with all the children of God, may not be made one loaf together with them, as must be true if one wishes truly to break bread according to the command of Christ.

9.6 Hans Denck, "Recantation," 1527, Fellmann, *Denck* I, 109-110

The Lord Christ took the bread in the Supper, blessed it and broke it. This was as if he meant to say: I have told you before that you should eat my flesh and drink my blood if you wish to be saved and indicated that this was to be done in a spiritual sense and not as flesh and blood understand it. Now I am emphasizing the same thing again here, how you ought to regard this bread and wine. For as this bread is the support of the physical life when it is broken and chewed, so also my body will support the life of your souls through the power of God as it is given, chewed and spiritually eaten, that is, as it is known and believed.

Again as this wine makes the heart of man fresh and glad, so also my blood which in the love of God I shed for you. If you so regard it, it will refresh you, make you joyful and fervent in love, so that you become completely one with me, and that I remain in you and you remain in me even as the food and drink are united with the nature of man.

9.7 Hans Schlaffer, "A Pleasant Letter of Comfort," 1527, Müller, *Glaubenszeugnisse*, 109

The body of Christ is the faithful community of Christ. Whoever eats of this bread in the Supper of the Lord, testifies that he desires to have fellowship with and to participate in all things with the body of Christ. That is, he commits himself to the community in all things, in love and suffering, wealth and poverty, honour and dishonour, sorrow and joy, death and life, indeed, that he is ready to give life and limb for the brothers, as Christ gave himself for him. Similarly with the cup in the blood of Christ: whoever drinks of this cup has first surrendered himself and testifies with it that he is prepared to pour out his blood for the sake of Christ and his church insofar as faith and the test of love demands it.

Whoever gives his body and pours out his blood as indicated, he does not give his own life nor spill his own blood, but rather the body and blood of Christ. For we are members of his body, indeed of his flesh and bone, says Paul. For this reason also Christ said to Paul when he called him on the way to persecuting the Christians: Saul, Saul, why do you persecute me? It is as if the Lord said: why do you kill my body and spill my blood? Thus it is among the true Christians. If one among them suffers, they all suffer since they are all members of one another and of Christ the head. Thus also the head always suffers the most. Thus the Lamb has been slain from the beginning of the world and will thus be persecuted and killed. For as many of us as partake of the one bread and the one cup are all one bread and one body.

This is the test in which a man must persevere. Is he ready to be thus minded toward Christ the head and all his brothers and sisters as his members? Is he ready to be one member of this body and to remain and persevere to the end in all things that concern this body?

And this means discerning the body of Christ. But whoever eats and drinks alone has fellowship with Judas who also ate and drank with the other disciples from the bread and cup of the Lord. But he did not wish to participate in the common brotherly love but went and sought his own gain and sold the Lord.

9.8 Attributed to Jörg Volk, 1528, Schornbaum, *Quellen*, 84

He taught that the flesh and blood of Christ was not changed into bread.... It must be understood spiritually. The bread which he broke was the gospel. If he had not broken it, it would not have come into the whole world. When they have the Word, receive it, and hide it in their hearts as Christ taught, they are receiving the body of Christ spiritually. The cup which Christ gave to his disciples means his suffering. The blood in the cup is the blood of Christ in the body of man. If a man is a Christian he has the blood of Christ. If suffering in the body comes, the cup is in the blood.

9.9 Melchior Hoffman, "Ordinance of God," 1530, Williams, *Spiritual*, 193-195

When now the bride of the Lord Jesus Christ has given herself over to the Bridegroom in baptism, which is the sign of the covenant, and has betrothed herself and yielded herself to him of her own free will and has thus in very truth accepted him and taken him unto herself, thereupon the Bridegroom and exalted Lord Christ Jesus comes and by his hand—the apostolic emissaries are the hand—takes bread (just as a bridegroom takes a ring or a piece of gold) and gives himself to his bride with the bread (just as the bridegroom gives himself to his bride with the ring) and takes also the chalice with the wine and gives to his bride with the same his true bodily blood, so that just as the bride eats a physical bread in her mouth and drinks the wine, so also through belief in the Lord Jesus Christ she has physically received and eaten the noble Bridegroom with his blood in such a way that the Bridegroom and the outpouring of his blood is [one] with hers—and the broken and crucified Christ Jesus. She [is] in him and, again, he is in her, and they together are thus one body, one flesh, one spirit, and one passion, as bridegroom and bride.

Yea, more. The bride is in truth assured the moment she takes the bread that she has accepted the true Christ for her Lord and Head and eternal Bridegroom in order that ever thereafter his will, spirit, mind, and good pleasure may be in her and that she on her part give herself over unto his will with all her heart, spirit, feeling, and will. It was in this sense that the disciples of our Lord Jesus Christ also ate when he sat bodily with them and they received him also bodily with the bread, as the bride receives the bodily bridegroom with the ring, that he in her and she in him may be one spirit, will, and mind. Moreover, a member and a bride of the Lord may well say, when she receives the bread, takes, and eats thereof, that she has bodily received, enjoyed, and eaten her Lord Jesus Christ, that the bodily Christ, who sits at the right hand of God, is in truth bodily her own and again that she is bodily his, yea with flesh and blood. And the two are thus one, and two in one flesh. While she has her house, habitation, tabernacle, and dwelling in Christ, for his part Jesus Christ has in her complete authority, sovereignty, habitation, and dwelling. Therefore Saint Paul writes to those of Corinth [1, ch. 11:28] that they should search themselves and prove whether Christ had his dwelling in them.

. . . .

It was surely in this sense that the apostles of the Lord Jesus Christ likewise understood the words when the Lord took the bread and gave therewith his body and with the wine his own quickening blood. [They also surely understood] that he did not for this reason corporally exist in the bread, and that the physical bread was not he himself, that his blood was not in the wine, nor did the wine become his physical blood. Instead, [they understood] that through the bread and belief in the Word they should receive that body which sat by them there, that that same body should be their own which would be burned at the cross. And [they believed] that theirs also was the physical blood which would be poured out from the cross. Such a simple explanation stolid fisherfolk could well understand even when they were still in the first birth, but one over which the wise and greatest scholars of Scripture for their part have become fools and madmen, and still are. They clash and break themselves over such simple words which were said and enacted in a quite straightforward way as by any other human being.

9.10 Pilgram Marpeck, "Confession," 1532, *The Writings*, 148

Fourthly, in the commemoration of the body of the Lord, a testimony for us to his death, the believers and baptized are to remind one another to be mindful of such love and of his new and eternal commandment. He is the first among them; he died and was given for us for the sake of love in order that we might live eternally. He commanded that we love one another as he loved us, and he goes on to point to death as the culmination of his love: no one has greater love than he that stakes his soul on behalf of his friend. That is why Paul commands the proclamation of the death of the Lord until he comes. In this bond of love, the Lord keeps his own in the unity of faith, which is the fellowship of the saints. In this fellowship, forgiveness and remission of sins through the Holy Spirit are practiced. He gives the life of the resurrection from the dead, an eternal life. In this commemoration, according to the practice of Christ, bread and wine are used as a parable of the mystery of Christ's body and blood, as a spiritual food which is eaten in faith and not in bread and wine. According to the opinion of Martin Luther and others, he would be of little use to us in bread and wine. Whoever thus eats of his body and drinks of his blood has eternal life through this Spirit who brings to life. And whoever walks among this people of God and true Israelites with an uncircumcised heart, the same shall be rooted out from among the people, that is to say, from the remembrance of the Supper of our Lord Jesus Christ.

9.11 Bernhard Rothmann, "Confession of Faith," 1533, *SBR*, 176-177

The Last Supper of Christ is a loving gathering and a common eating and drinking of those who believe in Christ, which was commanded by Christ to be observed to his remembrance. For this purpose the Last Supper was established and commanded by Christ and for no other as the evangelists, Paul, and also the ancient teachers testify. The evangelists, especially John, testify that the Lord, gathered with his own in the Last Supper, graciously communed with them in words as well as with actions, and never ceased to serve them as a proof of the great love which he had for them. For he was not satisfied to speak graciously to his own, to comfort and admonish them, indeed, to vow to die for them; he also humbled himself and washed the feet of his disciples. Therefore it is not by chance that John begins the words of the Last Supper and says: As he loved his own who were in the world, so he loved them to the end. Thus you will see, if you continue to read in John, how the Lord Christ adorned and strengthened the gathering with his disciples with sublime confirmations of his love. Therefore, in order to preserve rightly the Lord's Supper, we must diligently observe and follow the example of our Master with love to each other. For after Christ had washed his disciples' feet he said among other things: I have left you an example, that even as I have done to you, you do likewise. Without doubt the meaning is, that although it was given especially for the understanding of the apostles, nevertheless the Lord exemplified and commanded it as a model of love for all his disciples who would observe the holy Supper in his memory. From this we judge that the Lord's Supper may rightly be called and understood as a loving gathering, for all those who thus gather must be equipped with love to each other even as Christ is to them. The reason for specifying "those who believe in Christ" is that no one has the true love except the believers; unbelievers may in no way come to the Supper. That is why we say that the Supper is a loving gathering of those who believe in Christ.

9.12 Bernhard Rothmann, "Restitution," 1534, *SBR*, 257-258

The text indicates that Christ observed the Supper with his disciples and surrendered his body and blood to them with great desire and love. He instituted and commanded the eating and drinking of his body and blood in remembrance of him. He commanded: This do in remembrance of me. We understand this to mean that as Christ did with his disciples, we do with each other, that is, to take bread, break it, share it, eat it with one another, and all drink out of one cup. This is not the common natural usage, but in remembrance of our Lord and Saviour Jesus Christ. We understand the text to mean that we do as Christ did.... If we are to remember Christ properly we must remember two things: what he has done for us, and what we in gratitude should again do for him. He gave his body unto death and shed his blood for us and shared them with us for the forgiveness of our sins. For this we should heartily thank him and for the sake of his name and our neighbor to remember and be inclined to do the same, and to share with our brothers in Christ's church what we have and are. This is our understanding of the text, and since God's kingdom does not consist in words but rather in power and act, we conclude that much fighting about the words such as whether the bread be the body or the body in the bread ... is useless and offensive. Rather, in true remembrance of Christ we do as he did. Everything depends on this. Whoever is thus minded will receive a true understanding of the words of Christ. Whoever wants to understand the Scriptures should do what the Scriptures command. Then he will receive the key of David, and the coffer[47] of mystery will be opened. That is why we avoid getting involved in the argument about the words. Do, do, do what the Lord commands. Then you won't need to argue.

Now regarding the usage of the Supper. The Scriptures indicate that Christ used it in a common room and after the supper in simple manner while he had his disciples and those who loved him gathered together. Similar is the witness of Paul. Those who believed in Christ came together, ate of one bread and drank from one cup. This was not to nourish their bodies; for this they ate at home before or after, whenever they wished. Rather they came for a holy remembrance of the death of Jesus Christ and in the bond of unadulterated Christian love. This use of the Supper is now the practice among us. We gather together in a convenient place and expect that we will come each with examined heart so that we may approach worthily to proclaim the death of the Lord in true faith and to break the bread with one another in true love to each other. After that we fervently pray to

God for all necessities but especially for our dear brothers and sisters who are still subject to the dragon, etc. Then any need in the congregation is looked after and corrected. Thus the Lord has again restored the Supper and whenever we have been gathered together he has granted us to be richly quickened with heavenly blessing and other spiritual gifts. From now until eternity we will never be able to thank him enough.

9.13   Peter Riedeman, *Account*, 1542, 85-87

CONCERNING THE SUPPER OF CHRIST

The Lord Christ, the salvation of the world, was sent by the Father that those who believe on his name might have eternal life and be renewed into the divine likeness and grafted into his nature; which access to the Father and his grace he won through his death for us, who bear the likeness of his death. Therefore when he desired to go again to the Father from whom he had come, he wanted to show this to the disciples whom he had chosen from the world and to impress it on their inner being, so that after he had gone from them they might remember his grace and know for what purpose they had been chosen and accepted by God, that they might not be without hope like the rest, who know nothing of God.

Therefore he took a loaf of bread, thanked his Father, broke it and gave it to his disciples and said, "Take, eat: this is my body, which is broken for you: this do, as oft as ye do it, in remembrance of me." He took the cup in the same way and said, "Drink ye all of it. This is the new covenant in my blood, which is shed for you for the forgiveness of sins: this do in remembrance of me."

Now, in taking the bread and giving it to his disciples, Christ desires to show and explain the community of his body to his disciples, that they had become one body, one plant, one living organism and one nature with him, as Paul interprets it, "We who are many are one bread and one body; we, who all partake of one bread." He, however, in saying this, does not give them his body, his flesh and blood, to eat, as it has been twisted by the deceiver and made into idolatry; but, as we have said, he teaches them that they

202

are members of his body, and as the bread is made a loaf by the bringing together of many grains, even so we, many human beings, who were scattered and divided, of many minds and purposes are led by faith into one, and have become one plant, one living organism and body of Christ, cleaving to him in one Spirit, as the Lord pictures more clearly for them in still another parable, when he says, "I am the vine. Ye are the branches." Here he shows once more distinctly and clearly that they are one plant, organism, matter, substance and body with him. Therefore it is sufficiently clear that none other than this alone is Christ's meaning.

In that he breaks the loaf for them, however, and commands them to eat, he shows that they must bear the likeness of his death: be ready to die like him, if they would partake of his grace and become heirs of God. As Paul also says, "We are heirs of God and joint-heirs with Christ, if so be that we suffer with him, that we may be raised to glory with him."

That it has the above-mentioned meaning, and that this is truly what Christ means, is proved by his own words, in that he says, "This is the new covenant in my blood that is shed for you." Here he does not say, "This is my blood. Drink ye all of it," but, "This is the new covenant." What is then the new covenant? Is it to eat the body of Christ and drink his blood? On the contrary, show where that is anywhere promised! O, what great folly—that one does not want to see and know! We find indeed that God has promised a new covenant, not of the body or of eating flesh and blood, but of the knowledge of God, as the word says, "This shall be the covenant that I will make with them: I will give my law into their mind and write it in their inner members, that they shall all know me." Through this knowledge, however, man is led to God, is grafted into and becomes a fellow-member of his nature and character, whereby we are also all led into the one mind and will of Christ. For this reason he gives them wine, since many grapes have become one drink, and says, "This is the new covenant in my blood," as though he means to say, That is ratified or made strong and confirmed by my blood. For I have led you into such a covenant of grace and made you partakers of it, that you now have become one bread and one body with me through faith; that from henceforth, led by one Spirit, you be of one mind and purpose to prove that you are my disciples.

Thus, the meal, or the partaking of the bread and wine of the Lord, is a sign of the community of his body, in that each and every member thereby declares himself to be of the one mind, heart and spirit of Christ. Therefore Paul says, "Let a man truly examine himself before he eats of this bread and drinks of this cup, for he that eats and drinks unworthily thereof, eats and drinks judgment to himself," as though he would say, Let the man consider, examine and search himself well to see if he is partaking of this grace of Christ and is a true member of Christ, as he declares himself to be. For where this is not so he brings judgment upon himself in that he eats and drinks.

9.14 Dirk Philips, "The Lord's Supper," 1564, Kolb/ Klaassen, *Philips*, 68-71, 74-75, 78-81

[Philips has cited all the major texts concerning the Supper.] When we examine and look closely into the above words of Scripture in order to understand them thoroughly, and to lay hold of the true sense and understanding of it that accords in all cases with the Scriptures, and is contrary to no Scriptures or the faith we find the following. The Lord Jesus Christ, out of his great, overflowing love, gave his body for us, and shed his blood for us. He instituted the Supper with bread and wine as a memorial, that through the bread of his body given for us, and the wine of his blood shed for us, we might with thanksgiving remember. Hence the words of Christ at the Supper: "This is my body," "this is my blood," must be understood spiritually, for how else could it be that in the Lord's Supper the bread and wine were at the same time bread and wine, the body and blood of Christ, the communion of his body and blood, and a memorial of his suffering and death, a new testament or the blood of the new testament, and that at the same time all Scripture be reconciled? We will now look carefully into all these Scripture passages and by God's grace thoroughly explain them.

In the first place the Lord Jesus Christ instituted his Supper with bread and wine, and this accords perfectly with the statement, that he is himself the living bread, come down from heaven, by which souls are spiritually nourished by faith unto eternal life (Jn. 6:33). He is also the true vine (Jn. 15:7), planted by the true husbandman, God his Father. His Word is the pure wine (Is. 55:1), by which the believing soul is refreshed and made joyful in the Holy Spirit. Hence, as often as Christians eat of the bread of the Supper and drink of the wine, they are admonished and reminded of this.

After giving thanks, Christ broke the bread, gave it to his disciples, and said: "Take, eat, this is my body which is broken for you." On account of these words there is much dispute and chatter both among the learned and unlearned. Many firmly maintain that Christ is bodily in the bread. With this we do not agree, and do not understand the words cited above literally, but spiritually. The reasons that lead us, indeed force us, to this conclusion are many, and we will here present and point out a few:

First, the word eating in the Scripture is often synonymous with believing and drinking with trust. But the food and drink that are eaten and drunk is the bread of heaven, the word of God, the waters of the Holy Spirit, yea, the flesh and blood of Christ. This is evident in the sixth chapter of John, where the Lord says: "I am the bread of life. He that comes to me shall not hunger, and he who believes in me shall never thirst again" (Jn. 6:51[35]). And again he says: "I am the living bread which came down from heaven: if anyone eats of this bread, he shall live eternally. And the bread that I will give is my flesh, which I will give for the life of the world." And again: "My flesh is the true food, and my blood is the true drink. Whoever eats my flesh, and drinks my blood, remains in me, and I in him," etc. From all this it follows incontrovertibly that he who believes in Jesus Christ, the Son of the living God, who died for us, has eaten the flesh and drunk the blood of Christ.

Thus in the Scripture, eating often signifies believing. For Christ is the true bread of heaven (Jn. 6:51), which is eaten. The bread of heaven is God's Word, and the Word became flesh (Jn. 1:14), and the flesh of Christ was sacrificed and given for us. Thus the soul who believes in the crucified Jesus Christ is fed with the bread of heaven (Jn. 6:31), with the Word of God, yea, with the flesh and the blood of Christ. For these three, the bread of heaven, the Word of God, and the flesh and the blood of Christ, are all alike called the food of life. Christ himself in the gospel speaks of the one as of the other without any distinction. First, he speaks much about the bread of heaven and calls it the bread of life. Further he speaks in the same way and manner of his flesh and blood and calls his flesh the true food, and his blood the true drink. Finally, when some of his disciples understood his words literally, and therefore could not believe or endure them, he explained all that he had said of the bread of heaven, of the eating of his flesh and the drinking of his blood, he said in conclusion: "The flesh is of no use; it is the spirit that brings to life. The words that I speak are spirit and life" (Jn. 6:63), as much as to say: All that I have said of the bread of heaven, likewise of eating my flesh and of drinking my blood, is said, meant, and is to be understood of my words, for they are spirit and life, and food for believing souls.

Therefore, whoever believes in the Lord Jesus Christ, the Son of the living God, who was crucified and died for us (Mt. 26:25), and trusts in him, receives Jesus Christ, the Word of the Father. He is fed with the heavenly manna; indeed, he eats the flesh and drinks the blood of Jesus (Ex. 16:15; Num. 20:13), but spiritually with the mouth of the soul, and not physically, with the mouth of the body. For spiritual food—that is what the body and blood of Christ are—must be spiritually received.

. . . .

Thus Christ, in the Supper, calls the bread his body, and the cup his blood. He does not mean that his natural body is actually in the bread and the cup. However, both bread and blood mean and signify that Christ gave his body and shed his blood for us, and that we, through the power and consequence of his one holy sacrifice—namely, the offering of his flesh for us, and the shedding of his blood for our sin, once for all (Heb. 9:12; 10:10)—in the spirit, have eternal life by true faith. Therefore when he gave the bread and the cup to his disciples, and said to them, "Take and eat; this is my body. Drink of it, all of you. This is my blood of the New Testament," he added, "which is given or shed for you." By these words he meant us to understand that by means of the bread and the cup of the Supper we are to remember and be assured of our redemption and reconciliation with God the Father through the offering of the body and blood of Jesus Christ. By it we become renewed in and reminded of the spiritual fellowship which we have with Christ Jesus, namely, that he is in us with his Spirit through faith and we in him. He is our head (Eph. 4:15, 5:30) and we his members, flesh of his flesh, and bone of his bones, and therefore also partake of all that he has bought through his sacrifice and shedding of his blood, which is peace with God, forgiveness of sins, righteousness, salvation, and everlasting life.

. . . .

This communion and incorporation with Christ is confirmed and renewed through the Supper in that Christians in true unity of the Spirit and of faith break the bread and drink the wine. These point to and remind them of the fellowship of Christ and participation in all his merits, his righteousness, his holiness, indeed, all that is his. All this they partake of together to eternal salvation. The fellowship of Christ consists in this that all the treasures of Christ are given to, and possessed by, each Christian, and have thus become generally available. Therefore Paul says: "The cup of blessing which we bless, is it not the communion of the blood of Christ? The bread which we break, is it not the communion of the body of Christ? For we being many are one bread, and one body, for we are all partakers of the one bread" (1 Cor. 10:16).

. . . .

Hence they break the bread and drink from the cup as a testimony that they are in the communion of the body of Christ, into which they have entered by the grace of God and election by faith. They are confirmed in it by the true baptism, and preserved and confirmed in it by the Supper of the Lord. By this communion they are also made partakers of all that belongs to Christ, as the sons of Aaron in partaking of the altar were therefore partakers of all that God had given, and committed to Aaron, their father.

The harmony and fellowship of the believers are also portrayed and typified in the bread and wine of the Supper. In order to show the significance of this fellowship, the Lord chose and ordained such signs in the Supper as are everywhere available, and which by their form alert and persuade people toward such a communion. For as the bread is made of many grains broken and ground together, and out of many grains has come one loaf of bread in which every little kernel has lost its individual body and form; and likewise as the grapes, by changing their form become the body of a common wine and drink, so also must all Christians be united with Christ and with one another.[48] First they must be united with Christ, whom they receive by faith and who becomes their nourishment. For there is no closer intimacy nor anything more inseparable than the union of food with those who are fed, for the food is taken and becomes changed in its nature, and becomes one with the one fed. Thus also true Christians by faith in Jesus Christ are wholly united with and incorporated in him, yea, transformed and changed so as to be like him in kind and nature. Therefore Christ takes such an interest in their behalf that he who harms them harms Christ himself. Again, he that does good to them does it to Christ, as he himself says: "What you have done to one of the least of my brothers, you have done it to me" (Mt. 25:40).

Through this fellowship and love of Christ love must in turn be so enkindled in Christians that they consider the infirmities and needs of all Christians as being common to all, taking to themselves their condition and needs and thus becoming a community through the love which bears one another's burdens, and thus fulfills the law of Christ (Gal. 6:2).

· ·

Third, the bread and wine in the Supper are a token of remembrance of the bitter suffering and innocent death and shedding of blood of Jesus Christ, namely, that by it we remember that Christ Jesus in his great love gave his body and shed his blood for us. "He has made it to be a remembrance, and the gracious, merciful Lord has given food to those who fear him" (Ps. 111:3[5]). He has instituted a Supper with the bread and wine for the believers that thereby they should remember his suffering and death.

9.15   Menno Simons, "Distressed Christians," 1552, *CWMS*, 515-516

Similarly we believe and confess concerning the Lord's holy Supper that it is a holy sacramental sign, instituted of the Lord himself in bread and wine, and left to his disciples in remembrance

208

of him. Mt. 26; Mk. 14; Lk. 22; 1 Cor. 11. It was also taught and administered as such by the apostles among the brethren, according to the commandment of the Lord, in which in the first place the Lord's death is proclaimed. 1 Cor. 11. And it also serves as a remembrance how he offered his holy flesh and shed his precious blood for the remission of our sins. Mt. 26:27; Mk. 14:24; Lk. 22:19.

Second, it is an emblem of Christian love, of unity, and of peace in the church of Christ. Paul says, For we, being many, are one bread and one body; for we are all partakers of that one bread. 1 Cor. 10:17. For as a loaf being composed of many grains is but one bread; so we also being composed of many members are but one body in Christ. And as the members of a natural body are not disharmonious, but are altogether united and at one among themselves; so it is with all those who are in Spirit and faith true members of the body of Christ. For this reason this same supper was called by Tertullian a brotherly meal or love feast.

Third, it is a communion of the flesh and blood of Christ. As Paul says, The cup of blessing which we bless, is it not the communion of the blood of Christ? The bread which we break, is it not the communion of the body of Christ? 1 Cor. 10:16. This communion consists in the fact that Christ has accepted us in his great love, and we are become partakers of him. As Paul says, We are made partakers of Christ, if we hold the beginning of our confidence steadfast unto the end. Heb. 3:14.

Since it is a sign of such force which is left of Christ, that it is to represent and admonish us of his death, the love, peace, and unity of the brethren, and also the communion of his flesh and blood as was said, therefore none can rightly partake of this Supper except he be a disciple of Christ, flesh of his flesh, and bone of his bone, who seeks the forgiveness of sins in no other means than in the merits, sacrifice, death, and blood of Christ alone; who walks in unity, love, and peace with his brethren, and who leads a pious, unblamable life in Christ Jesus, according to the Scriptures.

Here you have the true Supper of our Lord Jesus Christ with its symbolism and mystery briefly stated, which the mouth of the Lord has left and taught you by his holy Word. If you would be a proper guest at the Lord's table and would rightly partake of his bread and wine, then you must also be his true disciple, that is, you must be an upright, pious, and godly Christian. Therefore prove yourself according to the doctrine of Paul before you eat of this bread and drink of this cup, for before God no feigning counts. He did not institute this ceremony as though mere bread, wine, and eating are pleasing to him. Oh, no. He has left this sacrament with you in order that you might by it faithfully observe and carefully conform yourself to the mystery represented by this sign or sacrament. For not the ceremony itself but the matter represented by it, if rightly understood and fulfilled in actions, constitutes a sincere Christian.

For further reading:

Beachy, *Grace*, 103-116.
Clasen, *Anabaptism*, 110-117.
Keeney, *Dutch Anabaptist*, 100-106.
Littell, *Church*, 98-101.
Gerhard J. Neumann, "The Anabaptist Position on Baptism and the Lord's Supper," *MQR* XXXV (April 1971), 140-148.
Wenger, *Even Unto Death*, 75-78.

X

Church Discipline

Virtually all the Anabaptists we know by name had experienced church discipline at the hands of the Catholic and Protestant church authorities. We know their names precisely because they appear in official records which describe the disciplinary action. What we today call persecution was regarded in the sixteenth century by those who did it as church discipline. Anabaptists were always regarded as members of the church, Protestant or Catholic, who had gone astray. The church authorities therefore felt responsible for them.

This discipline was often severe, involving imprisonment, torture, exile, deprivation of property, and even death. The death sentence as the ultimate act of discipline had a long history. In a society in which everyone was regarded as Christian there was no longer a world into which the offending member could be excommunicated. The only way of getting rid of an incorrigible heretic was to put him to death. This was duly justified from the Scriptures.

Anabaptists said that physical violence was not permitted the Christian. Therefore torture, imprisonment, and death were rejected as legitimate means of discipline. Moreover, Anabaptists saw a clear distinction between church and world. When, therefore, someone was excommunicated, that person was sent out of the church, God's kingdom, into the world, the kingdom of Satan. In this they followed the practice of the pre-Constantinian church which, too, had not resorted to violence in its church discipline.

Anabaptists argued that the physical sword has no place in the church since it belonged to the function of government. The function of government was strictly separated from that of the church. Government officials, therefore, had no right to exercise discipline in the church in their official role. That was the prerogative only of the congregation itself. Moreover, the sword was a punitive instrument. Church discipline, however, should not be punitive in its final purpose, but redemptive. Any disciplinary action, therefore, was designed to bring an erring member back to the fold of the church.

The following selections, however, reveal a considerable variety of views on the question of discipline. All accept its necessity; they do not agree on the manner of carrying it out. There was always a strong tendency to legalism, in part because the unity and purity of the church were such high priorities.

The first controversy within Anabaptism regarding church discipline is revealed in the letters which Pilgram Marpeck wrote to the Swiss Brethren (selection 10.12 is part of one of these letters) in which he censured them for their harsh, legalistic way of exercising discipline in their congregations. Not only was the end result harsh, but they did not properly follow the various steps of "the rule of Christ." Marpeck's own view was that there is much to do at the first, that is, the admonition stages, but that the final stage of excommunication should be only rarely resorted to. Marpeck had a fine sense of the reality of human growth of which failure is a part, of the difficulty of accurately assessing human motivation, and of the trauma of exclusion. We don't know what the Swiss wrote since we do not have their letters.

Selection 10.16 reveals that within North German and Dutch Anabaptism too, questions were raised about the degree to which church discipline ought to be exercised. The argument of Menno Simons and Dirk Philips that commitment to the church outweighed commitment to the marriage partner is specifically rejected. Among the Dutch the practice of discipline became excessively legalistic, even to the point of completely avoiding a spouse under discipline. There, too, the process seems frequently to have neglected the first, private stages of the "rule," and moved immediately to the public stage where it produced anger, dissension, and separation. Thus, even though physical violence was rejected, what we today call psychological violence was very much in evidence.

It must be remembered, however, that the motive for discipline was the preservation of the integrity of the church. It must always be

212

seen in the context of their time. Compared to the disciplinary measures of the established churches, Anabaptist church discipline was relatively benign.

It can be demonstrated that the Anabaptist emphasis on church discipline had its effect especially upon Martin Bucer, the reformer of Strassburg. It is also likely that Bucer was influential in the shaping of Marpeck's moderate position on the issue.

10.1 Interrogation of Hans Bichter, 1525, Muralt und Schmid, *Quellen*, 65

If anyone transgresses against the promise and commandment which they give to those whom they baptize, him they exclude and put out from among them.

10.2 Balthasar Hubmaier, "Basis and Cause," 1526-1527, *Armour*, 46

Whatever importance one attributes to fellowship with God the Father, the Son, and the Holy Spirit, to communion with all the heavenly hosts and the whole Christian church, even to the forgiveness of sins, so much ought he to attribute to water baptism. For through this baptism one enters and is incorporated into the universal Christian church, outside of which there is no salvation.

Not that remission of sins is to be attributed to the water, but rather to the power of the keys, which Christ in the power of his Word gave to his Spouse and unspotted Bride, the Christian church for the time of his physical absence, hanging these keys at her side when he said to her, "Receive the Holy Spirit...."

Here one should note carefully that the universal church now has the power on earth to loose or bind sins, which power Christ had when formerly a man bodily present here. Whoever believes the Word of God now enters the ark of Noah which is a true type of water baptism, and thus he will not drown in the flood of sins outside the ark.

10.3 Balthasar Hubmaier, "A Christian Instruction," 1526-1527, Davidson/Klaassen, *Hubmaier*, 290-294

Leon: What power have those in the church over one another? *Hans:* The power of fraternal punishment. *Leon:* What is fraternal punishment? *Hans:* When one sees his brother sin, he should go to him lovingly and reprove him fraternally in secret, that he may cease from his sins. If he does so cease, his soul has been won. If he is not successful, let him take two or three witnesses with him, and reprove the offence before them on the second occasion. If the man submits, all is well; if not, let it be told to the church. The church will call him to appear before it and reprimand him a third time. If he desists from his sin you have won his soul. (Mt. 18). *Leon:* Whence has the church this power? *Hans:* From the command of Christ when he said to his disciples: all that you bind on earth shall be bound in heaven also, and all that you loose on earth, shall be loosed also in heaven (Mt. 18, Jn. 20). *Leon:* On what basis may a brother use this power over another? *Hans:* On the basis of the baptismal vow, whereby man submits himself to the church with all its members, according to the word of Christ. *Leon:* How if the reproved sinner will not amend? *Hans:* Then the church has the power and right to exclude him as a perjurer and an oath-breaker, and to put him under a ban. *Leon:* What is a ban? *Hans:* It is an exclusion and separation of such a nature that from then on no Christian may have fellowship with such a man, not in words, meat or drink, in grinding or baking, or in any other way. He must consider him as an heathen and publican, that is, an offensive, disorderly and poisoned soul, who is bound and given over to the devil. One must avoid him and flee from him, lest by fellowship with him, the whole church visible be evil spoken of, shamed, despised and deteriorated through his evil example. Rather a man is to be shocked through this punishment that he may examine himself, and die to his sins. For truly as God lives, what the church binds or looses on earth is bound or loosed in heaven. *Leon:* What are the causes for exclusion? *Hans:* Not being willing to be reconciled to one's brothers, or not desisting from sin. *Leon:* Why do they exclude a man? *Hans:* Not on account of six shillingsworth of hazelnuts, as the papists have done up to now, but on account of grievous sin. It is done for the good of the sinner, that he may look into his own heart, take stock of himself, and abandon sin. *Leon:* If he abandons sin, and avoids all paths on which he might fall and amends, how does the church treat him? *Hans:* It receives him again joyfully, like a father receives a lost son, as Paul did with the Corinthians (Lk. 15, 2 Cor. 2), opens the doors of heaven to him, and lets him reenter the fellowship of the Lord's Supper.

10.4   Michael Sattler, Schleitheim Confession, 1527, *Legacy*, 36-37

II. We have been united as follows concerning the ban. The ban shall be employed with all those who have given themselves over to the Lord, to walk after [him] in his commandments; those who have been baptized into the one body of Christ, and let themselves be called brothers or sisters, and still somehow slip and fall into error and sin, being inadvertently overtaken. The same [shall] be warned twice privately and the third time be publicly admonished before the entire congregation according to the command of Christ (Mt. 18). But this shall be done according to the ordering of the Spirit of God before the breaking of bread, so that we may all in one spirit and in one love break and eat from one bread and drink from one cup.

10.5   Hans Denck, "Concerning True Love," 1527, Fellmann, *Denck* I, 82

For the children of love may not for the sake of love act against love. Here all the wise need wisdom and all the friends of God need love so that they do not prefer the love of man to the love of God. For whoever loves someone, but not according to God's truth and love, hates him. But if someone hates another for the sake of divine love, he loves him more than the former. But for the sake of love one may not hate another beyond earnestly admonishing him, and if he will not hear, to avoid him with a sorrowing heart. This is also loving in truth. Herein consists the separation of the children of God from the children of the world, and also the ban or exclusion of false brethren. This too must happen only for the sake of true love, unless indeed one wishes to deny the basis of the covenant of the children of God.

10.6 Hans Denck, "Concerning the Love of God," 1526, Fellmann, *Denck* I, 50

When you hear your brother say something that is strange to you do not immediately argue with him, but listen to see whether he may be right and you can also accept it. If you cannot understand him you must not judge him, and if you think that he may be in error, consider that you may be in greater error.

10.7 Melchior Hoffman, "Ordinance of God," 1530, Williams, *Spiritual*, 196-197

And the bride has now so covenanted herself with the Lord under the sign of the covenant [baptism] and so given herself over to him, and he to them, through his Word and again with the bread, that many brides are become one congregation and bride of the Lord, and he the husband and the Bridegroom. And if then the bride in the future should come to conduct herself improperly so as not to be fully obedient and faithful to her bridegroom but rather with a hard heart should come, against her vow, to attach herself to another and commit adultery with the same, and bespot herself (and be that whatever it may to which she attach herself) and thus turn away from obedience to her bridegroom and then if after warning no improvement should take place [—then, certainly the husband should eject her].

Likewise the [heavenly] Bridegroom [who], through his apostolic emissaries, would thereupon let her be thrown out of the congregation again, by his consent, yea, altogether out of his house, and would divorce her from his fellowship and would take from her the bread and wine, thereby indicating that she had no portion or should have any of him or of his blood, also that their vow had been broken,

216

and that he had treated her, just as a bridegroom would take away his ring from his wayward bride and divorce her and spurn her.

Therefore it has been held [in respect to] the ban from the time of the apostles that they who would live according to the will of Satan (as Saint Paul in Gal. 5:19-21 on the first fruits clearly indicated), after three warnings [Mt. 18:15-18] were ejected from Christ Jesus and his kingdom and delivered over into the kingdom of Satan and the devil. But in so far as the same turned back in their hearts and gave themselves over to improvement of their wicked way of life, they were again accepted by the congregation through the servants of God and received again into the congregation of the body of Christ Jesus and into the fellowship of his blood. O how well it went when such an ordinance was maintained in the true fear of God!

10.8 "Zofingen Colloquy," 1532, Haas, *Quellen*, 115-116

You have heard what gems adorn the church of God. Here is another in Matthew 18[15]: If your brother sins against you, go and chastise him in private. There you may hear the command which God has given to those who claim to be his. But that among you this does not function, we will show. When people, papists and Lutherans assemble in the drinking-houses, where is the chastisement? If someone blasphemes the name of the Lord no one admonishes him. Nor, if he does not improve his ways after admonition with two witnesses, does anyone take the matter to the congregation and thence to a servant of the Word! This is the task not of specially appointed men such as the so-called "marriage-judges." Rather each brother must and may do it according to the rule of Christ. It is this way, dear brothers. If someone has gambled, spoken profanity, etc.; if he has been admonished, and there is no fruit, we exclude him. We no longer consider him a brother until he improves, abandons his evil and receives God's grace. Whether you use this ban among yourselves can be clearly seen.

10.9 Menno Simons, "Admonition on Church Discipline," 1541, *CWMS*, 411-413

Dear brethren, this is the true nature and mind of the children of God, who are by grace converted in their hearts and with Christ born of God the Father. Therefore I beseech you as my sincerely beloved brethren, by the grace of God—nay, I command you with holy Paul, by the Lord Jesus Christ, who at his coming will judge the living and the dead—diligently to observe each other unto salvation, in all becoming ways teaching, instructing, admonishing, reproving, warning, and consoling each other as occasion requires, not otherwise than in accordance with the Word of God and in unfeigned love, until we increase in God and become united in faith and in the knowledge of the Son of God, into one perfect man and according to the measure of the gift of Jesus Christ. Eph. 4:7.

Therefore take heed. If you see your brother sin, then do not pass him by as one that does not value his soul; but if his fall be curable, from that moment endeavor to raise him up by gentle admonition and brotherly instruction, before you eat, drink, sleep, or do anything else, as one who ardently desires his salvation, lest your poor erring brother harden and be ruined in his fall, and perish in his sin.

. . . .

But do not have anything to do, as the holy Paul has taught and commanded, and do not eat, with people who being of age and driven by the Spirit were baptized into the body of Jesus Christ with us, that is, the church, but afterwards, whether through false doctrine or a vain and carnal life, reject and separate themselves from the body and fellowship of Christ, no matter whether it be father or mother, sister or brother, man or wife, son or daughter, no matter who he be, for God's Word applies to all alike and there is no respect of persons with God. We say, avoid him if he rejects the admonition of his brethren, done in sighing, tears, and a spirit of compassion and of great love, and if he nevertheless continues in his Jewish doctrine of sword, kingdom, polygamy, and similar deceptions; in the doctrine of shameless confession to each other, of no shame [for shameful acts], of nakedness; as well as a doctrine that contradicts the cross of Christ, as, for example, that impurity is pure to the pure—all

218

fellowship with evil work such as attending the preaching of worldly preachers, infant baptism, worldly Lord's Supper, and similar abominations, as also drunkenness, avarice, fornication, adultery, unseemly conversation, etc.

But if he affectionately receives the admonition of his faithful brethren, confesses his fall, is truly sorry, promises to do better, and brings forth fruits worthy of repentance, then no matter how he has transgressed, receive him as a returning, beloved brother or sister. But let him beware lest he mock his God, for restoration with the brethren does not avail without restoration before God. Let him be sure that his heeding the admonition, his sorrow, his promise of reformation, and his penitence, are sincere before God who searches the hearts and reins and knows all inward thoughts of men. If his heeding the admonition, his sorrow, promise, and penitence, are not sincere and from his heart, but halfhearted, put on, mechanical, and of a hypocritical exhibition, just because he does not want to be thrown out of the community of the brethren, he is still excommunicated by Christ, and is a hypocrite in the sight of God. Nor will he be rated or judged by God as anything else. For God the righteous Judge does not judge according to the outward appearance, but according to the inward intention of the heart.

. . . .

Wherefore, brethren, understand correctly, no one is excommunicated or expelled by us from the communion of the brethren but those who have already separated and expelled themselves from Christ's communion either by false doctrine or by improper conduct. For we do not want to expel any, but rather to receive; not to amputate, but rather to heal; not to discard, but rather to win back; not to grieve, but rather to comfort; not to condemn, but rather to save. For this is the true nature of a Christian brother. Whoever turns from evil, whether it be false doctrine or vain life, and conforms to the Gospel of Jesus Christ, unto which he was baptized, such a one shall not and may not be expelled or excommunicated by the brethren forever.

But those whom we cannot raise up and repentingly revive by admonition, tears, warning, rebuke, or by any other Christian services and godly means, these we should put forth from us, not without great sadness and anguish of soul, sincerely lamenting the fall and condemnation of such a straying brother; lest we also be deceived and led astray by such false doctrine which eats as does a cancer (2 Tim. 2); and lest we corrupt our flesh which is inclined to evil by the contagion. Thus we must obey the Word of God which teaches and commands us so to do; and this in order that the excommunicated brother or sister whom we cannot convert by gentle services may by such means be shamed unto repentance and made to acknowledge to what he has come and from what he is fallen. In this way the ban is a great work of love, notwithstanding it is looked upon by the foolish as an act of hatred.

10.10 Peter Riedeman, *Account*, 1542, 131-133
CONCERNING EXCLUSION

Paul says, "Put away from among yourselves what is evil." Therefore in the fear of God we observe and watch over one another, since the one would protect and keep the other from all wrong and from such evil as deserves exclusion. Therefore do we watch over one another, telling each his faults, warning and rebuking with all diligence. But where one will not accept the rebuke, but disregards it, the matter is brought before the church, and if he hear not the church, then he is excluded and put out.

If, however, one be discovered in the gross and deadly sins of which Paul says, "If any man that is called a brother be a fornicator, or covetous, or an idolater, or a railer, or a drunkard, or a thief or a robber, with such an one ye must not even eat." Such an one is put out and excluded or separated from the church without admonition, since the judgment of Paul is already spoken.

And if one is so excluded, we have nothing to do with him: have no company with him, that he may be ashamed. Yet is he called to repentance, that perchance he may be moved thereby and return the more quickly to God; and where not, that the church may remain pure and innocent of his sin, and bear not guilt and rebuke from God on his behalf.

In all such cases, however, a distinction is made, that he who sins willfully be punished according to the weight of his sin; and the more willful the sin, the sharper the punishment. If, however, he sin in the haste of the flesh and not willfully or recklessly, but through the weakness of the flesh, he is punished, but not completely separated from the church or excluded from all fellowship; but he is not permitted to use the Lord's greeting, to give or accept "Peace," that he may humble himself before God for his sin, and thereafter watch all the more carefully against it.

CONCERNING READMISSION

Now when one is excluded we have no fellowship with him until he has truly repented: though he may run with entreaty and desire, he is not accepted until he has received from the church the good report of a truly repentant life; yea, he is not accepted until one senses that the Lord has again drawn nigh to him, been gracious to and accepted him. When, however, this is recognized, the church likewise offers him the hand, that is, she does what she has been commanded by God, so that he is accepted by her and is counted once more a member of the church. But as in the beginning one is received into the church by means of a sign (that is baptism), so also after he fell and was separated from the church he must likewise be received by a sign, that is through the laying on of hands, which must be done by a servant of the gospel. This indicates that he once more has part and is rooted in the grace of God. When this has taken place he is accepted again in full love; all suspicion, complaint and disinclination are swept away and cut off—lest Satan should get the advantage of us—and one has a right and completely trusting heart toward him as toward all the other members of the church. Therefore is it so long postponed until, as has been said, the grace of God is once more felt to be at work in him, drawing the confidence of the church once more toward him.

10.11   Peter Riedeman, *Account*, 1542, 44
THE FORGIVENESS OF SINS

We acknowledge also that as Christ received from the Father might and power to forgive the sins of whom he will, he has likewise committed power to his bride, spouse, consort and church, as he himself says, "Receive ye the Holy Ghost: whose soever sins ye remit here on earth, they are remitted also in heaven; and whose soever sins ye retain here on earth, they are retained also in heaven." Thus the words of Christ show that he gives his church power here on earth to forgive sins.

But that this power and key is given to the church and not to individual persons is shown by the words of Christ when he says, "If your brother sins against you, go and tell him his fault between you and him alone: if he hears you, you have won his soul. But if he will not hear you, then take with you one or two more, that in the mouth of two or three witnesses every word may be established. And if he neglect to hear them, tell it unto the church, but if he neglect to hear the church, regard him as a taxgatherer and sinner."

Here it is, indeed, allowed the individual, if anything be done against him personally, to forgive his brother if he betters his way; but the full power of the key of Christ, that is to exclude and to accept, he has not given to individuals, but to the whole church. Therefore whatsoever she excludes is excluded, but whatsoever she forgives is forgiven here and in eternity, and apart from her there is no forgiveness, no goodness, no healing and salvation, no true comfort or hope. For within her and not without her is and dwells the Father, Son and Holy Ghost who makes all things good, and justifies.

10.12 Pilgram Marpeck, "Judgment and Decision," 1542, *The Writings*, 323-327, 356-357

First of all, every individual must possess true and diligent discernment of conscience and heart if he is to have a true and certain judgment that the self-made freedom of the flesh be not taken for the liberty of Jesus Christ. This self-made freedom is and remains the most profound slavery from which release is never possible. To act in accordance with self-made freedom is to sin, and to be led into wickedness and the hardest slavery of sin, for whoever commits sin is the slave of sin. It makes no difference that this self-made carnal freedom always adorns itself with the dead letter and, posing as the true liberty of Christ Jesus the Lord, covers itself with a false, lying appearance. It finally brings forth no fruit except open depravities, sin, and shame. Such is the case with the hypocrites who, by their own choice to live according to human law and its coercion, strut about and, without knowing anything about it, assume the appearance of the Spirit.

Now the true believers are forbidden to condemn all these people before the right time (1 Cor. 4[5]) that is, until their fruit, which is open vice, appears. Christ says: "By their fruits (he does not say by the blossoms or the foliage) you shall know them." For the day of the Lord will reveal everything. But some vices are revealed and clear before that time, for every man expresses that which is within the treasure of his heart. Whether it be before or at the time of the last day, to cover or reveal sin is in God's hands. For no one may judge the heart until the fruit appears or until the outpouring of the treasure of the heart occurs. Only God, through the Holy Spirit, may judge.

. . . .

Whoever, therefore, establishes, commands, prohibits, coerces, drives, punishes, or judges before the time the good or evil fruit is revealed, lays claim to the authority, power, and office of the Holy Spirit of the Lord Jesus Christ and, contrary to love, goodness, and grace, runs ahead of Christ Jesus. For the Son of God himself has committed this office and work to the Holy Spirit of God, and the office is to be carried out after his earthly, human life. With reference to this work, he says: "The Holy Spirit will come and judge because of sin, judgment, and righteousness." This Spirit now does the judging and searches the hearts, for the Holy Spirit has his work and good fruit in the children of light in order to reveal them before men. Similarly, the spirit of wickedness, who often and in many ways disguises himself as a spirit of light, has his work in the children of darkness. These, too, are driven by the Holy Spirit to do their own works in order that by the power and finger of God they may be known and revealed by their fruits.

Therefore, even if one is concerned about a lapse and sees the leaves and blossoms of evil appearance, one ought to warn and admonish, but not judge, before the time of the fruit.

The Lord does not say: "By their blossoms or leaves," but rather, "by their fruits you shall know them." For love also covers a multitude of sins (1 Pet. 4[8]) and judges all things in the best light. Even though it is concerned about evil appearances and evil fruit, it nevertheless always hopes for the best.

In the same way, Christ covers our sin and shame in the love and grace which leads to improvement. Whoever presumes to decide and judge, before the revealing of guilt, is a thief and a murderer (Jn. 10[1]). He runs ahead of Jesus Christ, who alone is the revealer of good and evil in the heart.

On the other hand, if the sin and wickedness, evident from the revealed fruit, is revealed through wrath in the righteousness of Christ, one must be ready to judge and decide with Christ, the true Judge; otherwise, he too, is a thief and a murderer. He runs behind Jesus Christ and not with Christ. All the elect of God, with Christ, judge in this time with the sword of the Spirit through the Word, and not, as the world does, with the carnal sword. They will also decide at the last judgment.

. . . .

No one may judge except he who has first judged and sentenced his own life through the grace and mercy of God, whereby he has pulled the beam out of his eye. Then, very properly, in patience, humility, meekness, and love, he may with the greatest care pull the sliver out of his brother's eye without hurting or irritating the eye. That is, after all, how he has been treated by God. And whoever brings someone to Christ in a different way for judgment, as the Jews brought the adulteress to him in the temple, will find himself, together with the hypocritical Jews, running from Christ and the adulteress in the temple. Open sinners will enter the kingdom of God before these do. Christ tolerated them less than the adulteress. All transgression is adultery before God, to whom man is betrothed.

. . . .

Even the world does not judge anyone on the basis of hearsay, suspicion, or appearance, but only on the words of the accused and of reliable witnesses. Christ also commands his own that all testimony must be substantiated by two or three witnesses. Only when evidence has been presented before the church, and he will not hear, does the judgment begin with tribulation, anxiety, sorrow

224

The other members of the body of Christ experience great pain and suffering for at stake is a member of the body of Christ the Lord. They must lose a member in order that the other members, who are well, are not hurt and the whole body destroyed, be it eye, foot, or hand. It should be pulled out or cut off according to the commandment of Christ, our Head: "If your eye offends you, or your hand, or foot," etc. The other members of the body of Christ will not be able to do this without great pain and tribulation. If the member is honourable and useful to the body, the tribulation is so much greater. It cannot possibly happen easily or simply. The natural body cannot lose a member without pain. Nor does it immediately cut it off, even if it is failing and weak; rather it uses all kinds of medicines. As long as it is not dead and is only painful, the body bears it with patience ~nd long-suffering, and delays the penalty to allow for improvement. If, however, it allows the body no rest, nor improves by any medicine from the Lord Jesus Christ, through suffering and pain, it must be cut off in order that the other members of the body of Christ remain healthy in the fear and love of God and the neighbor, to whom alone the judgment to retain and to forgive sin has been committed (Mt. 16[19]; 18[15-19]; 20[23]).

10.13 Dirk Philips, "Concerning the Ban," 1558, "The Church of God," 1562, "The Evangelical Ban and Shunning," 1602, Kolb/Klaassen, *Philips*, 233-234, 391-393, 525-526

Thereby he teaches expressly that believers shall have nothing to do with one who calls himself a brother, but is a fornicator, or covetous, or idol worshipper, or a reviler, or a drunkard, or a thief; with such the Christians shall have no fellowship (1 Cor. 5:10; 2 Thess. 3:6), nor to eat with them. Rather, they must be separated, and afterward shunned, and this for three principal reasons: first, that the church may not become a partaker of the sin of outsiders, and that a little leaven may not leaven the whole lump (2 Jn. 1:11; 2 Cor. 5:5; Gal. 5:9); second, that the person who has sinned may be ashamed and his flesh be thus punished, and his spirit saved in the day of the Lord Jesus; third, that the church of God be not blasphemed on account of the evils in it, and be not guilty on their account before the Lord (Ezek. 36:30[?]; Rom. 2:24; Josh. 7:20).

From all this it follows that the wicked and open sinners must be separated from the church of the Lord. For if their fellowship is not with God, if they are banished from, separated, and rooted out of the literal Israel (1 Jn. 1:3; Deut. 13:8; 17:7; 19:19); if they know not Jesus Christ (2 Jn. 1:7), if they have no part in the kingdom of God and Christ (Eph. 5:5), if they are not to inherit or possess the same (Gal. 5:21), and if Christians are to have nothing to do with them (1 Cor. 5:10; 2 Thess. 3:6), how then may they continue to be in the Christian church, be called holy brethren (Heb. 3:1), be greeted with the peace of Jesus Christ and the kiss of love?

. . . .

Now, what those sins are which must be punished with the ban are shown us by the evangelists and apostles in express words (Mt. 18:15; Rom. 16:16[17]; 1 Cor. 5:10; 1 Thess. 5:15; 1 Tim. 3:5; Tit. 3:19[10]; 2 Jn. 10). In our confession regarding the evangelical ban we have carefully explained it. What the church of the Lord thus judges by the word of God, the same is judged before God. For this reason Christ gave his church the keys of the kingdom of heaven (Mt. 16:19) that they might punish, exclude and put away the wicked and receive the penitent and believing. What the church thus binds upon earth shall be bound in heaven. What she looses on earth shall be loosed in heaven. This must not be understood to mean that men have power to forgive sins or to retain them as some imagine, and therefore deal with the confessional and absolution as with merchandise. No minister of Christ may do this, neither is the church of the Lord to admit any simony (Acts 8:21[18]). For no prophet or apostle on earth has presumed to forgive sin, to hear confession and to grant absolution to the people, although Christ said to his disciples: "Receive the Holy Spirit: those whose sins you forgive, they are forgiven; those whose sins you retain, they are retained" (Jn. 20:[22]-23). The holy men of God did not assume divine honour, but confessed through the inspiration of the Holy Spirit, that God alone forgives sin, as the Scripture unanimously testifies. But the church has received the Holy Spirit and the gospel from Jesus Christ (Is. 43:28; Mt. 9:6; Ps. 51:4) in which forgiveness

226

of sins, reconciliation with God, and eternal life to all who truly repent and believe in Jesus Christ is proclaimed and promised. On the other hand, disfavour, wrath and damnation are threatened and announced against all unbelieving, rebellious, and obstinate people.

This word, together with the Holy Spirit, is the judge in the church of all false brothers (1 Cor. 5:5; Rom. 10:16; 2 Tim. 2:3; Tit. 3:19[10]), against all heretics, who after sufficient admonition do not improve, and all disorderly and disobedient persons. On the Lord's day no other sentence will be pronounced, as the Lord himself says. The church has received this word from God, by which, in the name of Jesus Christ, and in the power of the Holy Spirit she testifies, judges, receives and expels. Whatever on earth she thus binds or looses with the word and Spirit of the Lord, is bound or loosed in heaven.

. . . .

Then again brotherly love is shown in this that among us we serve one another with active goodwill, not only in spiritual matters, but also with temporal gifts. We have received them from God in order to minister liberally to the necessity of the saints (Rom. 12:13), according to our ability. Just as it was done in Israel of old, namely, he that gathered much manna had nothing over, and he that gathered little had no lack (Ex. 16:18; 2 Cor. 8:15). Thus the rich, who have received many temporal possessions from the Lord, are to minister to the poor therewith (Rom. 15:27; 1 Cor. 8:10) and supply their need, so that the poor in turn serve them as they may have need of their services.

. . . .

Should some one contradict this or even admit that the husband, on his part, passes judgment by the Word of God against his guilty wife and aids in putting her without the pale of the Christian congregation, but would nevertheless want the church to grant the husband the liberty to maintain the same relation and companionship with his wife as before, when she was not excommunicated, we answer that the church separates and excommunicates the sister that has sinned or become apostate, by the power vested in or bestowed by Jesus Christ, and in such a manner indeed that there shall be no outward fellowship with her until the time when she, upon true sorrow, repentance and amendment is again received into the church. And the husband must, under the same conditions, be dealt with in the same way, for the reason that he is not his own, but the Lord's and his church (1 Cor. 6:9 and 3:23), to whom he must be obedient and devoted and render or show more love than he does to his own wife.

If to this it be said that by marriage the husband is bound and united to his wife, because he is one body and one flesh with her, which he is not with the church, we reply that if the believing husband is united by marriage to his wife, so also is he spiritually united to Christ, the true Bridegroom of the church. And moreover, inasmuch as the believer is one body and one flesh with the church in Christ Jesus, therefore this spiritual bond and union with Christ is and must be firmer, stronger and more binding than natural or carnal matrimony (Eph. 5:3).

Again, if it should be said that the husband may be united to Christ and yet remain with his wife, even though she has fallen away from the truth, the answer is that this cannot be, because it is against the teaching and command of the Lord and his apostles, because by so doing he does not observe excommunication as instituted, for whence should such liberty come to him? Should it be simply because she is his wife? No, certainly not, for, as we have said above, carnal marriage and union cannot destroy, supersede and render invalid evangelical separation.

10.14   Menno Simons, "Account of Excommunication," 1550, *CWMS*, 471-472

Therefore, beloved brethren, let us keep this Passover holy and unspotted, to the utmost of our ability. And let us, in the name of our Lord Jesus Christ, put away from us the corrupting leaven, that is, all those that walk in the uncircumcision of their hearts, and all of impure life (understand, open and known transgressors), that we may be the holy Israel of God; sprinkled with the blood of the Lamb, free from the avenging angel of God so that we may rejoice before the Lord in sincerity and truth, and celebrate and serve all the days of our lives.

All the pious may also learn from these words of Paul—Know ye not that a little leaven leaveneth the whole lump?—the second reason why this excommunication is so proper and useful to the house of God, and why it cannot stand without it. This has been shown by the example of Israel. Moses, the faithful servant of God, had strictly commanded the people of God that they should, without mercy, destroy from among them the willful transgressors, when convicted by two or three witnesses. Also, that if any prophets should arise among them, with signs and miracles to lead them to other gods, that they should not hear them, but put them to death. A father should not shield his child, the husband his wife, etc., but their hand should be the first upon them. They had to destroy completely any city which went after other gods, and make it a heap, so that Israel might hear these things, fear God, and plan such evil no more. I think this was a strict ban which was commanded Israel. If they had stood firm and had followed the command, counsel, teaching, and admonition of God, according to the Scriptures, and had they destroyed the false prophets and idolaters, they should never have become so estranged from God, nor have come to such deadly adultery and degeneration (over against the law, I mean). For the rejection of the counsel and will of God will never go unpunished.

But now the Holy Spirit does not teach us to destroy the wicked, as did Israel, but that we should sorrowfully expel them from the church, and that in the name of the Lord, by the power of Christ and the Holy Spirit, since a little leaven leavens the whole lump. It is a common saying, One scabby sheep mars the whole flock. The lepers were not allowed among the healthy in Israel; they had to stay in segregated places until cured. O brethren in the Lord! The leprosy of the soul is a leprosy above all leprosy, whether it be in doctrine or in life. It eats like a canker, and, as Paul says, leavens the whole lump. Therefore the Holy Spirit has abundantly taught us to separate such from among us; not to hear the words of the false prophets, for they deceive us; to separate from such who, contrary to apostolic doctrine, cause offense and contention; to shun those who are not satisfied with the salutary words and doctrine of our dear Lord Jesus Christ, but are contentious and desirous of quarreling. We are taught to guard against dogs and the concision; to flee the voice of strangers; to shun a heretic or a master of sects, after one or two admonitions; not to greet nor receive in our houses those who do not teach the doctrine of Christ; and to withdraw from every brother who acts disorderly and walks not according to the apostolic doctrine. Would, says Paul, that they were cut off who disturb you!

Methinks, beloved brethren, the Holy Spirit of God has done well, and fully performed the duties of his office, and his faithful service of divine love toward his chosen people, by admonishing, warning, teaching, and commanding, in Moses and the prophets, in Christ and the apostles, in regard to the shunning of heretics and apostates. If we through obstinacy or disobedience still associate with the leprous against the faithful counsel, teaching, and admonition of God, and intermingle with them, then we may expect to be infected with the same disease. It is the recompense of those who know the nature of the disease, and yet neither fear nor avoid it.

10.15   Menno Simons, "Account of Excommunication," 1550, *CWMS*, 474-475

My understanding, therefore, of *commisceri* or *commertium habere*, of which Paul speaks here, is that it points to communion, company, walk, intercourse, presence, usage, conversation, and dealings. It does not refer to an occasional word spoken, or to necessary business, such as dividing a legacy, paying debts, and similar incidental matters. Nor does it refer to services rendered in time of need, for the word *commertium* does not have such a strict connotation. Therefore, in my opinion, they err not a little who give the saying, Have no company with them (Not means not, they say!), the same strength which they attach to, Thou shalt not steal, and, Thou shalt not commit adultery, matters of which Paul testifies that those who are guilty of them shall not inherit the kingdom of heaven. Brethren, if this were the situation, who could stand before his God?

Again, if the word *commertium*, which in our language means company of fellowship, is to be pressed so rigidly that we are not to speak a word with an apostate, and not to transact necessary business, with him; then the word *commertium* would be violated, many a pious child would be defrauded, and many an unscriptural procedure followed, and the faithful Paul rejected. For he says, Yet count him not as an enemy, but admonish him as a brother. 2 Thess. 3:15. Besides, it would reflect unfavorably upon the gospel of Christ.

10.16 Letter of Zylis and Lemke to Menno Simons, 1557, *Hulshof*, 227-228

Concerning shunning of brothers and sisters that have fallen away we should act as follows. First, the nature of the sin ought to be considered, and that any action is compatible with the Word of Christ and his apostles. We must make determined efforts for the purity and preservation of the church, and that the fallen brother and sister is prepared for repentance. This must be done with moderation according to the witness of Scripture, with aid, mercy, and helpfulness to them when necessary. Therefore, dear brothers, it is our fervent prayer, and request to you that, for the sake of God's honour and praise, you will be satisfied and content with this solution. Thus we may finally be one people, at unity and peace with each other. Then we may with one voice praise God, through Jesus Christ. Amen.

. . . .

We also fervently desire that the brothers in the Netherlands do not counsel husband and wife to separate in the ban. Damage and vice will follow from it rather than God's praise and the welfare of souls. The commandment regarding marriage outweighs the one regarding shunning.

For further reading:

Beachy, *Grace*, 117-122.
Clasen, *Anabaptism*, 106-109.
Keeney, *Dutch Anabaptist*, 155-174.
Walter Klaassen, "Church Discipline and the Spirit in Pilgram Marpeck," Horst, *Geding*, 169-180.
Franklin H. Littell, "What Butzer Debated with the Anabaptists at Marburg: a Document of 1538," *MQR* XXXVI (July 1962), 256-276.
Oyer, *Lutheran Reformers*, 101-106.
Wenger, *Even Unto Death*, 87-91.

XI

Economics

The following selections discuss an aspect of the Anabaptist understanding of mutual aid. They are an expression of the commitment to sacrificial giving of which the Lord's Supper is a sign (see Chapter 9).

The majority of Anabaptists believed that property could be held privately, but that it could never be absolutely private. Property was viewed as a trust from God. All the selections clearly state that such property should always be available to sisters and brothers in need.

In selection 11.8 Menno Simons severely criticizes the Reformed pastors and churches for not looking after the poor among their members, and specifically relates this matter with their Lord's Supper calling it a "barren bread-breaking" which bears no fruit in terms of material aid.

Anabaptists also condemned any participation in commerce for profit. Commerce was permissible as a way of making a living. But the making of profit and the charging of interest was seen by them as a way of defrauding and especially of exploiting the poor (11.3, 11.7, 11.9).

The longer selections by Ulrich Stadler (11.4) and Peter Riedeman (11.6) describe in considerable detail the Hutterite stand on the total renunciation of property. Riedeman's argumentation in particular is reminiscent of the golden age myth in the Greek and Roman classics, which enjoyed considerable popularity in the sixteenth century. This myth identified the golden age as the time at the beginning of history when there was no private property, no agriculture, and no commerce. The golden age disappeared with the appearance of the sins of covetousness and greed, which then destroyed human society causing poverty, illness, and war. The notion of covetousness as the original sin is strong in Hutterite writings. Rothmann's statement about the community of goods in Münster strikes similar notes.

A fascinating, quite modern thought is expressed by Riedeman in selection 11.6. Some of the resources which God had given for the common use of humankind such as the sun and the air had remained so only because man had not been able to gain control of them. In our day we can easily envisage even the energy from the sun and clean air being sold on the market for profit.

Anabaptist attitudes to economic issues as articulated in these selections represented a real threat to their contemporaries, especially the economic and political power holders. Anabaptists were frequently interrogated on this question because their interrogators saw revolution on the horizon. The reformers Zwingli and Luther were afraid of it partly because their own strongest support came from the well-to-do middle class in the cities. Thus even though Anabaptists often tried to separate themselves from the affairs of the world, their statements and actions had political consequences.

11.1   Balthaser Hubmaier, "Conversation on Zwingli's Book on Baptism," 1526-1527, Davidson/Klaassen, *Hubmaier*, 157

Bal: Always and everywhere I have said as follows about the community of goods: that each man should have regard for his neighbor, so that the hungry might be fed, the thirsty refreshed, the naked clothed. For we are not lords of our own property, but stewards and dispensers. Assuredly no one could say that we claim that one should take his own from anybody and make it common property; rather we would say: if anyone would take your cloak, give him your coat also.

11.2   Interrogation of Hans Hut, 1527, *Meyer*, 231

Regarding article 23: He persuaded no one to sell his goods. However he taught, that whoever had a surplus should help the needy. True, some who were well-to-do sold some acres, vineyards and other property and shared it with the brothers who were poor. However there were no plans to move to any designated place.

11.3   Bernhard Rothmann, "Restitution," 1534, *Zuck*, 100

The living communion of saints has been restored, which provides the basis of community of goods among us. For not only have we put all our belongings in a common pool under the care of deacons, and live from it according to our needs: we praise God through Christ with one heart and mind and are eager to help one another with every kind of service. And accordingly everything which has served the purposes of self-seeking and private property, such as buying and selling, working for money, taking interest and practicing usury—even at the expense of unbelievers—or eating and drinking the sweat of the poor (that is, making one's own people and fellow-creatures work so that one can grow fat) and indeed everything which offends against love—all such things are abolished amongst us by the power of love and community. We know that such sacrifices are pleasing to the Lord. And indeed no Christian or saint can satisfy God if he does not live in such community or at least desire with all his heart to live in it.

11.4   Ulrich Stadler, "Cherished Instruction," ca. 1537, Williams, *Spiritual*, 277-279, 284

THE TRUE COMMUNITY OF THE SAINTS

There is one communion *(gmain)* of all the faithful in Christ and one community *(gmainschaft)* of the holy children called of God. They have one Father in heaven, one Lord Christ; all are baptized and sealed in their hearts with one Spirit. They have one mind, opinion, heart, and soul as having all drunk from the same fountain, and alike await one and the same struggle, cross, trial, and, at length, one and the same hope in glory. But it, that is, such a community *(gmain)* must move about in this world, poor, miserable,

234

small, and rejected of the world, of whom, however, the world is not worthy. Whoever strives for the lofty things [of this world] does not belong. Thus in this community everything must proceed equally, all things be one and communal, alike in the bodily gifts of their Father in heaven, which he daily gives to be used by his own according to his will. For how does it make sense that all who have here in this pilgrimage to look forward to an inheritance in the kingdom of their Father should not be satisfied with their bodily goods and gifts? Judge, O ye saints of God, ye who are thus truly grafted into Christ, with him deadened to the world, to sin, and to yourselves, that you never hereafter live for the world or yourselves but rather for him who died for you and arose, namely, Christ. [They] have also yielded themselves and presented themselves to him intimately, patiently, of their own free will, naked and uncovered, to suffer and endure his will and, moreover, to fulfill it and thereafter also to devote themselves in obedience and service to all the children of God. Therefore, they also live with one another where the Lord assigns a place to them, peaceably, united, lovingly, amicably, and fraternally, as children of one Father. In their pilgrimage they should be satisfied with the bodily goods and gifts of their Father, since they should also be altogether as one body and members one toward another.

Now if, then, each member withholds assistance from the other, the whole thing must go to pieces. The eyes won't see, the hands won't take hold. Where, however, each member extends assistance equally to the whole body, it is built up and grows and there is peace and unity, yea, each member takes care for the other. In brief, equal care, sadness and joy, peace [are] at hand. It is just the same in the spiritual body of Christ. If the deacon of the community will never serve, the teacher will not teach, the young brother will not be obedient, the strong will not work for the community but for himself and each one wishes to take care of himself and if once in a while someone withdraws without profit to himself, the whole body is divided. In brief, *one, common* builds the Lord's house and is pure; but *mine, thine, his, own* divides the Lord's house and is impure. Therefore, where there is ownership and one has it, and it is his, and one does not wish to be one *(gmainsam)* with Christ and his own in living and dying, he is outside of Christ and his communion *(gmain)* and has thus no Father in heaven. If he says so, he lies. That is the life of the pilgrims of the Lord, who has purchased them in Christ, namely, the elect, the called, the holy ones in this life. These are his fighters and heralds, to whom also he will give the crown of life on the day of his righteousness.

Secondly, such a community of the children of God has ordinances here in their pilgrimage. These should constitute the polity *(policeien)* for the whole world. But the wickedness of men has spoiled everything. For as the sun with its shining is common to all, so also the use of all creaturely things. Whoever appropriates them for himself and encloses them is a thief and steals what is not his. For everything has been created free in common *(in die gmain)*. Of such thieves the whole world is full. May God guard his own from them. To be sure, according to human law, one says: That is mine, but not according to divine law. Here is this ordinance [in our community] it [the divine law] is to be heeded *(gilt es aufsehens)* in such a way that unbearable burdens be not laid upon the children of the Lord, but rather ones which God, out of his grace, has put upon us, living according to which we may be pleasing to him. Thus only as circumstances dictate will the children of God have either many or few houses, institute faithful house managers and stewards, who will faithfully move among the children of God and conduct themselves in a mild and fatherly manner and pray to God for wisdom therein.

In order to hold in common all the gifts and goods which God gives and dispenses to his own, there must be free, unhampered *(ledige)*, patient *(gelassene)*, and full hearts in Christ, yea, hearts that truly believe and trust and in Christ are utterly devoted. Whoever is thus free, unhampered, and resigned in the Lord from everything, [ready] to give over all his goods and chattels, yea, to lay it up for distribution among the children of God—it is God's grace in Christ which prepares men for it. Being willing and ready—that makes one free and unhampered.

. . . .

Again, it is contended that nowhere in holy Scripture can it be read that it is a command of the Lord to bring together all the goods and to place deacons and stewards over them.

Answer: It is true abandon to yield and dispose oneself with

236

goods and chattels in the service of the saints. It is also the way of love. Moreover, true friends have all things in common; indeed, they are called two bodies with but one soul. Yea, we learn it in Christ to lose oneself in the service of the saints, to be and become poor and to suffer want, if only another may be served, and further, to put aside all goods and chattels, to throw them away in order that they may be distributed to the needy and the impoverished. That is the highest part and degree of divine abandon and voluntary surrender to the Lord and to his people through the Spirit of grace.

In brief, a brother should serve, live, and work for the other, none for himself; indeed, one house for another, one community for another in some other settlement in the land, wherever the Lord grants it that we gather together, one communion, as a body of the Lord and members one to another. This we see in all the writings of the holy apostles, namely, how one brother, one congregation, serves the other, extends assistance and supplies to the other in the Lord. Such is the life of the elect, holy children of God in their pilgrimage.

11.5 Georg Schnabel, "Defence and Refutation," 1538, *Quellen: Hesse*, 174-175

Concerning the community of believers and their material goods we say that everyone willingly helps his poor brother in his need out of his surplus. Paul writes about this in Romans 15 [26, 27] that those from Macedonia and Achaia have willingly collected a common contribution for the poor saints at Jerusalem. They have done it willingly and are in debt to them. . . . The Apostle John also says in his first letter chapter 3 [17, 18]: But if anyone has the world's goods and sees his brother in need and yet closes his heart against him, how does love abide in him? Therefore, beloved, let us not love in word or speech but in deed and truth. . . .

But there is no need to write much about what it is like in the church of the new pope.[49] For the deed is the witness whereby the tree can and must be tested as Christ himself says in Matthew 7, 12. For among them the great usury has consumed the small. Whereas before under the old pope they took one guilder of twenty annually, one must now give one measure of corn which until now has cost two guilders or more. Dr. Iserman[50] (in his book on the common good) condemned this as unchristian. Indeed he says it is worse than heathen, for among the pious heathen such a thing was not known. And now, with the advice and assistance of his cronies, he expels us poor people from our homes and property, separates us from wife and child, and tortures us with dungeon and stock, who said only what he said (namely that they have a heathen and not a Christian congregation).

11.6   Peter Riedeman, *Account*, 1542, 88-90

CONCERNING COMMUNITY OF GOODS

Now, since all the saints have fellowship in holy things, that is in God, who also has given to them all things in his Son Christ Jesus—which gift none should have for himself, but each for the other; as Christ also has nothing for himself, but has everything for us, even so all the members of his body have nothing for themselves, but for the whole body, for all the members. For his gifts are not sanctified and given to one member alone, or for one member's sake, but for the whole body with its members.

Now, since all God's gifts—not only spiritual, but also material things—are given to man, not that he should have them for himself or alone but with all his fellows, therefore the communion of saints itself must show itself not only in spiritual but also in temporal things; that as Paul says, one might not have abundance and another suffer want, but that there may be equality. This he shows from the law touching manna, in that he who gathered much had nothing over, whereas he who gathered little had no less, since each was given what he needed according to the measure.

Furthermore, one sees in all things created, which testify to us still today, that God from the beginning ordained nothing private for man, but all things to be common. But through wrong taking, since man took what he should not and forsook what he should take, he drew such things to himself and made them his property, and so grew and became hardened therein. Through such wrong taking and collecting of created things he has been led so far from God that he has even forgotten the Creator, and has even raised up and honoured as God the created things which had been put under and made subject to him. And such is still the case if one steps out of God's order and forsakes the same.

Now, however, as has been said, created things which are too high for man to draw within his grasp and collect, such as the sun with the whole course of the heavens, day, air and such like, show that not they alone, but all other created things are likewise made common to man. That they have thus remained and are not possessed by man is due to their being too high for him to bring under his power, otherwise—so evil had he become through wrong taking—he would have drawn them to himself as well as the rest and made them his property.

That this is so, however, and that the rest is just as little made by God for man's private possession, is shown in that man must forsake all other created things as well as this when he dies, and can carry nothing with him to use as his own. For which reason Christ also called temporal all things foreign to man's essential nature, and says, "If ye are not faithful in what is not your own, who will entrust to you what is your own?"

Now, because what is temporal does not belong to us, but is foreign to our true nature, the law commands that none covet strange possessions, that is, set his heart upon and cleave to what is temporal and alien. Therefore whosoever will cleave to Christ and follow him must forsake such taking of created things and property, as he himself also says, "Whosoever forsaketh not all that he hath cannot be my disciple." For if a man is to be renewed again into the likeness of God, he must put off all that leads him from him—that is the grasping and drawing to himself of created things—for he cannot otherwise attain God's likeness. Therefore Christ says, "Whosoever shall not receive the kingdom of God as a little child shall not enter therein," or, "Except ye overcome yourselves and become as little children, ye shall not enter into the kingdom of heaven."

Now, he who thus becomes free from created things can then grasp what is true and divine; and when he grasps it and it becomes his treasure, he turns his heart towards it, empties himself of all else and takes nothing as his, and regards it no longer as his but as of all God's children. Therefore we say that as all the saints have community in spiritual gifts, still much more should they show this in material things, and not ascribe the same to and covet them for themselves, for they are not their own; but regard them as of all God's children, that they may thereby show that they are partakers in the community of Christ and are renewed into God's likeness. For the more man yet cleaves to created things, appropriates and ascribes such to himself, the further he shows himself to be from the likeness of God and the community of Christ.

For this reason the Holy Spirit also at the beginning of the church began such community right gloriously again, so that none said that any of the things that he possessed was his own, but they had all things in common; and it is his will that this might still be kept, as Paul says, "Let none seek his own profit but the profit of another," or, "Let none seek what benefiteth himself but what benefiteth many." Where this is not the case it is a blemish upon the church which ought verily to be corrected. If one should say, it was so nowhere except in Jerusalem, therefore it is now not necessary, we say, Even if it were nowhere but in Jerusalem, it followeth not that it ought not to be so now. For neither apostles nor churches were lacking, but rather the opportunity, manner and time.

11.7   Pilgram Marpeck, "Concerning the Lowliness of Christ," 1547, *The Writings*, 449-450

Would to God, for their sake, that it were not true that today there are worse and even more evil merchants than the Jewish Pharisees, who bought the Lord from Judas because of envy and hate. [But, today], whole lands, armies, and peoples (many hundreds of thousands of people, even though they are not good people),[51] are betrayed, sold, and bought by their loans, finance, and usury. It is done out of avarice, envy, and hate, an attempt to preserve their earthly pomp, pride, and vain honour. Moreover, all the actions, of both the old and new[52] forcers of faith, are done in the semblance of Christ and his gospel. I am concerned that, shortly, the words of James, "Howl and weep, you rich," etc., will be fulfilled in them.

240

11.8   Menno Simons, "Reply to False Accusations," 1552, *CWMS*, 559

Is it not sad and intolerable hypocrisy that these poor people boast of having the Word of God, of being the true, Christian church, never remembering that they have entirely lost their sign of true Christianity? For although many of them have plenty of everything, go about in silk and velvet, gold and silver, and in all manner of pomp and splendor; ornament their houses with all manner of costly furniture; have their coffers filled, and live in luxury and splendor, yet they suffer many of their own poor, afflicted members (notwithstanding their fellow believers have received one baptism and partaken of the same bread with them) to ask alms; and poor, hungry, suffering, old, lame, blind, and sick people to beg their bread at their doors.

O preachers, dear preachers, where is the power of the gospel you preach? Where is the thing signified in the Supper you administer? Where are the fruits of the spirit you have received? And where is the righteousness of your faith which you dress up so beautifully before the poor, ignorant people? Is it not all hypocrisy that you preach, maintain, and assert? Shame on you for the easygoing gospel and barren bread-breaking, you who have in so many years been unable to effect enough with your gospel and sacraments so as to remove your needy and distressed members from the streets, even though the Scripture plainly teaches and says, Whoso hath this world's good, and seeth his brother have need, and shutteth up his bowels of compassion for him, how dwelleth the love of God in him?

11.9   Menno Simons, "True Christian Faith," 1541, *CWMS*, 368, 369

Captains, knights, foot soldiers, and similar bloody men risk body and soul for the sake of gain, and swear with uplifted fingers that they are ready to destroy cities and countries, to take citizens and inhabitants, to kill them and take their possessions, although these have never harmed them nor given them so much as an evil word. O God, what cursed, wicked abomination and traffic! And they call that protecting the country and the people, and assisting in justice!

. . . .

The wicked merchants and retailers (I say the wicked, for I do not mean those who are righteous and pious), together with all those who are out to make money and to make their living that way, are so bent on accursed profit that they exclude God wholly from their hearts. They censure what they should properly praise, and praise what they should censure. They lie and swear; they use many vain words, falsify their wares to cheat the people, and strip them of possessions; they sell, lend, and secure the needy at large profit and usury, never seriously reflecting or taking to heart that is written, Let no man go beyond and defraud his brother in any matter. 1 Thess. 4:6.

. . . .

This I write as a warning to the God-fearing merchants and retailers, lest they be like the ungodly, and be overcome by avarice. But may they be circumspect in dealing and on the alert against moral danger.

For the sake of this accursed thirst for profit, some become thieves, some murderers, some holdup men; others become necromancers, sorcerers, some harlots and brothel keepers; others, gamblers, betrayers, executioners, and tormentors; also persecutors and slayers of the pious, etc., and all this, I say, for the sake of accursed profit. By these things they openly testify, since they walk in such a way and are so intent on unlawful gain, that they are of the devil and not of God, that they have not the faith and Word of Christ, but in every respect hate them.

Yes, good reader, the whole world is so affected and involved in this accursed avarice, fraud, false practice, and unlawful means of support; in this false traffic and merchandise, with this finance, usury, and personal advancement that I do not know how it could get much worse. Yet they continue to be the priests' and preachers' Christians, and then call this earning their bread honestly, and doing justice to all.

For further reading:

Clasen, *Anabaptism*, 183-199, 283-292.
J. Winfield Fretz, "Brotherhood and the Economic Ethic of the Anabaptists," Hershberger, *Anabaptist Vision*, 194-201.
Robert Friedmann, "Economic Aspects of Early Hutterite Life," *MQR* XXX (October 1956), 259-266.
_____, "The Hutterian Brethren and the Community of Goods," Hershberger, *Anabaptist Vision*, 83-92.
Horsch, *Hutterian Brethren*, 131-133.
Keeney, *Dutch Anabaptist*, 135-136.
Walter Klaassen, "The Nature of the Anabaptist Protest," *MQR* XLV (October 1971), 291-311.
Klassen, *Economics*.
Peter J. Klassen, "Mutual Aid Among the Anabaptists: Doctrine and Practice," *MQR* XXXVII (April 1963), 78-95.

XII

Government

Basic to the Anabaptist view of government was their version of the two kingdoms doctrine. In its basic ingredients it was virtually identical with Martin Luther's. Government was given because of man's sin; it belonged to law, while the church, which was given out of sheer grace, belonged to the gospel.

The kingdom of Christ was characterized by peace, forgiveness, nonviolence, and patience. The kingdom of the world, or Satan, was strife, vengeance, anger, and the sword which kills. Government belonged to this kingdom of the world.

Nevertheless, government, according to all Anabaptists, was appointed by God and performed a divine function whether it was benevolent or tyrannous. Its function was to reward the good and punish the evil. It kept order by force in a world in which the spirit of Christ had not yet captured all hearts and made them obedient. This use of basic force was never disputed by Anabaptists. Many even accorded the government the right to exercise capital punishment.

Because the government was instituted by God and acted in God's stead, it had to be obeyed. Taxes and dues should be paid without resistance. (Only the Hutterites refused to pay taxes for war or the executioner.)

At the same time, all Anabaptists were clear that God's authority exceeded that of the government. If a conflict of loyalties developed, God should unquestionably be obeyed. However, in the Münsterite kingdom the voice of God and the voice of government were virtually identical, as was also the case in most Protestant jurisdictions. That being the case, it was easy to deal with dissidents and heretics.

244

On all of this Luther and Anabaptists were agreed. Where they parted company was on the Christian's relation to government. Luther argued that a Christian must participate in government out of love for the neighbor. He must be prepared to coerce and kill to save the neighbor, and he could do it with a good conscience because he was carrying out a divine mandate. The Anabaptists, on the other hand, said that a Christian may not participate in government out of love for the neighbor. A servant of Christ had no liberty to use coercion and vengeance or to kill because it was contrary to the commandments of Christ.

Most Anabaptists therefore rejected all participation in government for the Christian for the reasons mentioned above, and also because any Anabaptist in government in sixteenth-century Europe would soon find himself prosecuting the members of his own church. However, some Anabaptist leaders sensed a contradiction between the assertion that government was ordained by God and the claim that no Christian could be a magistrate, with its corollary that no magistrate could be a Christian. Hubmaier resolved it by rejecting nonparticipation. Hans Denck (12.5), Pilgram Marpeck (12.17), and Menno Simons (12.13) either specifically allowed or implied that a Christian could be a magistrate. However, both Denck and Marpeck then went on to say that the conflict between the spirit of Christ and the methods of the world would not allow a Christian to survive as a magistrate.

Marpeck also replied to the Protestant argument that the best government was a Christian one. It really would not make that much difference, he argued, unless the methods used conform to the spirit of Christ. Since that could not be the case, the argument was not valid (12.16).

A prominent theme one encounters in almost all selections is that governmental activity should be strictly limited to its proper sphere. In particular, it should have no role in the life of the church. This was argued specifically because they said, in the words of the Schleitheim Confession, that government was "outside the perfection of Christ." Its means and methods were sub-Christian and not suited to the new community of love and forgiveness. Even Hubmaier was very emphatic about this point (12.1). Marpeck made a special point of saying that government exceeds its authority when it seeks to suppress false teaching (12.8). Menno Simons took the opposite view. One of the government's functions, he stated, was to suppress false teachers who lead others astray. By false teachers he meant many of the Protestant and Catholic clerics. He did, however, say that such suppression should be done "without tyranny and bloodshed" (12.13).

Balthasar Hubmaier was the one Anabaptist leader who argued strongly for Christian participation in government (12.3, 12.4). Because of this he has often been considered a marginal Anabaptist, especially after nonresistance had become a special mark of Anabaptism. However, the restrictions under which he places even a Christian government have often not been understood. He called for obedience to government but then qualified that by saying that only a just government deserved such obedience. Each magistrate acts in the place of God, wrote Hubmaier, and is responsible ultimately to God alone. He may not hide behind a superior's orders. If he is ordered to do something unjust, he must disobey (12.1).

Hubmaier also took a very strong stand against the use of the sword in a holy war as he encountered it in Hans Hut (12.6) (see also selections 17.4, 17.5). The sword is ordained only for the preservation of order. This may involve a just war of defence, but never a holy war. At this point even the magisterial Anabaptist Hubmaier differed basically from his Protestant and Catholic contemporaries, most of whom accepted the necessity of the war for the gospel. Rothmann and his fellow leaders in Münster, however, disagreed with Hubmaier at this point. Like other Christians in Europe at the time, they were ready for the holy war to which God would call them (17.18).

Anabaptists frequently called on governments to exercise their function justly. Where they saw abuses they were not slow to threaten governments with God's judgments (12.1, 12.11, 12.13).

12.1   Balthasar Hubmaier, "Short Explanation," 1526, Davidson/Klaassen, *Hubmaier*, 533-537

Yet I implore, admonish and warn, in the name of Jesus Christ and of his last judgment, all those whom God has girded with the sword, not to use it against innocent blood with persecution, imprisonment, hanging, drowning, or burning. Verily, verily, I say to them, that the shed and martyred blood will cry out against them to heaven with the innocent blood of pious Abel against the Cainites, murderers and shedders of blood, to God. God will demand it at their hands, and pour out his vengeance on them and on their children. He who sheds the blood of man (I mean contrary to the order of God's justice), his blood also, says God, shall be shed (Gen. 9). He who takes the sword and uses it shall perish by the sword (Mt. 26). Therefore attend, O you in power, to what you should do. . . . You are not exercising a human but divine office, and what you judge will be meted out to you. Take heed that the fear of God be in you, and do all things diligently. There is in God no wickedness, no accepting of persons, no covetousness for bribes. Take heed, take heed, O you in power, lest you defile and wash your hands in the blood of the innocent. . . . It will not help you to say: I was forced to do so; my master bade me do it; he would have it thus. Nay, not so. One must obey God rather than man. . . .

The emperor himself with all his might, power, offices, and goods could not help you or me with so much as a cool drop of water. . . . In short, to come to the point, God will excuse us for nothing on account of unjust superiors. . . .
[At this point Hubmaier quotes Isaiah 1:10-23.]

Observe here, O pious Christian, how severely God complains of unjust officials. In truth, a hard punishment will befall them. God will take vengeance on them, as on his enemies. . . .

Whereupon I admonish all emperors, kings, princes, lords, all in authority and rank, as Moses admonished his judges (Deut. 1), that they hear, indict, and see everyone, and that they condemn no one on the basis of false witness. Many a man is accused now as an heretic and an agitator, into whose heart heresy and rebellion have never entered. Satan acts thus, to deliver a blow at the gospel—to make it hateful to all authority. The spirit of God said through Moses: judge what is right between a man and his brother, and to strangers. Be no respecters of persons in judgment. Hear the small as well as the great, and fear the face of no one, for the judgment is of

God. Note that the judge sits in the stead of God. So it is important that he judge not contrary to God.

12.2   Interrogation of Ambrosius Spitelmaier, 1527, Schornbaum, *Quellen*, 52

All government which has been since the time of Adam and which exists today has been instituted by God. However it has not remained in God but has presumed on its power and still does today. The government or power was originally instituted by God in order to judge the words and works done against God and man. But the words and works done against God the government is not to judge. Therefore it is blind and a leader of the blind, for it seeks only its own interest and not the interests of God. Therefore its judgment is false. Now the government presumes to judge the words and works which it says are against God but which are for God. In this sense it is like Pilate who condemned Christ.

12.3   Balthasar Hubmaier, "Concerning the Sword," 1527, Westin, *Quellen*, 441

Even a blind man can see that a Christian may with a good conscience be a judge and a council member to judge and decide in temporal matters. Even though the contentious and the litigious sin, yet would they sin far more if they were to bring their matters before unbelieving judges. Now if a Christian may and ought to be a judge in his pronouncements in the power of the divine Word, so he may also be a protector with the hand of justice and a punisher of the unrighteous. For of what good were law, court, and judge if one were not obliged to execute and carry out the penalty on the wicked? What good is a shoe if one dare not wear it? Observe dear brothers, that councils, courts and laws are not unjust. The judge too may and ought to be a Christian even though the contentious parties sin and are not prepared to be wronged. Thus also a Christian may—according to the order of God—bear the sword in God's stead against the evildoer and punish him. For it has been so ordered by God because of wickedness for the protection of the pious (Rom. 13).

12.4   Balthasar Hubmaier, "Concerning the Sword," 1527, Davidson/Klaassen, *Hubmaier*, 717-718

If we take the words of Christ to heart and ponder them we shall not err. Christ says: You have heard that it has been said: You shall love your neighbor and hate your enemy. Notice this: who is an enemy? Why, a man whom one hates or envies. But a Christian should never hate or envy anyone, but love everybody. Thus a Christian magistrate has no enemy, for he hates and envies no one. What he does with the sword, he does not out of grudging or hate, but at the command of God. The punishing of the wicked is not hate or envy, or enmity. If it were, God himself would be a hateful and envious enemy of man. But he is not. When he punishes the evil, he does it not from envy or hate, but from justice.

Therefore a just and Christian judge does not hate those he punishes. He is sorry from his heart at the offences of such evil folk. Whatever he does is by the order and solemn command of God. God made him his servant, and gave him the sword for the execution of justice. He has to render an account on the last day, as to how he has employed that sword. His sword is nothing else than the beneficent rod and scourge of God, with which he is commanded to chastise the evil. Now what God calls good, is good; if he should bid you to slay your own son that would be a good work.

God does many things through his creatures as his instruments which he could do alone, without them. But he wants to employ us, that we may serve each other, and not be idle. He wants everyone to serve in the office to which God has called him. One must preach, another be a soldier, a third till the fields, a fourth work in some other way. . . .

12.5   Hans Denck, "Concerning True Love," 1527, Fellmann, *Denck I*, 85

It is not that power in itself is wrong seen from the perspective of the evil world, for [the government] serves God in his wrath, but rather that love teaches her children a better way, namely to serve the graciousness of God. For it is the nature of love not to will or desire the hurt of anyone, but as much as is possible to serve for the betterment of everyone. A housefather should treat his wife and child, menservants and maids as he would that God should treat him. That is not incompatible with love. And insofar as it were possible for a government to act in this way it could well be Christian in its office. Since however the world will not tolerate it, a friend of God should not be in the government but out of it, that is if he desires to keep Christ as a Lord and master. Whoever loves the Lord loves him regardless of his station. But he should not forget what characterizes a true lover [of God], namely that for the Lord's sake he renounce all power and to be subject to no one but the Lord.

12.6 Balthasar Hubmaier, "Justification," 1528, Westin, *Quellen*, 489

... We wish to be subject and obedient to the government and are always ready to prevent and reject all strife, rebellion, and discord. On this account I am very dissatisfied with Hans Hut and his following. Secretly and in dark corners they talk to and mislead the people, and make a conspiracy and rebellion under the appearance of baptism and the Lord's Supper, and talk about using the sword and similar things. No, no! Certainly not! A Christian does not fight, strike, or kill unless he is a magistrate or commissioned to do it by a proper authority. Otherwise a Christian will surrender his cloak and his coat before he takes the sword. He offers his cheek, indeed, life and limb. The Christian way is peaceful for that is the victory of the Christian, even faith which overcomes the world (1 Jn. 5).

12.7 "Zofingen Colloquy," 1531, Haas, *Quellen*, 165-167

According to Romans 13, the sword, the power, and the authority which is to be deployed and used in the world has been established to punish the evil and protect the good. Similarly we read in 1 Timothy [8] ... and 1 Peter 2 [13-14].... Here Peter teaches the faithful that they may not resist the order of God in those things which agree with the gospel because they have been made free through the blood of Christ. This freedom in Christ may not become a cover for license. Paul writes to Titus (3:[1]): Remind them to be subject to those set over them. Thus the apostles taught the churches everywhere that they should not resist the order of the Father and the law insofar as it agrees with the gospel because Christ had redeemed them from the law. We, therefore, confess and accept the government and authority of the world because it is everywhere ordained by God. That is why taxes and duties must be paid.

. . . .

However, the Christian church is to punish evil in its own house according to the order of the ban and the usage of the apostles. . . . [He quotes Matthew 20:25-27 and Mark 10:43-45.] After that Jesus spoke to them about the rulers of the heathen who rule with violence. But among you it may not be thus, he said. Rather, whoever wishes to be great must be the servant of all. . . . These testify to the institution of authority, which we have no desire to resist according to its legitimacy. Anyone among us who did it would be told that he was doing wrong. Christ, the true, undoubted Son of the Father, did not accept the order of his Father[53] for his disciples, but rather relegated it clearly to the world when he said: among you it must not be so. Because of this we cannot admit that the authority of material weapons may be used in the Christian congregation.

12.8   Pilgram Marpeck, "Confession," 1532, *The Writings*, 150

I admit worldly, carnal, and earthly rulers as servants of God in earthly matters, but not in the kingdom of Christ. According to the words of Paul, to them rightfully belongs all carnal honour, fear, obedience, tax, toll, and tribute. However, when such persons who hold authority become Christians (which I heartily wish and pray for) they may not use the aforementioned carnal force, sovereignty or ruling in the kingdom of Christ. It cannot be upheld by any Scripture. To allow the external authority to rule in the kingdom of Christ brings blasphemy of the Holy Spirit, who alone is Lord and Ruler without any human assistance. And if false teachers desire to lead astray, the true sheep do not listen to the voice of strangers; they are soon known by them. Where the governmental authority is used, as

251

it was in the Old Testament, to root out the false prophets, Christ's Word and Spirit are weakened, and are turned into a servile spirit designed to uphold insufficient and weak laws. For the Word of God is the sharp, two-edged sword, separating and chastising false and true, good and evil.

12.9 Jacob Hutter, "Plots and Excuses," Müller, *Glaubenszeugnisse* 186-187

They answer us and say that the saints also warred to protect their law, religion, and faith. They say that David and many others have also gone to war and try to defend their folly in this way. Our answer is that David and others did indeed fight. It was customary in their time. Indeed the Lord commanded them to hate their enemies and to exterminate them. We do not deny this. For at that time servanthood had not been distinguished from sonship and the road to glory had not yet been revealed. Thus the law was their schoolmaster and they were imprisoned under external statutes until the time of Christ. He was to liberate those who were under the law so that they too would receive sonship. . . .

Again the godless say: you do not want to be subject to the government nor to pay taxes, when after all it is written that one should be subject to all human ordinances and whoever resists the government resists what God has ordained.

To this we reply that we do not wish to resist the government. Far be it from us to resist what is neither against God nor our conscience. Rather we would suffer violence for the sake of truth, for through the grace of God we are prepared for all good works and to give to everyone what we owe them before God according to divine testimony ... be it taxes, interest, the tithe, service, and customs duty or whatever it is called—whatever does not contribute to the destruction of man. . . . We do it not because of the threat of penalty but for the sake of our conscience. However where the government or power expects something beyond the order of God and its demands which is not normally given and which afflicts our conscience such as taxes in war and similar things which contribute to the destruction of men, then we say with Peter that we must obey God more than man. We do this not from wantonness but because of our conscience and because we fear God in this matter. For how could we be innocent before our God if we did not go to war ourselves but gave the money that others could go in our place? We will give nothing nor help in such matter in order that we retain a clear conscience before God and not become partakers of the sin of others and dishonour and despise God.

12.10 Bernhard Rothmann, "Restitution," 1534, *SBR*, 277-278

[He quotes Romans 13, 1-4.]

In these words Paul expresses clearly enough what a true Christian government is. It is a servant of God, the protector of the innocent and the righteous, an avenger of evil, having received power from God on earth to use it accordingly. That is the true Christian government. But a government that oppresses the innocent and the righteousness and supports the godless, has not been ordained by God to do so, but by the devil whom it serves when it supports unrighteousness, even though it has received its power from God. All power is of God, not to do evil but to do good. Those who use the power to do evil turn away from God and serve the devil. God does indeed call and use such governments to his praise, but they will be repaid for their evil ways. Therefore God admonishes all governments to give just judgment, as in Ps. 2, [10], 81. [82,2], 51. [52,3] etc. Wisd. 6, [1-11].

It is further said about the government that it is to be God's servant, a contender for justice. For this the sword is to be used. For a long time the sword was misused among us. But almighty God, when his Word began to grow among us, has also renewed and reestablished the government among us according to his Word. We cannot thank the almighty eternal God enough for this. He has covered the dead bones with flesh and sinews, made them alive, and established a glorious kingdom among us. This is the kingdom and the throne of David, in which, through the sword of righteousness, the kingdom among us is to be cleansed and extended from now on. Thus the true and peaceful Solomon can enter it and possess it.

Whoever has ears to hear, let him hear, and whoever has the wit to understand, let him understand. For we know that it will be known in power rather than in words.

12.11 Jacob Hutter, "Letter to the Vice-Regent," 1535, Manschreck, *History*, 86-87

Woe, woe unto you, O ye Moravian rulers, who have sworn to that cruel tyrant and enemy of God's truth, Ferdinand, to drive away his pious and faithful servants! Woe, we say to you! who fear more that frail and mortal man than the living, omnipotent and eternal God, and chase from you, suddenly and inhumanely, the children of God, the afflicted widow, the desolate orphan, and scatter them abroad. Not with impunity will you do this; your oaths will not excuse you, or afford you any subterfuge. The same punishment and torments that Pilate endured will overtake you: who, unwilling to crucify the Lord, yet from fear of Caesar adjudged him to death. God, by the mouth of the prophet, proclaims that he will fearfully and terribly avenge the shedding of innocent blood, and will not pass by such as fear not to pollute and contaminate their hands therewith. Therefore great slaughter, much misery and anguish, sorrow, and adversity, yea, everlasting groaning, pain and torment, are daily appointed you. The Most High will lift his hand against you, now and eternally. This we announce to you in the name of our Lord Jesus Christ, for verily it will not tarry, and shortly you shall see that we have told you nothing but the truth of God, in the name of our Lord Jesus Christ, and are witnesses against you, and against all who set at nought his commandments. We beseech you to forsake iniquity, and to turn to the living God with weeping and lamentation, that you may escape all these woes.

12.12 "Justification of the Brothers," 1539, Müller, *Glaubenszeugnisse*, 199-200

It is asked whether a Christian may be a magistrate if he is elected to that position. To this we say: they tried to make Christ into a king. But he fled and did not acknowledge the order of his Father for himself.[54] He also says: whoever will follow me must deny himself, take up his cross and follow me. He himself forbids the power of the sword when he says: the princes of this world rule the peoples, and the lords exercise authority, but it shall not be so among you. Rather, if anyone wishes to be an authority he must be your servant, and if anyone will be first, he must be your slave. Those whom God foreknew he also foreordained that they should be conformed to the image of his son. Peter also says: Christ did not rule but suffered, and left us an example that we should follow in his footsteps.

Further it is asked concerning the sword whether a Christian should give judgments in worldly disputes and quarrels which the unbelieving have among themselves. We confess and testify as follows: Christ did not wish to judge between brother and brother concerning an inheritance but refused. We want to do likewise. Further we say that it is not proper for a Christian to be a magistrate. Why? The power of the world is according to the flesh but the Christian's power is according to the Spirit. The citizenship of the world is in this world, but the Christian's citizenship is in heaven. Their battles and weapons are carnal and used against the flesh; the Christian's weapons are spiritual and used against the fortress of the devil. The worldly are armed with armour alone against the flesh, but the Christians are armed with the armour of God that is truth, righteousness, peace, faith, salvation and the word of God. In short, whatever Christ our head desires of us the members of his body must do, fulfil and think. As Christ our salvation searched, so we should seek his great prize in all things in order that there be no growth in his body which would bring him shame. For every kingdom that is divided against itself will fall.[55]

12.13 Menno Simons, "Foundation," 1539, *CWMS*, 193-195

Therefore, dear sirs, take heed; this is the task to which you are called: namely, to chastise and punish, in the true fear of God with fairness and Christian discretion, manifest criminals, such as thieves, murderers, Sodomites, adulterers, seducers, sorcerers, the violent, highwaymen, robbers, etc. Your task is to do justice between a man and his neighbor, to deliver the oppressed out of the hand of the oppressor; also to restrain by reasonable means, that is, without tyranny and bloodshed, manifest deceivers who so miserably lead poor helpless souls by hundreds of thousands into destruction. Whether the deceivers are priests, monks, preachers, baptized or unbaptized, it is your task to restrain them so that they may no longer detract from the power of the almighty majesty of God, our only and eternal Saviour, Christ Jesus, the Holy Ghost, and the Word of grace; nor introduce such ridiculous abuses and idolatry under the semblance of truth as has been done until now. In this way, in all love, without force, violence, and blood, you may enlarge, help, and protect the kingdom of God with gracious consent and permission, with wise counsel and a pious, unblamable life.

. . . .

O highly renowned, noble lords, believe Christ's Word, fear God's wrath, love righteousness, do justice to widows and orphans, judge rightly between a man and his neighbor, fear no man's highness, despise no man's littleness, hate all avarice, punish with reason, allow the Word of God to be taught freely, hinder no one from walking in the truth, bow to the scepter of him who called you to this high service. Then shall your throne stand firm forever.

. . . .

Sirs, dear sirs, humble yourselves. Righteous is he who will hear your case, and mighty is he who will sentence. His name is the Ruler of rulers; He is the Almighty, the holy and terrible, the highly adorable and wonderworking God who has created heaven and earth, and grips in the hands of his strength all majesty, power, and dominion. Him learn to know; him learn to fear. Rouse yourselves; the time is not far off when you will hear, Give an account of your stewardship; for thou mayest no longer be steward. Lk. 16:2.

. . . .

O kings and rulers of the land, where indeed is your faith and

256

love with their pious nature? Where is the fear of your God, your burning lamp, your humble heart dead unto sin? Where is your blameless, godly life which is of God? Is it not Simon-pure world and carnality which you seek and protect? We find in your houses and courts nothing but sparkling pomp and showy dress, boldness and presumptuousness of heart, insatiable avarice, hatred and envy, backbiting, betraying, harloting, seduction, gambling, gaming, carousing, dancing, swearing, stabbing, and violence. This is your chivalrous custom and courtly conduct all the days of your lives. You never once reflect through what misery, tribulation, humility, love, and righteousness the Lord of lords and King of kings walked his way before you, what he taught the children of men, and what pattern or example he left them. The pitiful moaning and misery of the wretched men does not reach your ears. The sweat of the poor we find in your house, and the innocent blood on your hands. Their gifts and presents are received to pervert judgment and you take counsel against the Lord and his anointed. The prophets of Jezebel and the priests of Baal, men who talk to your taste and fawn all over you, these are in big demand and swarm all over you. These are in big demand with you, men who sit on easy cushions and have a fine time.

12:14   Menno Simons, "Foundation," 1539, *CWMS*, 204

Do not usurp the judgment and kingdom of Christ, for he alone is the Ruler of the conscience, and besides him there is none other. Let him be your Emperor in this matter and his holy Word your edict, and you will soon have enough of storming and slaying. You must hearken to God above the emperor, and obey God's Word more than that of the emperor. If not, then you are the judges of whom it is written in Micah, They all lie in wait for blood; they hunt every man his brother with a net. That they may do evil with both hands earnestly, the prince asketh, and the judge asketh for a reward; and the great man, he uttereth his mischievous desire: so they wrap it up. The best of them is as a briar; the most upright is sharper than a thorn hedge: the day of thy watchmen and thy visitation cometh; now shall be their perplexity. Mic. 7:2-4.

12.15   Peter Riedeman, *Account,* 1542, 102-108

CONCERNING GOVERNMENTAL AUTHORITY

Governmental authority is appointed and ordained by God as a rod of his anger for the discipline and punishment of the evil and profligate nation. Therefore Paul names it a servant of God's vengeance, by means of which God will avenge himself on their sins and bring the evil they have done upon their own head, that their wickedness might not continue to spread and that the whole earth might not on their account become blemished and unclean. Therefore one should be obedient and subject to rulers as ordained by God for the purpose of protection, in so far as they do not attack the conscience or command what is against God. As Peter exhorts us saying, "Submit yourselves to every ordinance of man for the Lord's sake: whether it be to the king, as supreme; or unto the governors, as unto them that are sent by him." And Paul says, "Remind them to be subject to the principalities and powers, to obey magistrates, to be ready to every good work."

Therefore is one rightly obedient and subject to them, and the more diligent one is therein, the better is it and the more pleasing to God. For whosoever resists this, resists the ordinance of God. Where, however, the rulers command and act against God, there one must leave their command undone, and obey God rather than man. For the conscience has been set free and is reserved for God alone, that he and no human being may be Lord of the same and ruler over, teach and direct it whithersoever it pleases him. Therefore wherever the government presumes to lay hands upon the conscience and to control the faith of man, there it is robbing God of what is his. Therefore it is wrong to obey it in this. Now, since the office of government is an ordinance and establishment of God and because it has been appointed and ordained by God, within its own limits it is right and good, but where it is abused, this same misuse is wrong. The office, nevertheless, remains as it was ordained. Therefore is the office to be honoured. For, even though godless men fill it, the office is not thereby annulled. And God permits this to the godless for the greater punishment of the people. But just as a godless government

258

is given to the nation by God as a punishment, even so is a disobedient nation given to the godless government, that they might tear and devour one another and at last be consumed together.

WHY GOVERNMENTAL AUTHORITY HAS BEEN ORDAINED

Governmental authority has been ordained by God because of the turning aside of the people, in that they turned away from him and walked according to the flesh. For God says, "My Spirit shall not always strive with men, for they are flesh." For this reason, after the flood, he ordained governmental authority for them to be a rod of the anger and vengeance of God, to shed the blood of those who have shed blood.

And again, when Israel had once more turned away from the Lord who was their King, had forsaken him and desired a king, God spoke to Samuel, "They have not rejected thee, but they have rejected me, that I should not reign over them. They do to thee as they have always done. Since the day that I led them up out of Egypt they have forsaken me and served other gods, therefore hearken unto their voice and give them a king."

From these words we see how governmental authority grew and from whence it came, namely, from the wrath of God; even as it is written, "You said, Give us a king. I gave you a king in my anger and took him away again in my wrath." Thus, it is evident that governmental authority is not of grace but is given in disfavour and anger, and that after the turning away of the people. Since they forsook God and followed the flesh, flesh had to have dominion over them.

Therefore the government is a picture, sign and reminder of man's departure from God, and ought well to be to all men an urge to retire within themselves and to consider to what they have come and to what they have fallen, that they might with all the more haste turn back to God to receive again the grace they had lost. There are few, however, who consider thus, therefore do they remain in their sins.

Over and above all this, because governmental authority is a servant of God's anger and vengeance, as long as it has being it indicates that God's anger and wrath is still over sinners and is not at an end.

WHETHER RULERS CAN ALSO BE CHRISTIANS

Here begins a quite other kingdom and reign, therefore that which is old must stop and come to an end, as also the symbol of the Jewish royal house signifies, which was there until Christ came, as the scriptures declare, "The sceptre shall not depart from Judah until the hero, Christ, shall come." Therefore it is ended, stopped and broken in Christ. He now sits upon the throne of his father, David, and has become a king of all true Israelites. He also has now begun a new regime that is not like the old one and is not supported by the temporal sword.

Now, since the regime of the Jews, who until then were God's people, came to an end in Christ, ceased and was taken from them, it is clear that it should be no more in Christ, but it is his desire to rule over Christians with his spiritual sword alone. That the power of the temporal sword was taken from the Jews and has passed to the heathen signifies that from henceforth the people of God ought no longer to use the temporal sword and rule therewith; but ought to be the ruled and led by the one Spirit of Christ alone. And that it has gone to the heathen signifies that those who do not submit themselves to the Spirit of Christ—that is, all heathen and unbelievers—should be disciplined and punished therewith. Therefore governmental authority has its place outside Christ, but not in Christ.

Thus God in Christ, alone, is king and commander of his people, as it is written, "God hath set a ruler over every people, but over Israel he alone is Lord." Even as he is a spiritual king, he also has spiritual servants and wields a spiritual sword—both he and all his servants—that pierces soul and spirit.

Now because the Son was appointed by the Father, as it is written, "I have set my king upon my holy hill of Zion," and given not in anger like the other but in blessing, and has become a source of blessing to us all (as, indeed, it had been promised that in him all peoples should be blessed), therefore, even as the other was ordained to shed the blood of him who sheds a man's blood, this king has been

260

ordained to preserve the souls of men; as the other to take vengeance on evil, this to recompense it with good; as the other hate the enemy, this is ordained to love. Thus is Christ King of all kings, and at the same time the opposite of all the rulers of this world; therefore he says, "My kingdom is not of this world: if my kingdom were of this world then would my servants fight for me."

Thus, he sets up quite a different kingdom and rule and desires that his servants submit themselves to it and become like him; therefore he says to them, "The princes of the world are called gracious lords, and the powerful exercise dominion over the people, but it shall not be so among you: but let him who is the greatest among you be your minister." Thus the glory of Christ and of his servants consists in the putting off of all worldly glory. And the more one puts this aside, the more glorious he becomes in Christ's kingdom, as the word shows, "Whosoever exalteth himself shall be abased, and whosoever humbleth himself shall be exalted."

Now because in Christ our King is the full blessing of God—yea, he is himself the blessing—all that was given in wrath must come to an end and cease in him, and has no part in him. But governmental authority was given in wrath, and so it can neither fit itself into nor belong to Christ. Thus no Christian is a ruler and no ruler is a Christian, for the child of blessing cannot be the servant of wrath. Thus, in Christ not the temporal, but the spiritual sword rules over men, and so rules that they deserve not the temporal sword, therefore also have no need of it.

If one were to say, however, "It is necessary because of evil men," this we have already answered in saying that the power of the sword has passed to the heathen, that they may therewith punish their evildoers. But that is no concern of ours; as Paul says, "What have I to do to judge them that are without?" Thus no Christian can rule over the world.

To this someone might say, "Then according to this view, the way to life is closed to those in governmental authority!" We say, "No", for Christ says, "Come unto me all ye that are weary and heavy laden. I will refresh you and give rest unto your souls." Therefore is this free to all—to rulers as well as to subjects. Whosoever comes to him will he in no wise cast out.

261

Therefore if rulers divest themselves of their glory as Christ did, and humble themselves with him and allow Christ, only, to use them, then the way to life would be as open to them as to others. But when Christ begins to work in men, he does nothing except what he himself did—and he fled when men sought to make him a king.

If, however, their spirits remain unbroken and they remain in their glory, Christ himself says, "Whosoever divesteth not himself of all that he hath—yea, of his own life also—cannot be my disciple." From this it is clear that not only governmental authorities but all who still cleave to created things, and forsake them not for Christ's sake, are not Christians.

12.16   Pilgram Marpeck, "Explanation of the Testaments," *The Writings*, 558

[If the pope has no right to exercise coercion in the church] much less ought worldly magistrates to be put into the holy place. Rather, as stated above, they should be allowed to remain in their proper service of God to fulfill it according to God's will through the fear of God and that wisdom which is necessary and requisite for all worldly pagan authority (whom Paul calls the servants of God regardless of faith in Christ as stated above) as wisdom herself says in Proverbs 8:[15-16]: "By me kings reign, and princes decree justice; by me princes rule justly and all the judges on earth exercise authority." Wisdom 6 also admonishes rulers concerning this wisdom. . . . But Saint Paul distinguishes this wisdom of the worldly magistrates from the wisdom of Christ when he says: It is not the wisdom of the rulers of this world. 1 Cor. 2:[6]. It is thus clear that the worldly rulers have a special wisdom for their service. For Christian wisdom is not relevant to their service nor will it serve them since it brings about only grace, mercy, love for the enemy, spiritual supernatural things, cross, tribulation, patience and faith in Christ without mastery, killing of the body and the external sword, but only through the Word of God. The wisdom of the office of the worldly rulers is designed to work through the external sword in vindictiveness, mercilessness, hate of sin, physical vengeance, killing of evildoers, worldly natural governments, judgments, and similar things. It is therefore without foundation to say that no one can exercise worldly government better than a Christian. That would imply that he needed the wisdom of Christ for it or that Christ's wisdom is the wisdom of his office. Christ's wisdom is merciful and will not serve him in his office because he is not merciful in his office but rather an avenger.

12.17   Pilgram Marpeck, "Defence," Loserth, *Marbeck,* 303-304

The kingdom of Christ is not of this world. For this reason no true Christian may administer cities and protect countries, nor people as an earthly lord. Nor may he use force, for that is the function of earthly and temporal rulers but never of true Christians under the cover of the faith in Christ. This is what many false [Christians] have undertaken to do in our time, among them the Papists and the Evangelicals (as they call themselves). Even today they demonstrate their attempt to exercise earthly power by protecting cities, rulers, and lords under the cover of the gospel. I fear that they will have another experience like that of the peasants' revolt....No true Christian may exercise force in the name or under the cover of Christ and the gospel or faith in Christ, nor must he do this as the worldly power and sword does and must do over the kingdom of this world....

It is difficult for a Christian to be a worldly ruler....And if he did, and if everything concerning the kingdom of this world was done properly according to the true human and divine order and he ruled and ordered everything without fault ... how long would his conscience allow him to be a magistrate, assuming that he did not want to forsake the Lord Jesus Christ and Christian patience and the true fight and knighthood in Christ, or at least that he did not want to sustain some injury to his soul or Christianity, since no one can serve two masters, that is the king or emperor in the worldly magistracy, and Christ in the spiritual, heavenly kingdom....

For further reading:

Clarence Bauman, "The Theology of 'The Two Kingdoms': A Comparison of Luther and the Anabaptists," *MQR* XXXVIII (January 1964), 37-49.

Clasen, *Anabaptism*, 172-182, 257-260.

Estep, *Anabaptist Story*, 179-202.

Friedmann, *Theology*, 36-48.

Hans J. Hillerbrand, "The Anabaptist View of the State," *MQR* XXXII (April 1958), 83-110.

Klaassen, *Anabaptism*, 48-63.

Robert Kreider, "The Anabaptists and the State," Hershberger, *Anabaptist Vision*, 180-193.

Littell, *Church*, 101-108.

Oyer, *Lutheran Reformers*, 92-98.

James M. Stayer, *Anabaptists and the Sword*.

Wenger, *Even Unto Death*, 86-87.

XIII.

Nonresistance

The selections in this section should be read continuously with those in Chapter 12 since there is extensive overlapping. Both the rejection of participation in government and nonresistance are a refusal to use the sword. Both are based on the distinction between the old and new covenants. The use of the sword was allowed in the old, but was not taken into the new covenant under Christ (13.14). The reason for separating the two is that nonresistance has been such an important identity symbol for Mennonites for so long.

There has been extensive discussion of this aspect of Anabaptist conviction recently. James Stayer has shown that the conviction about the total rejection of the sword came gradually among the Swiss (see reference to Stayer in the literature list at the end of the section). That the same thing happened among the South German and Dutch Anabaptists we have known for some time. Nevertheless, the very first witness to the total rejection of the use of the sword comes to us from Conrad Grebel (13.1). It was this position which, after some attempts at a middle position, prevailed and is articulated in the Schleitheim Confession (13.3).

It is instructive that the setting for the discussion is not the secular war of the twentieth century, but rather the holy war, the war for the defence of Christian faith (13.16). Anabaptists always think of the sword as turned against fellow Christians either on the field of battle or in the exercise of church discipline (see section 10). The sword is almost always opposed, not to nonviolent resistance, as we might think today, but to the ban. Persons who oppose the official decisions of the church, say Anabaptists, should not be proceeded against with the sword, but should be dealt with by the restoring process of church discipline, including the ban (13.3, 13.9). Thus nonresistance is not simply a matter of refusing to bear arms in wartime, although that is certainly included. Rather it is a totally new life orientation in which all human relationships are governed by patience, understanding, love, forgiveness, and a desire for the redemption even of the enemy. It is part of the new way of ordering human relationships under the new covenant (13.12).

One of the basic problems with the use of the sword, argued Anabaptists, was that killing a person destroyed any possibility of improvement or repentance. Robbing anyone of the freedom to decide for Christ was a grievous wrong, and constituted a usurpation of divine prerogative (13.9, 13.12). Basically, Anabaptists believed that the use of the sword in human relations was counterproductive. It served only to produce more hostility, more vengeance, more chaos. It was too final in its action, especially when such action was frequently unjust. Once the sword had spoken, the injury could not be rectified.

Hans Hut, who was a disciple of Thomas Müntzer, was not an absolute nonresistant. His position can be described as "interim-nonresistance." The sword, he argued, had been put away until God would tell them to take it out again. Until then they were to be nonresistant. Hut and his followers expected the world to end soon, and they believed that God would use them to destroy the ungodly. This use of the sword has normally, in Christian history, been called the holy war, that is, war in defence of God or Christian faith (13.8, 13.10). The Münsterites took a position very much like that, except that they considered the end-time to be already upon them (see selections 17.11-17.19).

Balthasar Hubmaier again deserves special attention, not only because he represents an exception to nonresistant Anabaptism, but also because he thought deeply and carefully on the question.

He clearly defended Christian participation in defensive war, much as Luther did. The motive was to defend and protect the neighbor. Such wars he regarded as just in keeping with traditional just war theory. However, he made room for the individual conscience; each person was obligated to judge the justice or injustice of a conflict, and so decide whether he should participate or not

266

(13.6). Moreover, he made room for removal of a government that obviously offended against justice, but using the principle of proportionality, that is, that the benefits of the revolt must outweigh the cost (13.6).

Hubmaier also dealt with the Word of Jesus, "All they that take the sword shall perish with the sword." The emphasis was on the word *take*. No one could take it by himself on his own judgment, and anyone who did would reap the consequences. Scripture, on the other hand, clearly shows that the sword of justice is given by God to government, and when that government calls its citizens to defend justice, they are *given* the sword (13.7).

Finally, the Hutterite Peter Riedeman responded to criticisms the Hutterites encountered about weapons and weapons making. They rejected all production of weapons, and when they were told that a man could also be killed with an agricultural instrument, Riedeman indignantly responded by saying that everyone should know that weapons of war were made specifically for destroying and killing, whereas a fork was made to serve peaceful purposes. Anyone who used a fork to kill someone else would himself be to blame. The maker could not be made responsible.

13.1   Conrad Grebel, "Letter to Müntzer," 1524, Williams, *Spiritual*, 80

Moreover, the gospel and its adherents are not to be protected by the sword, nor are they thus to protect themselves, which, as we learn from our brother, is thy opinion and practice. True Christian believers are sheep among wolves, sheep for the slaughter; they must be baptized in anguish and affliction, tribulation, persecution, suffering, and death; they must be tried with fire, and must reach the fatherland of eternal rest, not by killing their bodily, but by mortifying their spiritual, enemies. Neither do they use worldly sword or war, since all killing has ceased with them—unless, indeed, we would still be of the old law. And even there [in the Old Testament], so far as we recall, war was a misfortune after they had once conquered the Promised Land.

267

13.2 Felix Mantz, "Admonition," 1526, *Martyrs Mirror*, 415

Whenever a person brings forth genuine fruits of repentance, the heaven of eternal joy is, through grace, purchased and obtained for him by Christ, through the shedding of his innocent blood, which he so willingly poured out; thereby showing us his love, and enduing us with the power of his Spirit, and whoever receives and uses it grows and is made perfect in God. Only love to God through Christ shall stand and prevail; not boasting, denouncing, or threatening. It is love alone that is pleasing to God; he that cannot show love shall not stand in the sight of God. The true love of Christ shall scatter the enemy[56]; so that he who would be an heir with Christ is taught that he must be merciful, as the Father in heaven is merciful. Christ never accused anyone, as do the false teachers of the present day; from which it is evident that they do not have the love of Christ, nor understand his Word; and still they would be shepherds and teachers; but at last they will have to despair, when they shall find that everlasting pain shall be their recompense, if they do not reform. Christ never hated anyone; neither did his true servants, but they continued to follow Christ in the true way, as he went before them. This Light of life they have before them, and are glad to walk in it; but those who are hateful and envious, and do thus wickedly betray, accuse, smite and quarrel, cannot be Christians.

13.3 Michael Sattler, Schleitheim Confession, 1527, *Legacy*, 39-41

VI. We have been united as follows concerning the sword. The sword is an ordering of God outside the perfection of Christ. It punishes and kills the wicked, and guards and protects the good. In the law the sword is established over the wicked for punishment and for death, and the secular rulers are established to wield the same.

But within the perfection of Christ only the ban is used for the admonition and exclusion of the one who has sinned, without the death of the flesh, simply the warning and the command to sin no more.

Now many, who do not understand Christ's will for us, will ask:

whether a Christian may or should use the sword against the wicked for protection and defense of the good, or for the sake of love.

The answer is unanimously revealed: Christ teaches and commands us to learn from him, for he is meek and lowly of heart and thus we shall find rest for our souls. Now Christ says to the woman who was taken in adultery, not that she should be stoned according to the law of his Father (and yet he says, "what the Father commanded me, that I do") but with mercy and forgiveness and the warning to sin no more, says: "Go, sin no more." Exactly thus should we also proceed, according to the rule of the ban.

Second, is asked concerning the sword: whether a Christian shall pass sentence in disputes and strife about worldly matters, such as the unbelievers have with one another. The answer: Christ did not wish to decide or pass judgment between brother and brother concerning inheritance, but refused to do so. So should we also do.

Third, is asking concerning the sword: whether the Christian should be a magistrate if he is chosen thereto. This is answered thus: Christ was to be made king, but he fled and did not discern the ordinance of his Father. Thus we should also do as he did and follow after him, and we shall not walk in darkness. For he Himself says: "Whoever would come after me, let him deny himself and take up his cross and follow me. He himself further forbids the violence of the sword when he says: "The princes of this world lord it over them, etc., but among you it shall not be so." Further Paul says, "Whom God has foreknown, the same he has also predestined to be conformed to the image of his Son," etc. Peter also says: "Christ has suffered (not ruled) and has left us an example, that you should follow after in his steps."

Lastly one can see in the following points that it does not befit a Christian to be a magistrate: the rule of the government is according to the flesh, that of the Christians according to the Spirit. Their houses and dwelling remain in this world, that of the Christians is in heaven. Their citizenship is in this world, that of the Christians is in heaven. The weapons of the Christians are spiritual, against the fortification of the devil. The worldly are armed with steel and iron, but Christians are armed with the armor of God, with truth, righteousness, peace, faith, salvation, and with the Word of God. In sum: as Christ our Head is minded, so also must be minded the members of the body of Christ through him, so that there be no division in the body, through which it would be destroyed. Since then Christ is as is written of him, so must his members also be the same, so that his body may remain whole and unified for its own advancement and upbuilding. For any kingdom which is divided within itself will be destroyed.

13.4   Michael Sattler, "Trial," 1527, Williams, *Spiritual*, 141

Eighthly, if the Turks should come, we ought not to resist them. For it is written [Mt. 5:21]: Thou shalt not kill. We must not defend ourselves against the Turks and others of our persecutors, but are to beseech God with earnest prayer to repel and resist them. But that I said that, if warring were right, I would rather take the field against so-called Christians who persecute, capture, and kill pious Christians than against the Turks was for the following reason. The Turk is a true Turk, knows nothing of the Christian faith, and is a Turk after the flesh. But you who would be Christians and who make your boast of Christ persecute the pious witnesses of Christ and are Turks after the spirit!

13.5   Hans Denck, "Concerning True Love," 1527, Fellmann, *Denck I*, 84

No Christian, who wishes to boast in his Lord may use power to coerce and rule. For the realm of our king consists alone in the teaching and power of the spirit. Whoever truly acknowledges Christ as Lord ought to do nothing but what he commands him. Now he commands all his disciples to teach evildoers and to admonish them for their improvement. If they will not listen we should allow them to be heathens and avoid them . . . .

270

13.6 Balthasar Hubmaier, "Concerning the Sword," 1527, Westin, *Quellen,* 455-456

This Scripture Romans 13, dear brothers, is enough against all the gates of hell to confirm government. For Paul says plainly that everyone should be subject to the government. Obedience and subjection are called for whether it be believing or unbelieving. The reason is that there is no government except from God. This obedience consists in all those things that are not contrary to God, for God has not established government against himself. Thus if the government wants to punish the wicked as they are obligated to do by their soul's salvation, but cannot manage it by themselves, the subjects are obligated by their souls' salvation to assist and help their rulers if they call them through alarm signals, letters, or other means that the wicked may be destroyed and rooted out according to the will of God. However, the subjects should first carefully test the spirit of their rulers whether they are motivated by arrogance, pride, greed, envy, hate, or self-seeking rather than by love of the common good and the peace of the land. For that would not be bearing the sword according to the order of God. If you conclude, however, that the government punishes the wicked only in order that the pious may be at rest and without harm, then help, advise, assist as often and as much as you are called on. In doing so you are carrying out the order of God and doing his will and not the work of man. If, however, a government is childish or foolish or even not equipped to rule, that government may justifiably be put away and another chosen. For because of a wicked government God has often punished a whole nation. If, however, such putting away cannot be done legally and peacefully without great harm and insurrection, one must be patient. God has given it to us in his wrath and desires to punish us for our sins as those who deserve nothing better.

Whoever will not help the government to rescue widows, orphans, and other oppressed people and to punish destroyers and aggressors, opposes God's order and will receive his judgment. For he acts against the command and order of God who desires that the pious be protected and the wicked punished. But if you are obedient, know with certainty that you render such obedience not to government or to man but to God himself. You have become a servant of God even as the government itself is nothing but God's servant.

13.7 Balthasar Hubmaier, "Concerning the Sword," 1527, Westin, *Quellen*, 436-437

Jesus said to Peter: Put your sword in its sheath, for whoever takes the sword will perish by the sword. Do you think that I cannot ask my Father that he send me more than twelve legions of angels? But how would the Scriptures be fulfilled? It must be so. Mt. 26. Take careful note of the words of Christ, pious Christian, and you will have an answer to the charge of the brethren.[57] First Christ says: Put your sword in its sheath. You have no right to use it. You do not have the authority. It has not been committed to you. You are not called nor chosen for it. For whoever takes the sword shall perish by the sword. They *take* the sword who use it without commission against all order and in their own authority. But no one may *take* the sword himself. However, if one is chosen and commissioned to it he takes it not of himself, but it is given to him. Now he may say: I have not *taken* the sword. I would rather not take it since I myself am all too guilty. Since, however, I have been called to it I pray God that he will give me grace and wisdom to bear it and to govern according to his Word. Thus Solomon prayed, and he was given great wisdom to bear the sword rightly.

Now you may understand why Christ says to Peter: put your sword in the sheath. He does not say: get rid of it. Christ chastises him for using it and not because it was hanging at his side. Otherwise, if that had been wrong, he would have chastised him earlier. It follows further that whoever takes the sword will perish by the sword, that is, he comes under the judgment of the sword although he is not necessarily always judged by the sword for good reason. Do you notice how Christ here confirms the sword and that one should punish those who with it support their own power and wantonness? And that must be done by those who are called to it whoever they are. However it is certain that the more pious they are the better and more properly they will bear the sword according to the will of God for the protection of the innocent and to the fear of the wicked. To this end God has ordered and instituted it.

13.8   Interrogation of Hans Hut, 1527, *Meyer*, 241-242

Matthew the 24th chapter: Whoever has two coats, let him sell one and buy a sword; item, when Peter cut off Malchus' ear Christ said that he should put up his sword, for whoever fights with the sword shall be punished with it; item, when Christ said that he had not come to send peace but a sword; item, the last Psalm: [Psalm 149]: Let the praises of God be in their throats and two-edged swords in their hands, to wreak vengeance on the nations among the peoples, to bind the kings with chains and the nobles with iron fetters, to execute on them the judgment that is written; item, Jeremiah 48:[10] cursed is he who does the work of the Lord unfaithfully, and cursed be he who holds back his sword from the penalty. These verses he had pointed out to them and explained to them. They now see that the peasants were not right about their uprising, for they had sought their own and not God's honour.[58] About the first verse he had said: a Christian may well have a sword but that it must remain in the scabbard until God tells him to take it out. Before then they would all be scattered and tried. Finally the Lord would gather them all together again and himself return. Then the saints would punish the others, namely, the sinners who had not repented. Then the clergy who had preached falsely would have to answer for their teaching and the mighty for their use of power. Whoever had done well would be able to stand before God. He also referred to the passages in Wisdom 2 and 3: the righteous will be rulers over nations and have power over the peoples; then the Lord would make an end of all sinners. The fifth chapter of Wisdom adds to it and explains that the just will prevail against those who have tormented them with great steadfastness and they will say: behold, these are they whom we formerly despised, how highly they are accounted now, their names are among the children of God, we have erred. Finally he also added the sixth chapter; the Lord will upturn the thrones of the mighty and they will suffer mighty torment, so that the Lord will make an end of the whole world.

13.9   Geiser, *Witness*, 1529, 68, 69

From all this it is easy to determine who is a Christian and not a Christian, for our neighbors, the sword users (*Schwärtler*), also think

273

they are Christians, but their works and deeds prove something much different. Their life accords very little and not at all with the teaching and life of Christ. Yea, they are neither heathen, Jews, nor Christians, they do not know themselves what they are, for they mix and patch the one to the other, namely, the sword of the world, of Moses, and of Christ together. That fits well together, cabbage, peas, and turnips, that this should all be one thing. O blindness, blindness! Through these testimonies one can be reminded still more that worldly government with its bloody judgment and condemnation, also the law of Moses, neither can nor dare be found in the Christian church, for the worldly sword and also the law of Moses kill and do not free the sinner. But Christ in his church forgives the sinner his sins when he renounces his sins. But he who will not renounce his sins, such an one he (Christ) commands to excommunicate and not to kill according to the body as the law of Moses and the worldly sword does.

. . . .

But the law and the sword of this world sever a man from his life in body and soul, even though he should desire to amend his life immediately. Hence, there is a difference as great as between heaven and earth between Christ and Moses, between the church and the children of this world. Therefore, if Christ is really to count for something *(gelten)* here in his kingdom, which is not material but spiritual, Moses, the servant *(Knächt)* must give way, with his literalistic law, for a spiritual kingdom cannot carry nor use a material sword. Worldly kings carry a material sword because their kingdom is material, but our king Christ is a spiritual king and has an eternal kingdom, wherefore his sword dare not be material but spiritual.

13.10 Interrogation of Georg Nespitzer, 1530, Schornbaum, *Quellen*, 188

Concerning the article that Christ would give the sword and vengeance to the Anabaptists to punish all sin, to abolish all government, to make all things common, and to kill all those who have not been rebaptized. He admits to the article. Hans Hut taught this article, namely, that it would happen three and one-half years after the revolt.[59] God would give them vengeance. He had believed it, accepted it and kept it. Had it come to pass that Christ would have given such a command he would have carried it out.

13.11   Jacob Hutter, "Letter to the Vice-Regent," 1535, Manschreck, *History*, 86

We desire to molest no one; not to prejudice our foes, not even King Ferdinand. Our manner of life, our customs and conversation, are known everywhere to all. Rather than wrong any man of a single penny, we would suffer the loss of a hundred gulden; and sooner than strike our enemy with the hand, much less with the spear, or sword, or halbert, as the world does, we would die and surrender life. We carry no weapon, neither spear nor gun, as is clear as the open day; and they who say that we have gone forth by thousands to fight, they lie and impiously traduce us to our rulers. We complain of this injury before God and man, and grieve greatly that the number of the virtuous is so small. We would that all the world were as we are, and that we could bring and convert all men to the same belief; then should all war and unrighteousness have an end.

13.12   Menno Simons, "Blasphemy," 1535, *CWMS*, 46[60]

All of you who would fight with the sword of David, and also be the servants of the Lord, consider these words, which show how a servant should be minded. If he is not to strive, and quarrel, how then can he fight? If he is to be gentle to all men, how can he then hate and harm them? If he is to be ready to learn, how can he lay aside the apostolic weapons? He will need them. If he is to instruct in meekness those that oppose, how can he destroy them?

If he is to instruct in meekness those that oppose truth, how can he angrily punish them that do not as yet acknowledge the truth? Paul says: if God peradventure will give them repentance.

275

13.13 Menno Simons, "Foundation," 1539, *CWMS*, 198, 200

Our weapons are not weapons with which cities and countries may be destroyed, walls and gates broken down, and human blood shed in torrents like water. But they are weapons with which the spiritual kingdom of the devil is destroyed and the wicked principle in man's soul is broken down, flinty hearts broken, hearts that have never been sprinkled with the heavenly dew of the Holy Word. We have and know no other weapons besides this, the Lord knows, even if we should be torn into a thousand pieces, and if as many false witnesses rose up against us as there are spears of grass in the fields, and grains of sand upon the seashore.

Once more, Christ is our fortress; patience our weapon of defense; the Word of God our sword; and our victory a courageous, firm, unfeigned faith in Jesus Christ. And iron and metal spears and swords we leave to those who, alas, regard human blood and swine's blood about alike. He that is wise let him judge what I mean.

. . . .

We teach and acknowledge no other sword, nor tumult in the kingdom or church of Christ than the sharp sword of the Spirit, God's Word, as has been made quite plain in this and our other writings: a sword which is sharper and more penetrating than any sword, two-edged, and proceeding from the mouth of the Lord. With it we set the father against the son and the son against the father, the mother against the daughter and the daughter against the mother; the daughter-in-law against the mother-in-law. But the civil sword we leave to those to whom it is committed. Let everyone be careful lest he transgress in the matter of the sword, lest he perish with the sword. Mt. 26:52.

. . . .

Murder is unknown to us, much less inculcated and permitted, for we believe of a truth that a murderer has neither lot nor part in the kingdom of God. Gal. 5:21. O dear sirs, how could we desire the blood of any man since we have to die daily for man's sake before the Lord who created us and knows that we seek nothing but that we might instruct and lead the world with doctrine, life, blood, and death so that they might reflect, rouse themselves, repent, and be saved? For this is the nature of pure love, to pray for persecutors, to render good for evil, to love one's enemies, to heap coals of fire upon their heads, and to leave vengeance to him who judges rightly. Rom. 12:20.

13.14   Peter Riedeman, *Account*, 1542, 108-109
CONCERNING WARFARE

Now since Christ, the Prince of Peace, has prepared and won for himself a kingdom, that is a church, through his own blood; in this same kingdom all worldly warfare has an end, as was promised aforetime, "Out of Zion shall go forth the law, and the word of the Lord from Jerusalem, and shall judge among the heathen and shall draw many peoples, so that they shall beat their swords into ploughshares and their lances or spears into pruning hooks, sickles and scythes, for from thenceforth nation shall not lift up sword against nation, nor shall they learn war any more."

Therefore a Christian neither wages war nor wields the worldly sword to practise vengeance, as Paul also exhorts us saying, "Dear brothers, avenge not yourselves, but rather give place unto the wrath of God, for the Lord saith, Vengeance is mine; I will repay it." Now if vengeance is God's and not ours, it ought to be left to him and not practised or exercised by ourselves. For, since we are Christ's disciples, we must show forth the nature of him who, though he could, indeed, have done so, repaid not evil with evil. For he could, indeed, have protected himself against his enemies, the Jews, by striking down with a single word all who wanted to take him captive.

But though he might well have done this, he did not himself and would not permit others to do so. Therefore he said to Peter, "Put up again thy sword into his place." Here one can see how our King sets out with a powerful host against his enemy; how he defeats the enemy and how he takes vengeance: in that he takes Malchus' ear, that had been struck off, and puts it on again. And he who did this says, "Whosoever will be my disciple, let him take his cross upon him and follow me."

Now, therefore, Christ desires that we should act even as he did, so he commands us, saying, "It hath been said to the men of old, 'An eye for an eye, and a tooth for a tooth,' but I say unto you, that ye resist not evil: but whosoever shall smite thee on thy right cheek, turn and offer to him the other also." Here it is clearly to be seen that one ought neither to avenge oneself nor to go to war, but rather offer his back to the strikers and his cheeks to them that pluck off the hair—that is, suffer with patience and wait upon God, who is righteous, and who will repay it.

If one should say that David, who was loved by God, and other saints, went to war, and therefore one should still do so when one has right and justification thereto, we say, "No." That David and other saints did this, but that we ought not so to do, can be seen by all from the words quoted above, "To them of old is said, 'An eye for an eye and a tooth for a tooth', but I say unto you, that ye resist not evil!" Here Christ makes the distinction himself. There is therefore no need for many words, for it is clear that Christians can neither go to war nor practise vengeance. Whosoever does this has forsaken and denied Christ and Christ's nature.

13.15   Peter Riedeman, *Account,* 1542, 111-112
CONCERNING THE MAKING OF SWORDS

Since, as has been said above, Christians should beat their swords into ploughshares and take up arms no more—still less can they make the same, for they serve for nothing else than to slay, harm and destroy men—and Christ has not come to destroy men— therefore his disciples, also, refuse to do so; for he says, "Know ye not of what Spirit ye are the children?" as though he would say, "Doth the Spirit of grace teach you to destroy, or will ye walk according to the flesh and forsake the Spirit, whose children ye have become? Know ye not that I am not come to destroy men? If ye will be my disciples, ye must let my Spirit rule over you and not walk after the flesh. For he who obeyeth the flesh cannot please God."

Now, since Christians must not use and practise such vengeance, neither can they make the weapons by which such vengeance and destruction may be practised by others, that they be

278

not partakers of other men's sins. Therefore we make neither swords, spears, muskets nor any such weapons. What, however, is made for the benefit and daily use of man, such as bread knives, axes, hoes and the like, we both can and do make. Even if one were to say, "But one could therewith harm and slay others," still they are not made for the purpose of slaying and harming, so there is nothing to prevent our making them. If they should ever be used to harm another, we do not share the harmer's guilt, so let him bear the judgment himself.

13.16   Pilgram Marpeck, "Concerning the Love of God in Christ," *The Writings*, 539, 540

Far be it from us that we should seek to be redeemed like the Jews and these present alleged Christians who comfort themselves and hope to be redeemed by human power and the arm of man. The Jews, contrary to Christ and his own, claim to expect a Messiah or Christ who will redeem them from all power of the Gentiles by means of the arm of man and carnal weapons and lead them into the promised land. Thus also the alleged Christians are now blinded by this Jewish error (contrary to the bright light and Word which they claim to have and of which they boast), [and assume that] with the carnal sword and the arm of man Christ will release and redeem them from those who justifiably coerce and frighten them through the appearance of his coming. The old Latin Roman Church, which is ruled by imperial power, also hopes that the emperor will achieve the victory in the semblance and name of Christ against all those who resist her, and rigidly insists that this will happen. [It will happen] in order that all those will be punished who, in the semblance of Christ, suppose that they will decide with the carnal sword.

. . . .

Christ himself, in his holy Manhood, submitted to every authority in patience, who himself had and has all authority in heaven and on earth. For whoever takes the sword to make decisions about Christ and himself in the semblance of the Word, takes and uses it like Peter, who cut off Malchus' ear, which Christ put back on and healed. If someone today takes and uses the sword thus and fights for

Christ the same must and will, according to the words of the Lord, perish by the sword. The guilt rests on their heads as long as they boast of Christ and do not believe his words. The Jews boasted that they were children of God and Abraham and did not believe the words of his Christ but crucified him under the authority of Caesar. They set themselves against the imperial authority deliberately and with a perverted mind. Into [this perverted state] God delivered them and has to this day abandoned them. Because of this they are coerced by the authority of Caesar with great persecution, interrogation, and destruction.[61]

13.17　Menno Simons, "Reply to False Accusations," 1552, *CWMS*, 554, 555

The Scriptures teach that there are two opposing princes and two opposing kingdoms: the one is the Prince of peace; the other the prince of strife. Each of these princes has his particular kingdom and as the prince is so is also the kingdom. The Prince of peace is Christ Jesus; his kingdom is the kingdom of peace, which is his church; his messengers are the messengers of peace; his Word is the word of peace; his body is the body of peace; his children are the seed of peace; and his inheritance and reward are the inheritance and reward of peace. In short, with this King, and in his kingdom and reign, it is nothing but peace. Everything that is seen, heard, and done is peace.

. . . .

O beloved reader, our weapons are not swords and spears, but patience, silence, and hope, and the Word of God. With these we must maintain our heavy warfare and fight our battle. Paul says, The weapons of our warfare are not carnal; but mighty through God. With these we intend and desire to storm the kingdom of the devil; and not with sword, spears, cannon, and coats of mail. For he esteemeth iron as straw, and brass as rotten wood. Thus may we with our Prince, Teacher, and Example Christ Jesus, raise the father against the son, and the son against the father, and may we cast down imagination and every high thing that exalteth itself against the knowledge of God, and bring into captivity every thought in obedience to Christ.

True Christians do not know vengeance, no matter how they are mistreated. In patience they possess their souls. Lk. 21:18. And they do not break their peace, even if they should be tempted by bondage, torture, poverty, and besides, by the sword and fire. They do not cry, Vengeance, vengeance, as does the world; but with Christ they supplicate and pray: Father, forgive them; for they know not what they do. Lk. 23:34; Acts 7:60.

13.18 Wismar Articles, 1554, *CWMS*, 1042

Article VIII. In the eighth place, touching weapons, the elders are unable to consider it impure when a believer traveling on the roads, according to the conditions of the land, carries an honest staff or a rapier on his shoulder, according to the customs and the manner of the land. But to carry weapons of defense, and, to present them according to the command of the magistracy, this the elders do not consider permissible—unless it be in case of soldiers on guard.[62]

For further reading:

Beachy, *Grace*, 167-172, 219-226.
Harold S. Bender, "The Pacifism of the Sixteenth-Century Anabaptists," *MQR* XXX (January 1956), 5-18.
Brock, *Pacifism*, 59-113.
James M. Stayer, "The Doctrine of the Sword in the First Decade of Anabaptism," *MQR* XLI (April 1967), 165-166.
————, "Melchior Hoffman and the Sword," *MQR* XLV (July 1971), 265-277.
————, "Hans Hut's Doctrine of the Sword: An Attempted Solution," *MQR* XXXIX (July 1965), 181-191.
Wenger, *Even Unto Death*, 99-102.

XIV

The Oath

The Anabaptist refusal of the oath was based in the first place on the words of Jesus which forbade any swearing at all. That, in itself, would have been sufficient ground for refusal by most Anabaptists. The arguments of the Swiss Brethren beginning with the Schleitheim Confession (14.1), of Menno Simons (4.7, 4.8), and of the Hutterites (14.5) were for the most part a rehearsal of Jesus' words in the Sermon on the Mount.

However, these statements must also be considered in the context of the Anabaptist attitude toward societal relationships. They stressed truthfulness as a prime prerequisite for the proper functioning of society, and argued that the oath could too easily become the refuge of the lie (14.5).

Again there are exceptions to this general position. Hubmaier does not even discuss the matter, nor do the Münsterites. For them it was evidently not an important issue, or they accepted it without question as part of their view of government and society.

Hans Denck would not adopt what he obviously saw in the Swiss as a legalistic position. He allowed for the swearing of oaths, but warned that one should swear only concerning those things that one could carry out. That which is the truth, he allowed, could also be confirmed by an oath (14.2). Hans Hut, likewise, did not object to oaths in the course of normal human affairs (14.3).

Marpeck once more appears to have taken a mediating position, trying to hold to a rejection of the oath as used in some respects, but rejecting what he considered the legalistic position of the Swiss Brethren. The one discussion of the oath by Marpeck that we know of is lost (see *The Writings*, 368, footnote 6). We know from the

Strassburg sources that he did oppose the oath, but that his view was not that of the Swiss Brethren. The selection (14.6) by Jörg Maler who belonged to the Marpeck circle sheds a little light on what Marpeck may have thought. Maler's view allowed for oaths in the normal conduct of societal affairs. Marpeck's objection may have been specifically to the oath of allegiance to the city of Strassburg which had to be sworn annually, and which was associated with the readiness to defend the city with weapons (See *Quellen: Elsass I*, 360).

14.1   Michael Sattler, "Schleitheim Confession," 1527, *Legacy*, 41-42

VII. We have been united as follows concerning the oath. The oath is a confirmation among those who are quarreling or making promises. In the law it is commanded that it should be done only in the name of God, truthfully and not falsely. Christ, who teaches the perfection of the law, forbids his [followers] all swearing, whether true nor [sic] false; neither by heaven nor by earth, neither by Jerusalem nor by our head; and that for the reason which he goes on to give: "For you cannot make one hair white or black" You see, thereby all swearing is forbidden. We cannot perform what is promised in swearing, for we are not able to change the smallest part of ourselves.

Now there are some who do not believe the simple commandment of God and who say, "But God swore by himself to Abraham, because he was God (as he promised him that he would do good to him and would be his God if he kept his commandments). Why then should I not swear if I promise something to someone?" The answer: hear what Scripture says: "God, since he wished to prove overabundantly to the heirs of his promise that his will did not change, inserted an oath so that by two immutable things we might have a stronger consolation (for it is impossible that God should lie)." Notice the meaning of the passage: God has the power to do what he forbids you, for everything is possible to him. God swore an oath to Abraham, Scripture says, in order to prove that his counsel is immutable. That means: no one can withstand and thwart his will; thus he can keep his oath. But we cannot, as Christ said above, hold or perform our oath, therefore we should not swear.

Others say that swearing cannot be forbidden by God in the New Testament when it was commanded in the Old, but that it is forbidden only to swear by heaven, earth, Jerusalem, and our head. Answer: hear the Scripture. He who swears by heaven, swears by God's throne and by him who sits thereon. Observe: swearing by heaven is forbidden, which is only God's throne; how much more is it forbidden to swear by God himself. You blind fools, what is greater, the throne or he who sits on it?

Others say, if it is then wrong to use God for truth, then the apostles Peter and Paul also swore. Answer: Peter and Paul only testify to that which God promised Abraham, whom we long after have received. But when one testifies, one testifies concerning that which is present, whether it be good or evil. Thus Simeon spoke of Christ to Mary and testified: "Behold: this one is ordained for the falling and rising of many in Israel and to be a sign which will be spoken against."

Christ taught us similarly when he says: Your speech shall be yea, yea; and nay, nay; for what is more than that comes of evil. He says, your speech or your word shall be yes and no, so that no one might understand that he had permitted it. Christ is simply yea and nay, and all those who seek him simply will understand his Word. Amen.

14.2   Hans Denck, "Recantation," 1527, Fellmann, *Denck I*, 110

The Lord Christ says: You shall in all things not swear in the same way in which he also forbids us to be angry, to cast judgment or to call someone a fool. Not that it is wrong in itself, but in order that no occasion or cause be given to all flesh to use the same and expect it to be pleasing to God, since in fact everyone misuses them however good the appearance might be. For this is the way in which everyone uses his oath as though what one says can never fail. Thus people often contract together what is openly contrary to Christ without daily swearing in a frivolous and thoughtless way. But whoever has the mind and spirit of Christ confirms, promises or swears nothing than that which he may in fact do with a good conscience, namely what he is obligated to do on the basis of the teaching of Christ, such as not stealing, not killing, not committing adultery, not taking vengeance and the like. In any case, he will not affirm these things except on the basis of God's grace; not what he will do but what he desires to do so that he does not make any unwarranted assumptions.

In summary, whatever anyone may in truth speak he may in fact also call God to witness for it. Much more may he do this with preachers as with holding up his hand and the like, and it makes little difference whether one calls it swearing or not; it was never in the mind of Christ to forbid this. Paul says: I call on God to witness as though he meant to say: God may call my soul to account if I do not speak the truth. It is no different than when we swear today and say this or that I will or desire to do so help me God. And that also means that if it is in fact not my intention may God not help me.

14.3 Interrogation of Hans Hut, 1527, *Meyer*, 227

Regarding the 60th article; he does not agree with this article. Indeed Kirschner and others have talked about it, but he admonished them and rather showed them the Scriptures which say that swearing at the behest of the government is not against God. He will not swear, however, in anything that is against God.

14.4 "Conversation with Hans Marquart," 1532, Fast, *Quellen*, 659, 668

I concede that one may call God to witness concerning what is past or present, but one may not swear. . . . Further one may promise and pledge faith concerning the past and the present, but never concerning the future. That is because nothing is in our power but everything depends on the will of God. Christ says in Matthew 5:[36] that we should not swear by our heads since we cannot make a single hair white or black. How much more terrible it is to swear by the name of God to do something in the future which is not in our power, since we are not certain of life for one minute.

. . . .

Christ wanted a pure people who had put off all uncleanness. That is why he gave a clear commandment regarding the oath. The faithful were not to swear at all but yes should be yes, and no, no. Thus all who were planted into the body of the church through faith in Christ, would not swear as the children of the world do. Rather they would confess and live the truth without additions with a pure heart.

14.5   Peter Riedeman, *Account*, 1542, 114-117

CONCERNING SWEARING

Even as the law was an introduction to the greater grace and knowledge of God, likewise also are the commandments. For this reason God, the Lord, desired nothing else by swearing in the old covenant than to direct and bring men to his name; that they might learn to know him aright, to cleave to give him alone the honour. For God, who is the truth, by commanding his people Israel to swear by his name, means to teach them to speak the truth and cleave to the same; therefore also he forbade them to speak his name vainly or lightly—as though he would say that they be careful in all that they say to be found servants of truth, that is of God. For this reason doth he also threaten not to hold him guiltless who speaks his name vainly and lightly, that is, who is careless about the truth. That it is true, however, that through the command to swear in the old covenant God has chosen in the new (since the will of God is fully revealed) the speaking of truth and walking therein, or the knowing of God aright and cleaving to him, may be seen from David's words when he says, "The man that swears by God is praised; but the mouth of them that speak lies must be stopped." Who, then, can say anything else than that here "swearing" means speaking the truth and cleaving to the same?

But that by means of the command to swear in the old covenant, we in the new are to understand to know God aright and cleave to him, is shown by the words, "Unto me every knee shall

286

bow and by me every tongue shall swear saying: Surely in the Lord is my righteousness and strength." This word is thus treated and explained by Paul, "Every knee shall bow to me, and every tongue shall confess to God." Here it is evident that swearing in the old covenant means in the new knowing God and cleaving to him alone. Thus, the law is now a guide to a better knowledge and hope; by the which we draw nigh to God.

Now, since the light of divine grace has appeared and been revealed more brightly in Christ, the servants of the new covenant lay no longer upon us the shade but the glory of the light of truth in its clarity. Therefore Paul says plainly, as one who has no veil before his face, "Put away lying and speak every man truth with his neighbour; for ye are members one of another."

If one should say, "But Israel was also commanded to speak the truth, and hate lies, so this is not the meaning." We say, it is true that Israel was also commanded to speak the truth, but since at that time sonship had not been distinguished from the state of bondage, and the spirit of bondage cannot attain the real truth, God desired to show them by means of swearing by his name that there is no other truth, and that he who would walk in the truth must enter through the name of God and be established therein. That is what God desires to teach us by means of swearing in the old covenant.

. . . .

For this reason Christ says, "It was said to them of old, Thou shalt not forswear thyself, but I say unto you, Swear not at all; neither by heaven; for it is God's throne: nor by the earth; for it is his footstool: neither by Jerusalem; for it is the city of the great King. Neither shalt thou swear by thy head, because thou canst not make one hair white or black. But let your yea be yea; and your nay be nay: for whatsoever is more than these cometh of evil." The evil one, however is the devil, who works in men everything whereby God is reviled.

Now it cannot be denied, for it is clear to all men, that God desires from us Christians a true worship performed in spirit and truth and more perfect than the service of the old covenant. Therefore we are not only not to forswear ourselves, but we are not to swear at all. Christ thereby teaches us to give and ascribe honour to God alone, and to humble ourselves before him, as those who of themselves can do nothing; for we can do nothing, not even promise to do something of ourselves—let alone swear to do it. Thus, it is evident that on account of our weakness and unprofitableness we swear not, for we will not rob God of his honour.

14.6 Interrogation of Jörg Maler, 1550, Fast, *Quellen*, 238

He said that he had disagreed with the brothers in Switzerland on a few points and had left them. Those brothers had agreed that one ought never to swear an oath. He, however, believed, and still does, that a Christian may swear an oath for the sake of the brothers and of love, and for the maintenance of justice and truth.[63]

14.7 Menno Simons, "Epistle to Micron," 1556, *CWMS*, 924

The oath serves no other purposes than to make men testify truly. Can the truth not be told without oaths? Do all testify to the truth even when under oath? To the first question you must say yes, and to the last no. Is the oath the truth itself to which one testifies, or does the truth depend upon the man who takes the oath? Why does not the magistracy then accept the testimony confirmed by yea and nay as commanded of God instead of that confirmed by that which is forbidden? For it can punish those who are found false in their yea and nay as well as those who swear falsely.

14.8 Menno Simons "Distressed Christians," 1552, *CWMS*, 519, 521

We are aware that the magistracy claims and says that we are allowed to swear when justice is on our side. We reply with the Word of the Lord very simply. To swear truly was allowed to the Jews under the Law; but the gospel forbids this to Christians. Since Christ does not allow us to swear, and since the magistracy, notwithstanding, proceeds according to their policy, although contrary to Scripture, and since the Scriptures may not be set aside by man, what shall the conscientious Christian do? If he swears, he falls into the hand of the Lord. If he swears not, he will have to bear the disfavor and punishment of the magistracy.

. . . .

This is our position and understanding in regard to this matter. Inasmuch as the Lord has forbidden us to swear at all (understand in temporal matters) neither sincerely nor falsely, as was said; and has commanded that our yea shall be yea and our nay, nay; and since Paul and James also testify to this, and since we know that no man nor commandment of man may take the place of God and his commandment, therefore it is that we in temporal matters dare not affirm the truth in more than yea or nay as the case may be. For thus the Word of the Lord teaches us.

We say, in temporal matters, and for this reason: Because Christ sometimes in his teachings makes use of the word verily and because Paul called upon the Lord as a witness of his soul. For this some think that swearing is allowable; not observing that Christ and Paul did not do this in regard to temporal matters as in matters of flesh and blood or money or property but in affirmation of the eternal truth to the praise of God and to the salvation and edification of their brethren.

For further reading:

Beachy, *Grace*, 165-166.
Clasen, *Anabaptism*, 181-183.
Hans J. Hillerbrand, "Remarkable Interdependencies Between Certain Anabaptist Doctrinal Writings," *MQR* XXXIII (January 1959), 73-76.
Keeney, *Dutch Anabaptist*, 132-135.

XV

Religious Toleration

The selections in this chapter again overlap with the section on government (chapter 12) and the one on church discipline (chapter 10).

Anabaptists deserve an honourable place in the history of religious freedom, even though their espousal of it was stillborn. Religious toleration, let alone religious liberty, could not be tolerated in the sixteenth century. The Reformers condemned it as an invitation to social chaos, and political rulers rejected it because it would divide political loyalties. When religious liberty finally came it took its rise in seventeenth-century England and eighteenth-century France, and was transplanted from there to the New World. But Anabaptists were among the pioneers who first thought of it and who gave words to their convictions by appealing to authorities in church and state to grant liberty of faith.

The first appeal for religious liberty in the sixteenth century came from the eloquent pen of Balthasar Hubmaier. "The heretic," wrote Hubmaier, "is an invention of the devil" (15.1). This means, not that there cannot be any heretics, but that the word "heretic" conveyed immediately the vision of a flaming stake, invented and ignited by the leaders of the church. "To burn heretics," continued Hubmaier, "is to recognize Christ in appearance, but to deny him in reality . . ." (15.1).

Killing people for their faith was seen to be in direct contrast to the spirit of Christ. The impassioned statement of Hans Umlauft dwells on the contradiction between the discrimination of official Christianity and the unlimited acceptance of God. God, argues Umlauft, does not demand a certain theology or certain specific religious rites as conditions of his graciousness. If God does not do it, neither should his people. However, God's liberality and unconditional acceptance has always been a scandal to those who regard themselves as God's special spokesmen (15.6).

An argument often encountered among Anabaptist pleas for religious liberty was that faith, in order to be true faith, had to be free. The moving letter of Hans Müller to the clergy and Council of Zürich pleads that they would understand how faith is something that God gives which human beings cannot really account for. Since God gives to whom he will, faith cannot be forced by any human authority (15.3) Following Christ, stated Kilian Aurbacher, is a matter of free choice. It cannot be compelled (15.4).

A sophisticated defence of religious liberty was made by Leopold Scharnschlager in 1534. He drew to the attention of the Protestant leaders in Strassburg their own claim to toleration from the emperor, and that by those rules they ought either to go back to being Catholics or grant liberty to Anabaptists (15.5). However, persuasive as that logic may be to the twentieth-century Western mind, it was unconvincing in the sixteenth century. For the Strassburg Protestant leaders knew that only they were right and that both Catholics and Anabaptists were wrong. Hence they could demand toleration on one side and persecute the other.

The statement attributed to Hans Denck[64] (15.2) is far in advance of its time, for Denck anticipated a truly religiously plural society in which there would be not only varieties of Christians but also "Turks and heathen and Jews," living together unmolested (see also 16.2).

Menno Simons makes two important observations. The first is that when rulers persecute Anabaptists they are actually persecuting Jesus Christ because the church is Christ's physical body (15.7). The other is that Menno made room for some regulation of belief in the case of those whom he calls "manifest deceivers" (15.8). By allowing this he actually surrendered the case for religious liberty for which he pleaded so eloquently elsewhere.

Thus Anabaptists anticipated a pluralistic society, not because faith does not matter and is not worth anyone's attention, but precisely because it is of the highest importance and must be granted the right to express itself.

15.1 Balthasar Hubmaier, "Concerning Heretics and Those who Burn Them," 1524, Davidson/ Klaassen, *Hubmaier*, 30-33

So it follows that the slayers of heretics are the worst heretics of all, in that they, contrary to Christ's teaching and practice, condemn heretics to the fire. By pulling up the harvest prematurely they destroy the wheat along with the tares. . . . A Turk or a heretic cannot be persuaded by us either with the sword or with fire, but only with patience and prayer, and so we should wait patiently for the judgment of God. . . . It cannot serve as an excuse (as they claim) that they transfer the sinner to the temporal power, for he who so delivers them has the greater sin (Jn. 19). . . . Therefore let the temporal power duly slay evildoers (Rom. 13), and those who have attacked the defenseless. But the foes of God no one should harm, unless he insists and thus abandons the gospel. . . . So, to burn heretics is to recognize Christ in appearance, but to deny him in reality. . . . Now let this saying be evident to everyone, even to the blind: the heretic is an invention of the devil.

15.2 Hans Denck, "Commentary on Micah," 1527, Fellmann, *Denck II*, 66

Such a security will exist also in outward things, with practice of the true gospel that each will let the other move and dwell in peace—be he Turk or heathen, believing what he will—through and in his land, not submitting to a magistrate in matters of faith. Is there anything more to be desired? I stand fast on what the prophet says here. Everyone among all peoples may move around in the name of his God. That is to say, no one shall deprive another—whether heathen or Jew or Christian—but rather allow everyone to move in all territories in the name of his God. So may we benefit in the peace which God gives.

15.3 Letter of Hans Müller, from Aatal, to Council of Zürich, 1530, Muralt and Schmid, *Quellen*, 346-347

The saving grace of God be with you, honourable and dear sirs, and the inward peace of Jesus Christ be with all the children of God in the Lord. Amen.

Honoured, dear sirs, I beg you in all friendliness that you would have fatherly compassion on me as a father has compassion on his children. Please do not burden my conscience since faith is a free gift of God. It does not have its source in him who chooses or in him who runs the race but in the merciful God. Not all are able to believe as the Scripture says, for it does not come by the will of the flesh but must be born of God. They are the children of God who are driven by the Holy Spirit. . . . Again, no one comes to me unless the Father draw him to me. All good gifts come down from above, from the Father of lights. The mysteries of God are hidden and are like the treasure in the field which no one can find unless the Spirit of the Lord shows him.

So I beg you, you servants of God, that you will give me freedom for my faith. The Lord says, without me you can do nothing. If I should be mistaken, then I pray God to give me the spirit of understanding to recognize the evil and choose the good. For he says: whoever comes to me I will not cast out. . . . Have compassion on my four little children and let me go home for a little while. As you wish that men should do to you do also to them.

15.4 Kilian Aurbacher, 1534, *Hulshof*, 247. (Translation by H. S. Bender)

It is never right to compel one in matters of faith, whatever he may believe, be he Jew or Turk. Even if one does not believe uprightly or wants to believe so, i.e., if he does not have or want to have the right understanding of salvation, and does not trust God or submit to him, but trusts in the creature and loves it, he shall bear his own guilt, no one will stand for him in the judgment. . . . And thus we conduct ourselves according to the example of Christ and the apostles and proclaim the gospel according to the grace that he has entrusted to us; we compel no one. But whoever is willing and ready, let him follow him, as Luke shows in Acts. That this then also is an open truth, that Christ's people are a free, unforced, and uncompelled people, who receive Christ with desire and a willing heart, of this the Scriptures testify.

15.5 Leopold Scharnschlager, "Appeal for Toleration," 1534, Fast, *Der Linke Flügel*, 123

My dear Lords, I beg you to ask yourselves how things are with each one of you in the matter of faith. For I do not doubt that each one of you, if he love the truth, wishes to have free access to God, of his own will; indeed, to do God voluntary service, not under constraint, but uncoerced. And if you be urged to accept a faith of which you, and each one of you severally, cannot approve, you would never be able to accept such faith with a quiet conscience and would always wish to be free in the matter. Therefore I sincerely ask you consider and take to heart that the matter stands thus with me and those with me, and must so stand. Nor have we any intention to maintain ourselves and our faith with violence and military defence; but with patience and suffering even to physical death in the power of God for which we pray.

My dear lords, you tell and urge us to abandon our faith and accept yours. That is as if the emperor said to you that you should deny your faith and accept his. Now I appeal to your conscience: do you suppose that it is right before God to obey the emperor in this? In which case you may also say that it is right for us to obey you in the similar case. But then you must also declare that you are obligated to reintroduce all the idolatry, papist monasteries, also the mass and other things. If, however, you say that it is not right before God to obey the emperor in this, I beg and admonish you for God's sake and the sake of your soul's salvation as a poor Christian; please yield to your conscience in this, and have mercy on us poor people.

15.6 Letter of Hans Umlauft to Stephan Rauchenecker, 1539, *Quellen: Bayern II*, 68-69

You write further that we have no faith, word nor sacrament, and that we cannot pray nor be saved. Even if this were true—and may the kind Father preserve us from it—you should nevertheless not judge or condemn anyone, nor deny him salvation. Consider rather, that we are people and human as you and those of your kind, created in the image of God, a creation of God, having God's law, will, and word written in our hearts (Rom. 2:[15]). Therefore you should grant to us a gracious God as well as to yourselves, since God is also a God of the heathen. He is no respecter of persons, but whoever among all nations fears him and does right, is acceptable to him (Acts 10:[35]). From the beginning until the end (Dan. 11:[16, 30, 36, 41]) he has scattered his church among all the nations. At his appearing he will gather in the dispersed, true Israel from the four winds and corners of the earth. Ruth, the Moabite woman who was a heathen, was included in the genealogy of Christ (Mt. 1[5]). Therefore I believe that many children of Abraham are to be found among the heathen, carved in stone (Mt. 3:[9], Rom. 9:[8]). Similarly, this unpartisan God took pleasure in Adam, Abel, Enoch, Noah, Job, Abraham, who was a heathen before his circumcision, Naaman, Cyrus the Persian king, the Babylonian king Nebuchadnezzar, Nathanael, the Ethiopian eunuch (Acts 2:[9]), and Cornelius before and without the external circumcision in baptism. So little has God bound his grace and people to the external elements and ceremonies. We really ought to take this to heart and refuse to condemn anyone. We should allow God to remain unpartisan and accessible to all as one who is no respecter of persons. Certainly we should not, in a sectarian way, claim God as our own as the Jews did, implying that all others, who do not agree with us or belong to our sect, are simply heathen. God can make children of Abraham out of stones. We must listen to Christ when he says that many, who are today called Turks and heathen, will come from east and west and eat with Abraham in the kingdom of God. By contrast, the children of the kingdom, the so-called Christians and the Jews who presume to sit in the front and who believe that God belongs to them, will be thrust out. We heathen should be careful about such presumption since we are bastards and aliens in this Testament and covenant of grace.

15.7 Menno Simons, "Christian Baptism," 1539, CWMS, 284-285

Therefore I say, if you find in me or in my teachings which is the Word of God, or among those who are taught by me or by my colleagues any thievery, murder, perjury, sedition, rebellion, or any other criminal act, as were and are found among the corrupt sects—then punish all of us. We would be deserving of punishment if this were the case. I repeat, if we are disobedient to God in regard to religious matters, we are willing to be instructed and corrected by the Word of God, for we seek diligently to do and fulfill his most holy will. Or if we are disobedient to the emperor in matters to which he is called and ordained of God, I say matters to which he is called, then we will willingly submit to such punishment as you may see fit to inflict upon us. But if we sincerely fear and seek our Lord and God, as I trust we do, and if we are obedient unto the emperor in temporal matters as we should be according to the Word of God (Mt. 22:21; Rom. 13:7; 1 Pet. 2:13; Tit. 3:1), and if then we have to suffer and be persecuted and crucified for the sake of the truth of the Lord, then we should consider that the disciple is not above his Master nor the servant above his lord. If they have called the master of the house Beelzebub, how much more shall they call them of his household. Mt. 10:24, 25.

Yet you should know and acknowledge, O dear noble, illustrious lords, ye judges and officers of the law, that as often as you take, condemn, and put to the sword such people, that you thrust your tyrannical sword into the blessed flesh of the Lord Jesus Christ, that you break the bones of his holy body, for they are flesh of his flesh and bone of his bone. Eph. 5:30. They are his chosen, beloved brethren and sisters, who are together with him, born from above of one Father. Jn. 1:13. They are his dearly beloved children who are born of the seed of his holy Word. They are his spotless, holy, and pure bride whom he in his great love has wed.

15.8 Menno Simons, "Foundation," 1539, CWMS, 193

Therefore, dear sirs, take heed; this is the task to which you are called: namely, to chastise and punish, in the true fear of God with fairness and Christian discretion, manifest criminals, such as thieves, murderers, Sodomites, adulterers, seducers, sorcerers, the violent, highwaymen, robbers, etc. Your task is to do justice between a man and his neighbor, to deliver the oppressed out of the hand of the oppressor; also to restrain by reasonable means, that is, without tyranny and bloodshed, manifest deceivers who so miserably lead poor help-less souls by hundreds of thousands into destruction. Whether the deceivers are priests, monks, preachers, baptized or unbaptized, it is your task to restrain them so that they may no longer detract from the power of the almighty majesty of God, our only and eternal Sa-viour, Christ, Jesus, the Holy Ghost, and the Word of grace; nor in-troduce such ridiculous abuses and idolatry under semblance of truth as has been done until now. In this way, in all love, without force, violence, and blood, you may enlarge, help, and protect the kingdom of God with gracious consent and permission, with wise counsel and a pious, unblamable life.

· ·

O highly renowned, noble lords, believe Christ's Word, fear God's wrath, love righteousness, do justice to widows and orphans, judge rightly between a man and his neighbor, fear no man's high-ness, despise no man's littleness, hate all avarice, punish with reason, allow the Word of God to be taught freely, hinder no one from walk-ing in the truth, bow to the scepter of him who called you to this high service. Then shall your throne stand firm forever.

15.9   Menno Simons, "Foundation," 1539, *CWMS*, 201-202

Therefore, we pray and admonish you; yes, we counsel and request you, to contrast our desire with your desire, our spirit with your spirit, our doctrine with the doctrine of the learned, our conduct with your conduct, our poverty with your abundance, our disgrace and reproach with your selfish ambition, our affliction and sorrow with your ease and luxurious life, our patience with your tyranny, our cruel bonds and shameful death with your merciless fury and fierce cruelty (I speak of the guilty), and if then you should discover that your doctrine, faith, life, ambition, and conduct are in harmony with the Spirit, Word, and life of the Lord, and are better than ours, then instruct us with a fatherly spirit. We desire so fervently to fear and obey; for the truth we desire to obey unto death.

But if you cannot reprove us with Scripture, and acknowledge our [doctrine and conduct] to be best, then it would be heathenish, yes, ungodly and tyrannical, would it not, to crowd us out of life unto death, from heaven into hell, with the sword and violence! This you will have to acknowledge and confess. But so much decency I fear will not be shown us wretched children: to weigh the matter in the balance of the Holy Word, and to measure it with the standard of Christ.

15.10 Menno Simons, "Supplication to all Magistrates," 1552, *CWMS*, 530

And so we distressed and sorrowful ones humbly pray your Excellences for the third time for Jesus's sake to reflect carefully on the matter. And be pleased with Christian fidelity to compare us and the preachers with each other according to the tenor of the ensuing writing addressed to them and with the conditions therein stipulated, so that our innocence might at long last be heard, and the truth be established with the Word of God, so that the innocent may not be longer condemned, contrary to the Word of God, and the guilty no longer defended in their unrighteousness. Yes, kind sirs, if this might at long last come to pass, without partiality and in the fear of God, then you would, by God's grace, soon discover and without equivocation on whose side the truth is, and that the clerics' doctrine, sacraments, and conduct are not in accordance with the Scriptures but misleading and contrary to the Word of God.

15.11 Dirk Philips, "The Church of God," 1562, Kolb/ Klaassen, *Philips*, 397-399

True Christians must here be persecuted for the sake of truth and righteousness, but they persecute no one on account of his faith. For Christ sends his disciples as sheep among the wolves (Mt. 10:16). However, the sheep does not devour the wolf, but the wolf the sheep. Those who persecute others on account of their faith can nevermore be counted as a church of the Lord. In the first place, God, the heavenly Father, has committed all judgment to Jesus Christ (Jn. 5:22), to be a Judge of the souls and consciences of men, and rule in his church with the scepter of his Word forever (Lk. 2:29

298

[3]). Second, it is the office or work of the Holy Spirit to reprove the world of the sin of unbelief (Jn. 16:8). Now, it is evident that the Holy Spirit did not administer this reproof through the apostles and all pious witnesses of the truth by violence or with the material sword, but by God's Word and power. Third, the Lord Jesus Christ gave his church the power and established the rule to separate from her, avoid and shun the false brethren, disorderly and disobedient, contentious and heretical people, yea, all in the church who are found wicked, as has already been said (Rom. 16:16; 1 Cor. 5:10; 1 Thess. 5:15[13]; Tit. 3:19). What is done over and above this is not Christian, evangelical, nor apostolic. Fourth, the parable of the Lord in the gospel proves clearly to us that he does not permit his servants to pull up the weeds so that thereby the wheat be not pulled up also. They are to let the wheat and the weeds grow together in the world until the Lord shall command his reapers, that is, his angels, to gather the wheat into his barn and throw the weeds into the fire (Mt. 24:29[30]).

From this it is evident that no church may exercise dominion over the consciences of men with the carnal sword, or seek by violence to force unbelievers to believe, nor to kill the false prophets with sword and fire. With the Word of God she must judge and expel those in the church who are found wicked. What is done over and above this is not Christian, nor evangelical, nor apostolic. And if some one ventures to assert that the government has not received the sword in vain (Rom. 13:1), and that God through Moses commanded that the false prophets be put to death (Deut. 13:5), I will briefly give this answer: the higher power has received the sword or authority from God, not to judge therewith in spiritual matters (for these things must be judged by the spiritual, and spiritually, 1 Cor. 2:13), but to maintain a proper policy and keep the peace among its subjects, to protect the good and punish the evil. God's command to Moses to put the false prophets to death is a command of the Old, and not the New, Testament. By contrast we have received another command from God that we are to take heed of false prophets, that we are not to give ear to them, that we are to shun a heretic, and thereby commit them to the judgment of God (Mt. 7:15[13]); Jn. 10:5; Tit. 3:10). Now, if, according to the Old Testament command, false prophets were to be put to death, then this would have to be carried out, first of all, with those who are looked upon as false prophets and antichrists by almost the whole world. Likewise the higher powers would be obliged to put to death not only the false prophets, but also all image worshippers, and those who serve idols, and who counsel other people to commit sacrilege (Deut. 13:1; Ex. 22:18), and all who blaspheme the name of the Lord, and who swear falsely by that name, all who curse father or mother and profane the Sabbath (Ex. 20:7-10; Deut. 27:17); for they are all alike condemned to death by the law as well as the false prophets are.

15.12   Heinrich Bullinger, *Anabaptist Origins*, 1561, Horsch, *Mennonites*, 325-326

One cannot and should not use force to compel anyone to accept the faith, for faith is a free gift of God. . . . It is wrong to compel anyone by force or coercion to embrace the faith, or to put to' death anyone for the sake of his erring faith. It is an error that in the church any sword other than that of the divine Word should be used. . . . The secular kingdom should be separated from the church, and no secular ruler should exercise authority in the church. . . . The Lord has commanded simply to preach the gospel, and not to compel anyone by force to accept it. . . . It is the work of the great Judge to separate the tares from the good seed. This will be done by Christ at the last day only. For when in the parable of the tares among the wheat the servants came to their master saying, "Wilt thou that we go and gather in the tares?" his reply was, "Nay, lest while you gather up the tares, you root up also the wheat with them. Let both grow together until the harvest; then I will tell the reapers to gather together the tares and bind them in bundles to be burned." And since the field is the world and the tares are the children of the wicked one, or of the evil doctrine, and the Lord has clearly ordered, "Let both grow together," therefore the government should not undertake to destroy the tares by punishment and death. . . . Paul gives definite instruction regarding the attitude which the church should take toward a heretic, and says "A man that is an heretic after the first and second admonition, exclude." So Paul instructs the church

300

to exclude a heretic (Tit. 3:10), not to torture, maltreat, or kill him.... The true church of Christ has the characteristic that it suffers or endures persecution but does not inflict persecution upon any one.... To put to death an erring man before he has repented means to destroy his soul. Therefore one should not kill him but wait for his conversion, lest both body and soul be destroyed. Often a man who is in fatal error forsakes it and turns to the truth.

For further reading:

Harold S. Bender, "The Anabaptists and Religious Liberty in the Sixteenth Century," *MQR* XXIX (April 1955), 83-100.

Estep, *Anabaptist Story*, 194-198.

William R. Estep, "*Von Ketzern and Iren Verbrennern:* A Sixteenth-Century Tract on Religious Liberty," *MQR* XLIII (October 1969), 271-282.

James M. Estes, "Whether Secular Government Has the Right to Wield the Sword in Matters of Faith: An Anonymous Defense of Religious Toleration from Sixteenth-Century Nuernberg," *MQR* XLIX (January 1975), 22-37.

Paul Peachey, "Answer of Some Who Are Called (Ana)baptists—Why They Do Not Attend the Churches: A Swiss Brethren Tract," *MQR* XLV (January 1971), 5-32.

Wenger, *Even Unto Death*, 70-71.

XVI

Relations to
Other Christians

Anabaptists saw their relationship to other Christians in terms of the teaching about the two kingdoms (see introduction to Chapter 12). As the first selection in this section shows, they saw reality in terms of two distinct worlds, sharply separated, and clearly distinguishable from each other. Like all other Christian groups in the sixteenth century, they believed that they had the truth, and that all others were in error. Not only that, but the sixteenth-century mentality held that one could not be slightly in error. If one was in error, one was totally in error. Anabaptists conceived of only two realms of being, the kingdom of God and the kingdom of Satan. Truth was on God's side; error on Satan's. Catholics, Lutherans, and Reformed Christians, since they were in error, belonged to the kingdom of Satan (16.1, 16.4, 16.5).

There are evidences that even the Swiss and Menno, who expressed themselves most strongly on separation, realized that the reality was not quite like the theory. They admit that they learned from the Reformers, and Menno calls his admonitions to them "a brotherly warning." Pilgram Marpeck always spoke to Bucer and the other reformers of Strassburg as fellow-Christians. Their actions were therefore better than their theology.

Much of Anabaptist denunciation of other Christians was like that of the Old Testament prophets. They charged them with being meticulous about theology and ritual, but careless of ethical obedience. They claimed to be Christians but denied it by their lives (16.7).

They turned the charges of sectarianism against their opponents by charging them with having forsaken the biblical norms for the church (16.6), and did not hesitate to refer to Catholics and Protestants as sects (16.7). Peter Riedeman wrote about the pollution of Christianity through the deliberate use of pagan temples as churches. He claimed that doing this insured the survival of certain pagan practices in the church, a point that is historically accurate (16.6).

But the reason for the negative attitude of Anabaptists toward other Christians was not only their theology. In fact, their theology seems to have developed at least in part because of their experiences at the hands of other Christians. Selection 16.3 explains that good relations between Christians could hardly exist as long as one party had the power of life and death over the other. Threats of coercion and actual physical violence do not make for brotherly relations. Such treatment at the hands of the established churches at least explains in part why Anabaptists relegated them to the kingdom of Satan. Did they not use the methods which Augustine long before them and Luther their contemporary had identified as belonging to the kingdom of Satan? How could torture and killing be reconciled with the love of Christ?

Hans Denck was more directly aware of the inadequacies of the two kingdoms doctrine as a representation of reality. He was aware of the relativity of theological formulations and saw no need for separation because of such disagreements. With real sadness he, too, comments on the impossibility of brotherly relations when coercion and force are threatened or applied to questions of belief. He knew others could be in error because he was prone to it. Conversely he also knew that others could comprehend truth because he could, and that there was always some mixture of the two (16.2). As indicated in 15.2, Denck's sympathies were very wide. He could conceive of Turks and Jews having a measure of truth. These sentiments were also expressed by Sebastian Franck, a popular writer of that day. Anyone who fears God, should be acknowledged as a brother. But Dirk Philips would have none of that (16.7). If one is not born again, and does not know God through Christ, he cannot be a brother.

Thus Anabaptists shared in considerable measure in the intolerance of their age. To keep resentment and even hate for their persecuting enemies subjected to the love of Christ was a perpetual battle which they did not always win. The odds were against them, but they tried, and for this they deserve our respect.

16.1 Michael Sattler, Schleitheim Confession, 1527, *Legacy*, 37-38

IV. We have been united concerning the separation that shall take place from the evil and the wickedness which the devil has planted in the world, simply is this; that we have no fellowship with them, and do not run with them in the confusion of their abominations. So it is; since all who have not entered into the obedience of faith and have not united themselves with God so that they will to do his will, are a great abomination before God, therefore nothing else can or really will grow or spring forth from them than abominable things. Now there is nothing else in the world and all creation than good or evil, believing and unbelieving, darkness and light, the world and those who are [come] out of the world, God's temple and idols, Christ and Belial, and none will have part with the other.

To us, then, the commandment of the Lord is also obvious, whereby he orders us to be and to become separated from the evil one, and thus he will be our God and we shall be his sons and daughters.

Further, he admonishes us therefore to go out from Babylon and from the earthly Egypt, that we may not be partakers in their torment and suffering, which the Lord will bring upon them.

From all this we should learn that everything which has not been united with our God in Christ is nothing but an abomination which we should shun. By this are meant all popish and repopish works and idolatry, gatherings, church attendance, winehouses, guarantees and commitments of unbelief, and other things of the kind, which the world regards highly, and yet which are carnal or flatly counter to the command of God, after the pattern of all the iniquity which is in the world. From all this we shall be separated and have no part with such, for they are nothing but abominations, which cause us to be hated before our Christ Jesus, who has freed us from the servitude of the flesh and fitted us for the service of God and the Spirit whom he has given us.

304

Thereby shall also fall away from us the diabolical weapons of violence—such as sword, armor, and the like, and all of their use to protect friends or against enemies—by virtue of the word of Christ: "you shall not resist evil."

16.2 Hans Denck, "Recantation," 1527, Fellmann, *Denck* I, 108

Wherever I find hearts who honor this goodness of God through Christ and follow his footsteps I rejoice and love them according to my knowledge of them. But those who do not wish to listen to me and who will yet not let me be silent in matters that divide, it is not possible for me to have much fellowship with them. For I do not notice the mind of Christ in them but a perverted spirit that seeks to coerce me from my faith with violence and to convert me to another regardless of whether it is right or not. And even if he is right, his zeal may be good but it is used without wisdom. For he must know that in matters of faith everything must be free and uncoerced. Thus I separate myself from some, not because I regard myself as better or more just than them, but that I may search for the costly pearl free and without hindrance and insofar as I have found it, that I may keep the same in peace with everyone so far as it is possible. Persecution and other fears of that sort have separated me from some but my heart is not turned from them, especially not from any person who fears God. But so far as God wills I do not desire to have any fellowship with error or unrighteousness recognizing that all the time I am among sinners and among the erring. With this conscience I wait for the judgment of Jesus Christ gladly and without fear however much I may be afraid of men because of my timidity. And with all this I do not desire to justify myself but I recognize and know well enough that I am a man who has erred and who may still err.

16.3 Some Swiss Brethren, 1532-40, Peachey, *Answer*, 32

Further, some of you, our opponents, ask why we do not stand up and appear among the people, preaching openly, whether or not the world approves, thus awaiting the cross as did the apostles, when they were told no longer to preach in the name of Jesus; to which command they answered in Acts 4, "Whether it be right in the sight of God to hearken unto you more than to God, judge ye. For we cannot but speak the things that we have seen and heard."

Answer: it is good enough for the opponents to speak thus, but they are not in love and earnest. For if we were to appear in their church or congregation, and to speak to the salvation of souls, as has happened often already, they would be the first to cry out against us, and to seek to silence us, and so bring sorrow and persecution upon us. The point is that they speak such words only so as to have occasion to persecute us by bodily force. How can they be in earnest, when, as shown in the first book above, they resist us in their congregations, not permitting us to speak openly according to the practice and custom of the apostolic churches; though we shall not fail to do so nonetheless, when God moves one or more of us, but not at the behest or action of the opponents, rather only where and when the Holy Spirit instructs and moves us.

16.4   Martin Weninger, "Vindication," 1535, *Wenger*, 82-83

Christ commands us to guard ourselves from the mixed teaching of the Pharisees and the befuddled expositors who pose as teachers of the Scripture but know not what they set forth or say (Mt. 16, 1 Tim. 1) and teach what is not profitable—just as the teaching of the priests does not profit—for base gain. Titus 1: [They are] lazy bellies which may not produce works, all with deceitful minds, just like our priests. David says, They teach only sins, and glory in their pride and speak vain contradictions (Ps. 59), just as our priests also do now, teaching sins and hardening [people] in sins with their frivolous teaching, as it stands in Ezekiel 13 and Jeremiah 23. They minimize to the people the shadow of the wantonness of their life of sin (Jer. 8, 6, 2 Pet. 2), saying peace when there is no peace and promising freedom to those who ridicule God with their doings and walk after the lust and desire of their evil heart (Jer. 23, 2 Pet. 2), and they themselves are servants of corruption and sin (Rom. 6, Jn. 8). They are called the Christians, even pious Christians and Brethren, who walk in darkness and have no fellowship with the light of Christ (1 Jn. 1), and whom the apostle of God calls children of the devil, as he says: He who does the right is of God and has the new birth of the Spirit, but he who does not do the right, but commits sin, is of the devil and not of God, because sin is also not of God. He has never known God and will also not see him (1 Jn. 2, 3, 5 and 3 Jn. 1). He who transgresses the teaching of Christ has not God (2 Jn. 1), and all his piety will no longer have any significance (Ezek. 18, 33, Jas. 2).

By such evident witness it is now clear that the doctrine of the priests is not of God, and that it does not correspond with the doctrine of Christ and the apostles. Furthermore it is no wonder that such false apostles and deceptive workers pose as apostles of Christ, because the god and prince of this world himself (2 Cor. 4, Jn. 12, 14, Eph. 2), the devil, poses as an angel of light. It is no wonder that his servants also, who draw the wanton people to themselves (2 Pet. 2, Jer. 23) and harden them in sin so that they so much the less repent (Ezek. 13) and live, pose as preachers of light, whose end will be according to their works (2 Cor. 11).

Now when such hirelings, shepherds who have bargained for a definite wage, see the wolf coming they flee and do not lay down their lives for the sake of the sheep (Jn. 10). Such shepherds the little sheep of Christ will not hear. But the foolishness of such shepherds who are come as from Christ whether [or not] he sent them, will be manifested to many people in the Free Territories [of Argau], moved as they are by a seditious, blood-thirsty spirit which brought destruction in the rebellion of Korah, etc. Also many Zwinglian priests have turned back to the pope in Turgau, disregarding how it went with those for whom they had promised to stake their lives, and having been found to be liars (Apoc. 2). He who had not wished to recognize this must now see that it is true.

16.5   Menno Simons, "Foundation," 1539, *CWMS*, 207-208

And I turn to you, O learned ones, you who think that you have the keys of heaven and are the eyes and the light of the people. I will speak with you as with those whose salvation I seek with all my heart because I see plainly that both you and those you teach run confidently into the eternal destruction of your poor souls. Nevertheless you boast that you are the commissioned teachers, and your churches the churches of Christ. And I wish to admonish you in faithful brotherly spirit one and all, Roman Catholics, Lutherans, and Zwinglians, concerning the following articles.

Notice in the first place that your office and service are not of God and His Word but issue from the bottomless pit. For it is evident that you blaspheme and persecute Christ's Word, ordinances, and commands, and teach and promote the word, ordinances, and commands of Antichrist. You violate the temple of God, building and honouring temples of stone. You break the living images in which the Spirit of God dwells, making and adorning images of gold, silver, and wood. You hate a pious, blameless life, encouraging and defending by your frivolous example an unchecked wild life of the flesh. Dear sirs, where is there a single letter in the Scriptures enjoining all your ritual and worship, your masses, infant baptism, auricular confession, etc.? Is not all you do and promote deception, hypocrisy, blasphemy, abomination, and idolatry? Whence do your offices and services come and of whom are they? I would advise you in true love to reflect in the light of the Scriptures, and in the true fear of God.

. . . .

Dear me, what is your entire ambition and conduct if not world, carnality, belly, and a life of luxury? Who can fathom and describe your earthly mind and carnal life? Some of you parade in ermine, in silk and velvet, others live in headlong revelry, others are avaricious and hoard; some disgrace virgins and young women, others defile the bed of their neighbor, the chastity of others is like the chastity of Sodom. The doctrine of all of you is deceiving, your sacraments are superstitious, your piety is mostly wickedness, and your divine service is an open abomination and idolatry. Some of you fear neither God nor the devil. The name of God you blaspheme, his holy Word you falsify, his children and servants you persecute, and in response to his grace, you do all manner of evil. Just so you can lead a carefree life and have a good time, then all is fine. Tell me, is it not

308

so? Worthy men, is it not so? This is, is it not, your chief ambition and striving, great and small. You must acknowledge and grant it, for the fruit is manifest through all the world and cannot be longer hid.

Gentlemen, beware! If men could enter into life on this broad way which you teach and travel, and keep their souls in God, then we may well lament and say that the prophets, apostles, and all the witnesses of God and even Christ Jesus himself did not act wisely. Neither did they deal honestly with us when they travailed with so much anguish, oppression, sadness, and pain in this sorrowful vale of tears, nor when they directed us miserable weak children to such a way.

Oh, no, dear friends, no. Truth will remain truth forever. If you are not converted to a better and a Christian mind, if you do not die to your error and also to your vain, carnal life, if you do not repent and become like innocent, simple children, you cannot enter into the kingdom of heaven. For to be carnally minded, says Paul, is death.

16.6   Peter Riedeman, *Account*, 1542, 91-95

CONCERNING SEPARATION

Firstly, we say that God has taken and chosen a people for himself through his Christ to be his property, wherefore also he has bestowed on it his Spirit that they might be of his nature and character, and no longer carnal but spiritual, as Paul says, "Ye are not in the flesh, but in the Spirit, if so be that the Spirit of God dwell in you. But if any man have not the Spirit of Christ, he is none of his." Therefore the church of Christ is not carnal but spiritual, and there is no Church of Christ save that which the Holy Spirit gathers, rules, teaches and directs. Now those who surrender themselves to the Spirit that the same might rule over them, yield themselves to the church of Christ, in which the Holy Spirit works. But those who yield themselves to sin, to serve it and let the same rule over them, these separate themselves from the church of Christ and estrange themselves from her, and if so be that they leave her, they go even farther into destruction.

For this reason we by no means admit that we have separated ourselves from such a church of Christ, on the contrary we have drawn near to her, yielded ourselves to her, that he who works in her might also work in us, and that we through his working might be assured that we are God's children. Thus, we are in the community of the church of Christ or of the children of God, where there are no more servants, but all are children through faith in Jesus Christ.

Thus, we say and must say and confess, that not we but all baptizers of children have forsaken the church and community of Christ and separated themselves from the same. They have fallen away, and are become so corrupt that they neither know nor recognize what the true church of Christ is and in what way she proves herself the church of Christ. To which thing, if one ask them and tell them, they give the answer, "The saints did that, who had the Holy Spirit. But we are not able to do so." They know not that the church of Christ is a house of the Holy Spirit, and that none is therein unless he has the same, as also Paul says, "If any man have not the Spirit of Christ, he is none of his."

Since then God has chosen this church for himself and separated her from all nations that she might serve him with one mind and heart through the one childlike Spirit, there is, as has been said, no more a servant therein but only children. Nor have they separated themselves, but God has separated them from all other peoples, and has therefore also given them a sign of the covenant, that is baptism, whereby they receive all who surrender themselves to God into the church.

Since, however, God allowed us all to fall away because of our many sins, in that we had all turned from good to evil and had twisted the usage and order of the church into what was evil, and misused it, so that we all now walked in darkness until God, who desires not the death of the sinner, had mercy upon us and once more let the true light of his grace shine and brought his truth to light, we—as the wise man teaches, "My child, neglect not to turn back to the Lord, and put it not off from one day to the next"—have with haste turned again to the Lord, to keep his ordinances, which we had forsaken and from which we had fallen, and to thank God who has accepted us.

310

Thus, we have not turned away from the church of Christ, but to it; but we have left the soiled and impure assembly, and would wish that all men did so too. Therefore we call to repentance and tell whoever is willing to hear to harden not his heart and so bring the wrath of God upon him. Whosoever will not repent, however, and cleave to the true ordinances of God, but remains in his sins, we must let go his way and leave him to God.

CONCERNING THE TEMPLE AND THAT WE GO NOT THEREIN

God the Lord has built a temple for himself. That is his church wherein he desires to be honoured, and apart from it he desires to plant the memory of his name neither here nor there—for the ceremonial semblance has been brought to an end, and in Christ Jesus the real and true service of God has begun, which must take place through human choice is no service of God, however much it may deceptively seem to be, since there is no other divine service than in the church of Christ, which he himself has sanctified so that there is neither spot nor blemish in her. The assembly in the temple, however, is a rabble and gathering of whores and adulterers and of all unclean spirits, whom God hates; wherefore there is no divine service there, but on the contrary blasphemy and contempt of the Almighty, and this has moved us to flee from and avoid their assembly.

With regard to the buildings of stone and wood—these originated, as the history of several shows, when this country was forced by the sword to make a verbal confession of the Christian faith.[65] Further, men dedicated temples to their gods, and then made them "churches,"[66] as they are wrongly named, of the Christians. Thus, they originated through the instigation of the devil and are built up through sacrifice to devils, since as Paul says, "The things that the heathen sacrifice, they sacrifice to devils and not to God: and I would not that ye should be in the fellowship of devils." For that is also not God's will, for Christ has no fellowship with Belial. Therefore, also, he commanded in the Old Testament that they should utterly destroy and break down such places, that they might not share in

311

that fellowship. Nowhere does he say, change it and use it aright; but says break it down utterly.

Now, because the people did this not, but left the root in the earth, they not only brought not the heathen practices to the right usage, but they themselves forsook the right usage and surrendered themselves to all manner of idolatry, and they have now changed so much that they call "saints" what those called "gods." And for the same reason—because the root is left in the earth—they have gone farther and have built one house after another for their gods (or "saints," as they call them), and filled them with their gods and idols, and thereby show that they are the children of their fathers, and have not left their fellowship.

But because we know that God hated such places from the beginning, and still hates them, we likewise avoid and flee from them (as those who know most surely that therein is no true service of God, but on the contrary that he is continually dishonoured and despised) that we might not share their fellowship and again fall away from the truth we have recognized; since God might because of this turn from us as from Israel. We know well, however, that if a path goes through such a temple, if one goes straight through he makes himself not unclean before God. But to go in to partake of such fellowship, to hear anything therein, to learn or receive anything, of that Paul says, "I would not that ye have fellowship with devils."

16.7   **Dirk Philips, "A Loving Admonition," 1558, "The Second Admonition," "Refutation of Two Letters of Sebastian Franck," after 1563, Kolb/Klaassen, *Philips*, 425-426, 431, 437-438, 485**

Now, from this it may be easily deducted and clearly understood that there must be a separation from the temple of idols, from all ungodly preachers when they stand in the pulpit and pervert the word of God, and from all false worship, not in heart and spirit only, but also in body. Therefore those who profess such false liberty, referred to above, lie against the truth, deceive themselves and others. These are they of whom Jesus Sirach says: "Woe be to fearful hearts, and faint hands, and the sinner who walks on two streets.

Woe to him that does not remain in good heart! What will be their lot when the Lord comes in judgment?" (Sir. 2:12, 13). These are they of whom Peter says: "These are wells without water, clouds that are carried with a tempest; for whom is reserved deep darkness in eternity. For they speak courageous words, but do not follow them. Through wantonness they entice to lusts of the flesh those who had truly escaped, but now wander in error. They promise them liberty, while they themselves are the servants of destruction" (2 Pet. 2:17-19). Those are inconstant and apostate Israelites who try to carry water on both shoulders and swerve from side to side (1 Kings 18:21[22]), who intend partly to serve God, partly Baal. And thus they are led astray by the splendor and lecherous spirit of the prophetesses of Jezebel. They persuade them that sin is not sin, that unrighteousness is no unrighteousness (Rev. 2:20); but let every one take heed and beware of these prophetesses of Jezebel. Let no one be deceived by them; for the Lord will cast all them who have committed fornication with her into extremest torment, if they do not repent, and the whole church shall confess that he is the Lord, who rewards every man according to his works.

. . . .

Now, I know very well that all sects claim to be right, and are industrious in their ability to pervert the Scripture according to the way of Satan, in order to embellish their evil things and hide their wickedness, and do not see the blindness of their heart with which they are stricken by God, that they deny the confessed and accepted truth, that they despise and change the unchangeable counsel of God, revealed in Jesus Christ in the gospel and witnessed by the Holy Spirit, that they seek altogether the friendship of the world, which yet is enmity with God (Jas. 1[4]:4), that they try to preserve the temporal life, and therefore, according to the Lord's own Word, must lose eternal life (Jn. 12:25), that with Esau they sell their birthright for a morsel of meat (Heb. 12:16), and shall possibly never afterward be able to obtain it, yea, that they are again in their former uncleanness, which Jesus Christ had washed away by his blood and by the washing of water by the Word (Rev. 1:6; Eph. 5:26), and that the common proverb applies to them: "The dog is turned to his own vomit again; and the sow that was washed to her wallowing in the mire" (2 Pet. 2:22).

. . . .

Thus also may we glory in the Lord against all sects, namely, that the true and pure gospel of Jesus Christ is with us, the true priesthood with its true worship of God, the true ordinances of God, as those that have come down from heaven, given by God the Father, taught and commanded by Jesus Christ, testified to and confirmed by the Holy Ghost (Mt. 3:17), and practiced and declared by the apostles. But with our adversaries and the apostates are the golden calves of Jeroboam and his priests (Rev. 3) which he made contrary to the command of God. There offerings are made in the high places, there Baal is worshipped, the prophetess Jezebel reigns with her false doctrine, there the doctrine and way of Balaam is followed, who raised up an offence before the children of Israel, so that they committed fornication with the daughters of Moab, and worshipped Baal-peor (Num. 25:1-5). So also do these modern Balaamites, who practice hypocrisy to please the world and to mislead others, and use all diligence to destroy the church of God. Therefore let us sound the trumpet as one voice, and blow the trumpet of God, and the enemies shall be terrified when they shall hear the sound of the trumpets of God (Judg. 7:20); yea, then the cake of barley bread will fall upon the tents of Midian and destroy them, if so be that we sound the trumpet and break the earthen pitchers in pieces and let our light shine and strive manfully for the truth of God; then all who oppose the truth or depart from it and grieve and oppress the church of God must come to shame. For, because Pharaoh oppressed the children of Israel he was drowned in the Red Sea (Ex. 14:23). And because Jannes and Jambres withstood Moses (2 Tim. 3:8), they were brought to shame. And how many tyrants have been punished by God because they tyrannized over God's people; and how many false prophets who set themselves against the true prophets have been brought to shame! "They shall not succeed," says the apostle, for their folly shall be made manifest unto all men."

. . . .

From this it follows that it is nothing but foolishness for Sebastian Franck to profess and advise, that heathen, Turks, Jews and even all those who have no historical or scriptural knowledge of the Lord Jesus Christ, be acknowledged as brethren if they fear God. Dear reader, how shall a man who does not know God fear him? Or how shall or can a man fear and confess God the Father who does not believe in Jesus Christ whom the Father gave as a Saviour and Reconciler? (Jn. 1; 1 Jn. 5). Or how can a man be born of God except by faith in Jesus Christ? Or how can a man become our brother and fellow-member in Christ Jesus ([1] Jn. 2) who is not born of God? For this birth can not take place in any other way than in the way already mentioned, namely, that to as many as received the Word and Light, Jesus Christ, to them gave he power to become the children of God (Jn. 1:12). And again: "Whosoever believeth that Jesus is the Christ and the Son of God is born of God" (1 Jn. 5).

For further reading:

Robert Friedmann, "Ecumenical Dialogue Between Anabaptists and Catholics," *MQR* XL (October 1966), 260-265.
Walter Klaassen, "The Anabaptist Understanding of the Separation of the Church," *Church History*, XLVI (December 1977), 421-436.

XVII

Eschatology

Anabaptist theology was shaped to a considerable degree by the experience of repression and persecution. This was especially true of their eschatology, that is their doctrine of the last things.

The social and religious upheavals of the sixteenth century were regarded by most observers as signs of the end time. There was a mass of popular literature on the subject, much of it depending on earlier prophetic literature especially of the fifteenth century. The Reformers too, especially Martin Luther, had a lively interest in the subject. Anabaptist eschatology must therefore be seen and understood in the total context of the period.

As with other subjects above, there was great variety in interpretation among Anabaptists. They all agreed that they were living in the last days, but they disagreed in emphasis, specificity, and especially regarding their own attitude toward and participation in the expected events.

Most Anabaptists followed Luther in identifying the church of Rome as the Antichrist or the Babylonian harlot. The claim of the Papacy to be the voice of God on earth and/or the inseparable mingling of the spiritual and temporal powers were identified as the "abomination of desolation" (17.1, 17.14, 17.15, 17.21, 17.24). Even the Protestants are occasionally included in this identification (17.1).

There is only one selection from the Swiss Brethren which is attributed to Michael Sattler. It seeks to correlate the prophecies of Revelation 13-17 with contemporary events, thereby implying that the second coming cannot be far away (17.1). Most of the selections from Dutch Anabaptism (Menno Simons and Dirk Philips) are of the same general nature, Menno refraining from all detailed identification. The same is true of Peter Riedeman.

The early South German/Austrian Anabaptists and the early Dutch Anabaptists made many more specific contributions. Hans Hut, the disciple of Thomas Müntzer, contributed the first detailed calculations, identifying Pentecost, 1528, as the date of the second coming. This was taken over by his immediate disciples (17.4, 17.8). Another disciple shared Hut's *Sieben Urteile* (Seven Judgments) with his interrogators. These articles were a kind of summary of Christian faith, the first three dealing with the covenant, the kingdom of God, and the body of Christ, and the last four with eschatology (17.6). The distribution testifies to the preoccupation with the last things. Hans Hut and his earliest followers clearly expected to participate in God's punishment of the wicked at the end (17.4, 17.5). Leonhard Schiemer offers a fairly detailed chronology with calculations tying prophecy in with contemporary events (17.7). So does Hubmaier, who vigorously disputes the Hut-Schiemer calculations (17.8). In Jacob Hutter and Peter Riedeman, who also belonged to the Hut succession, we find only general expectation of the last days with their reward and punishment (17.9, 17.19).

The Melchiorite-Münsterite eschatology also represents a special approach. For Melchior Hoffman eschatology was in the very forefront of preoccupation from 1526 onwards. He saw Strassburg as the centre of God's activity and predicted that the end would come in 1536 (17.13). But even as he made this prediction the Anabaptists had succeeded in gaining control of the city of Münster in Westphalia. Bernhard Rothmann's interpretations regarded Münster as the centre of the coming kingdom. In fact, the Münsterites were convinced it had already begun with the reign of Jan van Leyden (17.14).

Rothmann described the fall of the church in some detail, to come, finally, to the restitution of all things, which, he confidently believed, had begun in Münster. God had begun his work in New Testament times with the poor and uneducated. The truth proclaimed by them had been destroyed by the learned leaders of the church. Until their own time the church had been in ruins until God, in a fine display of symmetry, had begun the restitution with the scholars, Erasmus, Luther, and Zwingli, and was now determined to

317

bring it to its fulfillment again through the poor and unlearned (17.14). Part of this restitution would be the execution of God's vengeance on the godless by his elect (the Münsterites). As a justification Rothmann quoted Joel 3:10, the exact opposite of the passage quoted by other Anabaptists as the most desired state (Is. 2:4). The restrained eschatology of Menno Simons and Dirk Philips was a direct consequence of the holy war theology of the Münsterites.

Coming back to the assertion made in the first paragraph of this introduction, it seems clear that the persecution of Anabaptism had much to do with their consciousness of living in the last days. They regarded their sufferings and martyrdom as the tribulation preceding the second coming. They were convinced, however, that they belonged to God's people and were thus at the centre of God's purpose. This purpose could not be defeated by earthly tyrants, and therefore the suffering and martyrdom would be only temporary. After that would come the judgment when they would be rewarded for their faithfulness, and their enemies would receive their deserved condemnation. The Anabaptists were, for the most part, not free to retaliate against the attacks of their enemies. They could not always resist expressing a certain degree of satisfaction at the prospect of the torments which would come on their enemies at God's hands (17.21, 17.27).

17.1 Michael Sattler (?), "On the Satisfaction of Christ," *Legacy*, 116-118

They say much about faith and yet know neither what Christ nor faith is. They reject works without faith in order to raise up faith without works. They would like to obey God with the soul and not also with the body, so that they might be without persecution. They believe that faith is a lazy and empty fiction, whereby they are also able to say that infants have faith, even though no works of faith can be discerned in them, even when they grow up. It would thus seem that the works of faith and the Holy Spirit were to curse when they hardly know how to speak, etc. Oh, the miserable blindness! Although they write all of this not because they do not know better, but in order that they provide for their belly and maintain their honour. Thus one sees here so clearly how the beast, with seven

318

heads and ten horns, recuperates from its mortal wound; according to which the Roman school or curia, from which the Bread-Lord-God[67] and infant baptism originally come, are again defended as truths by the scribes. To say nothing of many other things wherein the scribes again flatter the papists and set them up again as Christians. But that is how the second beast with the two horns, namely the band of the scribes, had to do, so that the earth and the men who live on it would again worship the first beast; they had to reestablish the popish oil idols,[68] that is the clergy; they had to throw down fire from heaven to banish and curse everyone who does not adhere to them, just as John had predicted it all. And this is precisely what he also saw, Rev. 17, how the ten horns on the beast would hate the harlot, and would leave her desolate and naked, would devour her flesh and burn her with fire, after God had put it in their hearts. The kingdom was to be given to the beast until the Word of God was all accomplished. Yea, that said ten horns, which [are] like kings, would take over the kingdom one hour after the beast, would come to an agreement to give power to the beast, would wage war with the Lamb and the Lamb would overcome them. That is how in the last days from all the high schools, awakened by the Spirit, the scribes were to arise and to attack with great zeal the Roman Church, the congregation of the work-saints, seize everything, and consume all the gold, silver, and other goods which she had brought together, condemn her as heretical, but soon after they would again take the side of the beast, that is the Roman school, and defend it, and again cast away the kingdom of God which previously had come to them. Yea, these would then defend the beast against the Word of God and those who adhere to it, and would violently strive against the Lamb (i.e., Christ). Nevertheless the Lamb, Lord of all lords, King of all kings, would overcome them, together with his called and believing ones. And is not that, together with the papists, the abomination of desolation of which Dan. 9, Paul in 2 Thess. 2; Peter in 2 Pet. 2, and Christ in Mt. 24; Mk. 13; Lk. 17, clearly spoke, which now sits in the place of the saints, lets itself be worshiped as either gospel or Christendom since the work-saints say, "Behold, here is Christ!" The scribes call, "Behold, here is Christ!" And therefore blessed is he who goes out from said Babylon. . . .

17.2 Balthasar Hubmaier, "Twelve Articles," 1526-1527, Davidson/Klaassen, *Hubmaier*, 217-219

I also believe and confess that you will come to judge the quick and the dead in the day of the last judgment, which, to all godly men, will be a chosen day, rich in joy. Then shall we see our God and Saviour face to face in his great glory and majesty, coming in the clouds of heaven. Then our carnal, sinful and godless life will have an end. Then will every man receive the reward of his works. Those who have laboured well will go into eternal life; those who have done evil into everlasting fire. O my Lord Jesus Christ, hasten that day and come down to us soon. . . .

But the fearful, the unbelieving, the accursed, the impure, adulterers, gluttons, blasphemers, the proud, the envious, the miserly, robbers, tyrants, magicians, idolaters and liars shall have their part in the lake of brimstone. From which preserve us ever, O blessed kind Lord Jesus Christ.

17.3 Statement of Hans Hut, November 26, 1527, *Meyer*, 239

It had been his view that God the Lord had given three and one-half years for repentance according to Revelation 13. Whoever repented would be persecuted and would have to suffer, as we read in [2] Timothy 3. All who would lead a godly life would have to suffer persecution. Daniel 12 says that they will all be scattered. He also talked about the three and one-half years and predicted famine, pestilence, and war. Only after these had happened would the Lord gather his own in all countries, and in each country they would punish the governments and all sinners. He based this on the passage where it says that the Lord would send his angels to the four corners of the earth to gather his elect. Then the new heaven and earth and a habitation for all the pious and elect here on earth would appear. This he called the future world according to Ezekiel 37 and Psalm 37, when the godless would be rooted out and the just would live in the land in perpetual peace.

Those who in these last times repent, remain steadfast to the end, and are not killed but remain, they will not die, but possess the earth and reign after the day and judgment of the Lord, as is stated in 1 Corinthians 15.

17.4   Eitelhans Langenmantel, 1527, *Armour*, 88

The Apocalypse tells of the seven angels who are commanded by God to pour seven plagues on the world in the last days. The Lord tells the first angel, "Do not harm the earth until I have sealed our brethren (*mitbrueder*) on their foreheads" (Rev. 7:3). The accused understands this to refer to all Christian men who have been and shall be baptized.[69]

17.5   Interrogation of Hans Hübner, 1527, Wappler, *Thüringen*, 244

The Turk will enter these lands and great war will come either from the south or Hungary, or from the north. When that happens, the gospel will be preached purely and clearly. When the Turk comes, the people will flee into the forests and hide themselves. But those who have bound (*verpunden*) themselves to Christ through this sign [of baptism] shall flee into the wilderness, and into Hungary. Then, if this judgment takes place, those who have accepted the covenant will root out all those who survive the Turks. Soon thereafter Christ will come and the last day. It is twenty-two months before the last day comes.

17.6   Interrogation of Ambrosius Spitelmaier, 1527, Schornbaum, *Quellen*, 55

This will happen when the end of the world really comes to its end. All the just who have remained will come together from the ends of the earth in a moment and kill all the godless. One will kill a thousand, two ten thousand. This commission will be given by God to his own (1 Cor. 15, the two epistles to the Thessalonians).

God will very soon raise up a people which we call heathen and enemies of the cross of Christ, namely the Turks. They will not bring the true cross, but there will be very little desire for it. All the people will be afflicted and afraid and the hearts of all men will despair and they will abandon their weapons. Then at one swoop will come plague, famine, war and heavy storms from the firmament. Then the rich of this world will consider their wealth, property and money as unclean and throw it out into the streets. They will put on hair shirts and do penance but to no effect since God will take no pleasure in it (Ezek. 7, Dan. 7, Lk. 21).

17.7 Interrogation of Ambrosius Spitelmaier, 1527, Schornbaum, *Quellen*, 50

Ambrosius Spitelmaier describes the Sieben Urteile[70] (Seven Judgments): The fourth judgment concerns the end of the world. The time is here in which God will purge all things through fire, earthquake, lightning and thunder. He will overthrow and destroy all buildings as happened in the great city of Babylon (Hab. 4, 6, 7) [Daniel?]. Then all the resistance and wisdom of the world with its wealth will be smelted down so that the kingdom of heaven can be erected (Ezek. 7, Jer. 30).

The fifth judgment concerns the future and the last judgment. After all things are thrown down and all men will die, then Christ will come (Mt. 25, 2 Cor. 5) in his glory to judge the living and the dead. Then each will be given according to his works (Mt. 20). He will reap there what he has sowed here. But none of the condemned have yet come into condemnation, nor have any of the blessed received anything.

The sixth judgment concerns the resurrection. All men will rise again in body and soul. The blessed will be resurrected to life for they have been dead here (Rom. 6), and the godless will be raised to death, for they have lived here (Ezek. 18). They have lived in peace and in the pleasure of this world and have had their kingdom of heaven (Mt. 19, Lk. 12, 16, 1 Tim. 6).

The seventh and last judgment concerns the eternal decision. The godless must come into condemnation and will go into the eternal fire (Heb. 4, Mt. 25) which never dies. Then the biting worm will begin to gnaw in the hearts of the godless and [there will be] crying, mourning, and gnashing of teeth, for here[71] they have laughed and had peace all their lives (Mt. 23).

17.8 Leonhard Schiemer, "A Letter to the Church at Rattenberg," 1527, Müller; *Glaubenszeugnisse*, 54-56

The Lord says: Sun and moon will be changed. Then all the generations on earth will wail and will see the Son of Man coming in the clouds of heaven. The wailing of the godless will continue for five months, but before that they will seize you. These days of the greatest tribulation are shortened, as Daniel says. Whoever reads it let him take notice. Daniel says further that 1290 days will transpire while the daily offering is removed (that is the killing of the Christians), the abomination of desolation is raised up and [he] takes his seat in the sanctuary of God. The man clad in linen is baptizing. It will last for 20 months, that is, a time, two times, and half a time. The woman, that is the church clad with Christ the sun, will flee from the dragon for 1200 days. She will be miraculously nourished by God in the desert where he has prepared her a place. That is 42 months. The judgment begins with the house and people of God. This refers to our day of greatest tribulation, to the time, year, month, and day according to the 7 parts of Scripture as mentioned above. But if someone takes days for years as with the 70 weeks, I say no. For the Scripture says that the days are shortened, and that it will last only a short while. If someone takes days for years the tribulation would not be short but very long, namely 1200 years. No persecution ever lasted that long. It has also been described in terms of days for years in the Fourth Book of Esdras and Daniel. The desolation of Jerusalem will also remain until the struggle has ended. He will make a strong covenant with many. And in the middle of the week he will remove the burnt offering and the food offering. But a time has been determined for the abomination of desolation which will come over him until it is all over. In the middle of the week, he says, that is three and one-half years from the end, the daily offering, that is the Christians, will be removed. The Lord says concerning the food offering: I have food and drink about which you know nothing. This is my food that I do the will of my Father who is in heaven. Work for the food which does not perish. Thus the faithful are the food offering. The food offering and the daily offering are the same thing.... They will lie buried for three and one-half days, that is three and a half years after which they will arise from the dead with all who sleep in the Lord. At exactly that time they began to kill the brethren of the community at Solothurn in Switzerland.... But when Esdras says in his fourth book: my son Christ will be killed after seven days, we must understand that Christ is not to be separated from his brethren, but rather to understand what is written that the lamb is slain from the beginning of the world, although Christ our head was slain only once and henceforth dies no more. But in his members it began with Abel and continues to the last half week. Thus is fulfilled the number of all the companions and brothers that have to be slain. Therefore the Lord says that there will be a tribulation the like of which has not been nor will be. After all this comes the resurrection of the dead.

17.9 Balthasar Hubmaier, "Justification," 1528, Westin, *Quellen*, 475

The day of the Lord is nearer to us than we expect. Therefore we should be prepared in daily worship, piety, and the fear of God.

Concerning this I very strongly opposed Hans Hut and his followers when they hoodwinked the simple people by claiming a definite time for the last day, namely next Pentecost. They convinced them to sell their property and leave wife and child, house and field behind, and are now without means of support. Thus the poor people were convinced to follow him by a seductive error which arose out of ignorance of Scripture.

The Scripture speaks of four years which Daniel calls a time, times, and half a time (Dan. 12). John in the Revelation calls the time 42 weeks which also make three and one-half years. That will be the time in which antichrist (whom Paul calls the man of sin and son of perdition, 2 Thess. 2) will move and reign. At the end of that time God will destroy him with the breath of his mouth (Is. 11, Dan.

8). Out of these three and one-half years which are sun and Daniel years, this ignorant Hut has made common years which is a great mistake. For a sun year is that time in which the sun makes one circuit which happens in one year with a little time remaining. That's where leap year comes from. Thus one common year is one day of the sun year. From this it follows that when Hut teaches about three and one-half years as in Daniel or the 42 weeks in the Revelation and regards them as common years he is mistaken. It is in fact according to the true understanding of Scripture three and one-half sun years which makes 1277 common years. By that much his calculations are in error which I seriously and openly flung into his face. I chastised him severely that he misled the simple people with his ungrounded claims.

17.10 Jacob Hutter, "The Fourth Epistle," Müller, *Glaubenszeugnisse*, 156-157

Be comforted, you chosen of the Lord, for the time of our deliverance is at hand. Lift up your heads to God the Lord in heaven and await your Shepherd and King from heaven with meekness, with great patience in righteousness and truth, in godly love and with strong faith and confidence. For he who is to come will soon come in the clouds of heaven with great power and glory, the King and comfort of Israel. He will rescue, save and liberate his own and will give them a glorious crown that will never fade. But before that there will be struggle and strife. Whoever battles like a true knight of Christ and is victorious will be crowned and will attain the prize. He will enter upon peace and joy, eternal rest and glory with all the chosen and with the heavenly host. He will be with the Father, his dear Son, and all the saints for ever and ever in the covenant of eternal life. . . .

O dear and elect children of the living God. I take joyful comfort in the assurance of God which he has promised us that we shall see him in his holy and beautiful temple. Our pain and distress will come to a final end, our weeping and crying will stop, and we will look upon and receive each other with great and unspeakable joy. No longer will anyone hurt or insult us for all tribulation and sorrow will pass away. For the curtain to the sanctuary which represents all earthly splendour and power will be removed by the power of the Lord. But the godly will rule and reign. Their mouth will be full of laughter as the Lord says; they will be joyful with the Lord and sing praises to him for ever and ever.

17.11   Melchior Hoffman, *Daniel XII*, 1526, A2b-B1b

The angel Michael [Dan. 12:1] must be understood to be a teacher who is now present in the Spirit and in the power of the Spirit's messenger, since in the Old Testament the spiritual angels led God's people and fought in their vanguard and protected them. Michael is called the chosen prince of the battle. Thus also now a teacher is at hand in power and in that same Spirit, who now leads God's people and fights for them with his angels and teachers.

The angel, Michael, the divine teacher, has arisen by God's mercy. For a long time he sat still in the Spirit because of God's wrath and displeasure, and permitted the prince of darkness to reign and to scatter the holy people and flock of Christ Jesus. But now God's wrath has declined and his grace has arisen. The time which was determined for and permitted to the prince of this world is now complete.

God is now again present with his Spirit and angel and intercedes for his children and chosen ones. He is again cleansing his holy temple, which the angels of God are now rebuilding and erecting again in a time of struggle. But however much the enemy of God's people with all his angels and false teachers seeks to prevent this rebuilding of God's temple, he will not succeed. It will be rebuilt. The last building of the physical temple was a figure, 1 Esdras 1[:1-4], of the spiritual temple which is now being built in the Spirit by means of God's Word for a spiritual dwelling of God. 1 Pet. 2[:4-5], 1 Cor. 3[:16-17], 2 Cor. 6[:16-17], Rev. 21[:1-8].

In order to help understand more clearly the truth concerning these present last times, the angel Michael is more clearly portrayed in the Revelation of John chapter seven. There we read about the power of his office, how, when, and with whom he struggles, namely with the dragon and his angels. The Spirit says it is a red dragon, by

326

which we must understand a kingdom of bloodshed.... This kingdom ruled over Christians during the time of the apostles. Similarly this great red dragon will quaff the blood of Christians. The woman, which is Christendom, will be persecuted by the dragon, who will attempt to drown her with a stream of water. However, she will be protected for three and a half times with two wings, about which we will speak later.

First we need to understand who this dragon and Satan is. We need to peruse and give attention to the words from God's mouth in Ezekiel 29[:2-5]....

Is it not remarkable that a prophet had to announce disaster and the punishment of God to the great king Pharaoh, and to chastise him by calling him a dragon, indeed, a great dragon, and that he would be cast away with his whole kingdom? From these words it is easy to judge who the great red dragon is. He is the sovereign who rules over the Christians in the flesh. But that he is called Satan must be understood as follows: Isaiah in the 14th chapter speaks about it, when he rebukes the king of Babylon as a devil and Lucifer. He is to be pulled from heaven into the abyss because he exalted himself above the stars and the clouds and made himself equal with God.... This prince of the world with his angels dwelt in the temple of God and ruled over the righteous by means of his fear and law, although only God's law as well as his staff and the heavenly bread should have been in them as it was in the ark of the Old Testament. That is what it means to become a devil and Satan who desires to rule in equality with God. He forbids whatever God commands....

. . . .

When the prince of this world is cast out with his teachers and angels by the angel Michael and his angels, the terror begins. Heaven must be understood here to mean all the elect of God, who in the Word of God are called heaven and a temple of God where God dwells. All people whom God has designated as his temple and his dwelling are heaven. It is as David said: the heavens declare your glory.

. . . .

When the Word of God enters this heaven of man, Satan and

327

his teaching has to be thrown out. This happened in the time of the apostles through the apostles; the devil had to leave God's heaven which he had occupied and make place for the Spirit of God to enter again into the hearts of the elect.

This is what is happening now through God's teachers and witnesses or angels. The hearts of the elect are again made free from the .devil, from unbelief, and from the fear of the world's tumult. They are again filled with the Spirit of God, and strengthened in steadfastness against all the attacks of Satan.

What has been written is now at hand.... The gospel of the kingdom will be preached to all nations as a witness. Then the end will come....

In these words [Rev. 14:6-7] we read about our own day and about the judgment which will come upon the world in power....

17.12   Interrogation of Melchior Hoffman, 1533, *Quellen*, *Elsass II*, 18

According to the Scripture there would be insurrection and unrest in the whole world, indeed, the time for it was there. The whole mob of the clergy would be destroyed. The true Jerusalem could not come into being or be built up until Babylon with all her mob and support would collapse and be brought to ruin.

17.13   Interrogation of Melchior Hoffman, 1534, *Quellen: Elsass II*, 393

All the prophecies, the old and the new, which concern this city,[72] were revealed through his brethren in the Netherlands, but hidden to this city. He would gladly reveal them to the city so that they too would know them. They knew in advance through the prophecies that many of his followers here would be scattered and at least a hundred would be driven out. But my lords had a schism in the council so it was not done. The time will come when they will buy with a lot of money a man whom they had driven out. Briefly, no detail was so small but they knew in advance. Hans Rebstock's wife of Esslingen is their chief prophetess; God had showed it to them. There are also many prophecies which concern him, Melchior Hoffman, and his work, in which one could find the secret. For everything he had said so far he had based on foreign prophecies as one could see from the book he had with him.

17.14 Interrogation of Melchior Hoffman, 1535, *Quellen: Elsass II*, 395

In Münster they have a prophet by the name of John Mathis who claims that he is one of the witnesses of God.[73] Münster will not be oppressed. We will have three kings here before this city. We wait for it every hour.

17.15 Interrogation of Melchior Hoffman, 1535, *Quellen: Elsass II*, 444-445

First he said that God was telling them to provide themselves with the Word of God.

Secondly God says, that they should supply themselves with food and other necessities, for the city would suffer hunger and need. Weapons also should be stocked. In the third year of his, Melchior Hoffman's imprisonment, God would come.

The city need not be afraid of the Anabaptists, and those Anabaptists who will not take the sword should be ordered to the moats, for they will do no harm. They should be concerned about those who are after the wealth of the clergy and who have no sense.

Item, the imperial cities will come under much attack, and this city is to be an example to all the imperial cities. This has not yet begun. But God is telling us that in the utmost extremity she should raise the banner of divine justice, namely the eternal son of righteousness. This must first be proclaimed here.

When the tumult has died down, this banner will flow from us into the whole world, and we will here send messengers into all the world.

. . . .

He would not take a sword into his hands, for he, Hoffman, would alone pray to God for us all. He has also warned his brothers about it.

329

17.16   Bernhard Rothmann, "Restitution," 1534, *SBR*, 216-219

The apostasy from Christ under the gospel was caused by human reason, wisdom, and desire when men depended rather upon their own wisdom and desire than to remain steadfastly with the teaching of Christ. Paul laments because he saw that Christians were thereby provoked to apostasy. Together with the other apostles he warned them earnestly. But all the warning and admonition did no good since human wisdom and good intentions and desire gained the upper hand. The teaching of Christ was mocked; opinion and hypocrisy possessed the field. Thus Christianity fell into the abyss and into the abomination of desolation. Since they were not willing to accept the love of truth that they might be saved God sent them a strong error that they listened more to the lie than to the truth. This apostasy took place not long after the ascension of Christ and the preaching of the apostles. For since the apostles lament about it, it happened in their time to their great sorrow as reported especially by Paul and John. During the apostles' time darkness and light struggled with each other and the gang of antichrist violently established itself against the sheep of Christ. Then, about one hundred years after the ascension of Christ, the truth had to yield to the establishment of the lie. Where Christ spread the truth through ignorant, poor, simple, uneducated fishermen and rustics, the old serpent darkened and confiscated the power and brilliance of the truth through the worldly wise, reasonable and educated ones of this world. Under the appearance of wisdom, holy divine wisdom and true holiness were suppressed and darkened. This did not happen all at once through one person. Rather one piece of Christian teaching, life, and faith after the other was gradually darkened and destroyed.... You will find that you cannot take up any of those who are called Scriptores ecclesiasticos[74] and read them with assurance and without any doubt, for you will find the problem now here, now there. All of them have departed from the true and sound teaching of Christ. This is without doubt because they sought praise and fame with their education and wisdom so that finally Christendom fell to the point where all the teaching of Christ was darkened. Only the learned ones, the men called theologians, and the spiritual decretals, councils, and opinions have possessed the field to the point where an aristotelian or thomist subtlety was considered more important than any passage of the holy Scriptures. Indeed they totally disregarded the Scriptures. This, we believe, is so clear and obvious that there is no need to prove it with many witnesses. If anyone wants more proof he should read the writings of the learned immediately after the times of the apostles. Their names are Linus, Clement, Marcellus, Dionysius, Tertullian, etc.,[75] some of whom lived in the time of the apostles and others shortly thereafter as one may read in the chronicles, especially in the book called De Scriptoribus Ecclesiasticis. Remember also the true teaching and manner of the pope, the pretended head of Christendom, and the schools which are called universities, and the matter will without doubt become as clear as the sun to you. Thus holy Christendom which was erected by the old-fashioned Christ and his simple uneducated apostles with the power of truth was perverted and made apostate by the educated and the worldly wise and their invented wisdom who did not seek God's glory and praise but their own. This happened at one point earlier, at another later, until no health remained in the whole of Christendom. Rather the abomination of desolation totally occupied the holy place, yes, completely inundated Christendom. What the Babylonian whore was not able to accomplish with her poisoned wisdom and invented holiness to bring about the apostasy of the Christians, the monarchs of the earth, who fornicated with her, have helped her accomplish with carnal violence. It was so complete that not one sign of true and sound Christian teaching, faith, and life remained.

Now we will consider briefly concerning the time and manner of the restitution.... Christ wants us to understand concerning the apostasy in the words: When you see, etc. [Mt. 24, 15]. In those words he also gives us a comforting account of the restitution. Among other things when he says: When you see, he should have said: When you have the grace to see the desolation and the abomination in the holy place, lift up your heads, for the time is near, and your salvation is not far off. Peter also speaks clearly regarding the restitution in Acts 3. Jesus Christ must take possession of heaven until the time of restitution about which God has spoken by the mouth of all his holy prophets from the beginning of the world. Then everything that the Father has not planted must be rooted out. Indeed, there must be one sheepfold and one flock in which, what was begun by Christ and his apostles will be restored, erected, and preserved. Concerning this much was taught at the time of the apostles, that is, regarding the day of the Lord.

They said that an apostasy would take place and that after that the Lord would come to bring to an end the abomination and again establish and restore his kingdom most gloriously in full power. For there were some who thought and tried to convince the people that it should happen immediately at the same time. To this Paul answered and chastised them saying in 2 Thess. 2,[3]: Let no one deceive you in any way, for he will not come before the apostasy takes place, etc., and the child of perdition is revealed. Rightly he should have said: When that happens, the Lord will come. From this you can see what was said at the time of the apostles.

Now concerning the time of restitution and its beginning. The Babylonian whore and the child of perdition, namely the Roman Antichrist, who from the beginning of his life had no other intention than the destruction of true Christianity and to exalt himself, has now become known. Regarding this reprobate and his manner enough has been written. Actually, in order to understand this rightly we say that God the almighty began the restitution when he awakened Martin Luther, who, by the grace of God (although sad to say he has not continued but remains stuck in his own pride and dirt) nevertheless identified the child of perdition, the true Antichrist, and began to introduce the true gospel.

It is now necessary, dear reader, that you consider the matter discreetly. We say that the restitution began in Luther's time, for then God revealed to us the abomination and the Antichrist. We do not say, however, that it has been concluded and fulfilled. Christ and his apostles had erected Christendom in perfection in all true teaching, faith, and life. Afterward the apostasy took place through the learned ones so that the most abominable lies ahd idolatry were introduced and erected by the most ignorant asses, the monks, popes, and godless theologians. Now comes the Lord, and where the old serpent used the learned ones to bring about the apostasy, the Lord

332

also uses the learned ones to restore that which has fallen away. He pays the devil in his own coin and measures to him with his own measure.... As the apostasy passed from the learned to the unlearned, so God has begun again with the learned. And now he wishes to set up the restitution most gloriously with the most unlearned according to the world that he alone may have the praise. Observe, therefore, that what was begun by Erasmus, Luther, and Zwingli has now been gloriously established in the truth first by Melchior and Jan Matthijs and now in our brother Jan van Leyden, who are quite unlearned as the world thinks.

17.17 Bernhard Rothmann, "Concerning Earthly and Temporal Power," 1535, *SBR*, 403-404

The fourth beast with the iron shins and feet is undoubtedly the Roman Empire. Concerning this beast we read that it was horrible beyond measure. It had iron teeth in its mouth and bronze claws and with its feet it destroyed what was left. Among its horns another small horn grew which spoke horrible mockeries. Here the prophet wants us to understand that the fourth kingdom shall be rent and divided, that it will be no longer one monarchy but many. This has in truth happened, for the Roman Empire has in many ways lost the unity of its great glory. The prophet also wants us to understand how this kingdom has been and will be against the truth and the saints of God, what is the source of its power and how it will be fulfilled. We will not reveal our understanding of it and wish that God will give to each to understand the truth. The horns and the iron toes are kingdoms which belong to the beast and do his will. Many kingdoms and powers belong to the Roman Empire and obey it in their temporal office. They have their foundation in God's order of temporal government. First, the clay toes which are totally without power; these are the so-called spiritual clergy. They are mixed with the iron, but it is crumbly dirt which does not stick. The power and glory which they use is covered by false names and titles. If they are uncovered one would find that there is no coincidence of the names with the essence. For although they call themselves spiritual and

333

claim and boast that they are incumbents, bishops, and shepherds of the truth of God for the shepherding of souls, in truth they are just as the other toes and practice violence like the kings of the heathen. These clay toes mix themselves with the iron of the fourth part of the image, that is the fourth great empire, which is the Roman Empire. This is also the horn of depravity that rose up among the others which speaks mockery against God. It claims to change laws and time and thrusts the other horns out of the way. This is the horn or beast with the three crowns, the pope, with his whole substance and nature. For he has elevated himself under the Roman Empire, taken his seat in God's place, given laws, and changed the time according to his will. He has seated himself above everyone, that is, that he has brought under his feet the temporal power, God's order, the Roman emperor. He rules in pride to blaspheme God, boast of his power, and to suppress the saints and the truth. The prophet quite properly marvelled at the proud scoffing of the horn until it perished with the beast and was cast into the fiery pit.

17.18 Bernhard Rothmann, "Restitution," 1534, SBR, 273

The Scriptures say that everything must be finished on earth. The Lord our righteousness will do justice and righteousness on earth. The mouth of the godless must be stopped on earth. All evil, and everything that the heavenly Father has not planted must be rooted out and done away with. There must be one sheepfold and one flock and one king who rules over all. All creatures must be set free. In summary: God's people which survive and which must remain unspotted and clean in all obedience will inherit the earth and will be at the service of Christ the King over all the earth. All this will happen in this time and on earth where righteousness shall dwell. Those who understand the Scriptures to say that this will happen after the judgment day and that it must be fulfilled then do not understand. For the Scriptures are written for men for the time of this life upon earth about which Christ says that every dot will be fulfilled. Peter says in Acts 3, [21]: Everything that the prophets have spoken will in the last days be erected and restored.

17.19 Bernhard Rothmann, "Concerning Vengeance," 1534, *SBR*, 292

There may be those who think that God himself will come down from heaven with his angels to avenge himself on the godless, and who confidently wait for it. No, dear brother. He will come, that is true. But the vengeance must first be carried out by God's servants who will properly repay the unrighteous godless as God has commanded them. God will be with his people and will give them iron horns and bronze claws against their enemies. For very soon we, who are covenanted with the Lord, must be his instruments to attack the godless on the day which the Lord has prepared. Thus God's strong arm will be with us and he will display his glorious power in his people who have so long been despised and cast out before the world. It is as Malachi says: You shall tread the wicked to death, for they will be as dust under your feet on the day which I make, says the Lord of hosts.

17.20 Bernhard Rothmann, "Concerning Vengeance," 1534, *SBR*, 296

After that the Lord will pour his wrath out on the head of the godless and he will not stop until he has finished everything that he has in mind. He will make the godless despair and take their power from them. He will strengthen the hand of David and will instruct his fingers for the battle. God will make for his people bronze claws and iron horns. They will make plowshares and hoes into swords and spears.[76] They shall choose a captain, fly the flag, and blow the trumpet. They will incite an obstinate and merciless people against Babylon. In everything they will repay Babylon with her own coin, yes, in double measure. These are the plans which the Lord has made against Babylon and the whole earth and his hand will be stretched out against all the heathen. For when the Lord of hosts decides something, who will be able to prevent it? Smoke will arise from the north. No one will be able to withstand his power. And what will the envoys of the heathen be able to bring for satisfaction? But God will fortify Zion and the poor of his people will be able to depend on her.

17.21   Peter Riedeman, *Account,* 1542, 32-34

FROM WHENCE HE WILL BE A JUDGE
OF THE LIVING AND THE DEAD

We confess also that the Father has committed judgment unto the Son, who will come, and that right terribly, namely with flaming fire, to take vengeance upon all that is ungodly and all the wrong brought by men, and to render praise, honour and an intransient nature to them, who with patience seek in well doing the eternal, immortal life.

But he to whom the Father has given the power and might to judge speaks thus, "I judge no man; but the word that I have spoken unto you will judge you in the last day." And this word will justify none save him who has surrendered with all his heart thereto, and now, in this life, allowed the same to judge, control and guide him. He, however, who has not listened to the Word and has been disobedient to it will be condemned.

For this reason we say that when the last trumpets sound, when the Son of Man will come into his glory from heaven with his holy angels, and those who are in their graves will arise to meet him, the sentence of each is already passed, as the word of Christ shows when he says, "He that believeth not is condemned already," and the place prepared, as we see when he speaketh of the last judgment with these words: "When the Son of Man will come in his glory and all the holy angels with him, then shall he sit upon the throne of his glory; and before him shall be gathered all nations; and he shall separate them one from another, as the shepherd divides the sheep from the goats; and he shall set the sheep on his right hand, but the goats on the left."

Thus we consider it to be clear enough that each one is already judged and sentenced: the devout to life, and the godless to death. It remained only that Christ speak this sentence and show each his place as the words indicate: "Come, ye blessed of my Father, inherit the kingdom prepared for you from the beginning: for I was an hungered, thirsty, naked, a stranger, sick and in prison and you ministered unto me," and to the others, "Depart from me, you cursed, into eternal fire, prepared from the beginning for the devil

336

and his angels, for I was in need of your help and you ministered not unto me."

As Daniel says, "The judgment was set and the books were opened," and after him John testifies that the dead were judged out of those things which were written in the books, and received according to their works, so we believe with our whole heart that all our words and works, be they good or evil, are preserved before God and his Son as though they were written in a book; and that when the time comes God will open his secret casket, and will show to each all his doings; as Paul says, "The day of the Lord will make all things manifest, that each may know why he is or will be blessed or condemned."

17.22 Pilgram Marpeck, "Concerning the Love of God in Christ," *The Writings*, 536-538

Time will cease to be. Sun, moon, stars, and everything that exists in time and for the sake of man (not created to remain eternally) must cease to be for the sake of that which is and must remain eternally (such as men and angels which are taken up into God and God into them). For there will no longer be any need for time nor the creatures of time such as animals, birds, fish, light, nor day. For in eternity time ceases, and God himself is day and light. Darkness and night will [depart] from the light, the incarnate Word and Spirit, and go to its eternal place where no grace or creaturely light will ever again be seen. Only the hellish and eternally deadly fire is the revelation and illumination of everlasting torment. They will suffer eternally, be and remain eternally in the darkness of God's wrath, yea, in eternal envy, hate, anger, murder, and in agonized crying because of the fire which will never depart from them.

For all their sin and guilt along with their wickedness remains eternally in them and with them. For salvation and mediation are no longer available so that they do not have even the smallest particle of comfort. . . .

The fallen angels and men are delivered over to each other as the greatest enemies with never-ending enmity, envy, and hate, in order completely to fulfill in one another their hellishly incorporated wantonness and their envious, hateful, and wrathful manner without the means of any adjudication, judgment, or restraint. Whatever in their greed and lustful wrath they invent and scheme to torment, insult, and to hurt each other they completely carry out. Beyond that all the evil they do to each other will be most bitterly salted with fire when the torment and great pain of eternal fire will be their arbiter. Thus the great pain of eternal fire together with everlasting despair will far exceed their own torment, and all this in immortality. It would be as though a mortal man had many deadly pains in his body, each pain far exceeding the other, with no surcease. Thus the lesser pains would be a small relief compared to the greater torment, but added to the greatest torment, even unto death. Thus not a single remedy will be available for all those condemned, each according to their deserts.

For all authorities are in this time gods and mediators between goodness and evil, between the just and the unjust, established to provide physical rest and peace and to restrain evil and protect the good. For evil and good now exist together in this physical life undifferentiated and [un]separated until the day when judgment takes place and good and evil are separated. This will take place when the last person to be saved is brought in. Then all worldly authority will be dissolved, one house will fall upon the other, there will be war and the cry of war without any means of peace or rescue, and all piety, faithfulness, love, truth, faith, and confidence will cease. For the pious and the godly, for whose sake the world with its wickedness is spared, will be saved. They will be separated from all wickedness and gain rest and eternal joy as Christ said: When you hear war and the cry of war lift your heads, for your salvation approaches.

Only then goodness and wickedness are separated one from the other, love and truth from envy, hate, and lying, hope from despair, faith from unbelief, peace from strife, patience from vengeance, joy and comfort from mourning and discouragement, mildness from greed, mercy from mercilessness, humility from arrogance, meekness from pride and haughtiness, and truth from lying.

That will be the salvation and final decision for all the godly who in themselves and among the wicked are now attacked, prone to fall, and imprisoned, afflicted, sorrowful, anxious, tormented, and

338

molested daily against their will by evil, abominable behaviour. Thus they will be redeemed and led out of all temptation.

17.23 Dirk Philips, "Concerning the Ban," 1558, Kolb/ Klaassen, *Philips*, 224-225

Beloved brothers and sisters and friends in the Lord:—I thank almighty God in this that I hear of your faith, of your love for the Lord Jesus Christ and for his saints, and of your patience and steadfastness in all the persecutions you endure, as an assurance of your salvation, which is a manifest token of the righteous judgment of God. He will recompense tribulation to them that trouble you, if they will not amend and sincerely repent. But you he will quicken and refresh when the Lord Jesus shall be revealed from heaven with his mighty angels, in flaming fire, taking vengeance on them that know not God, and that obey not the gospel of our Lord Jesus Christ. They shall be punished with everlasting destruction from the presence of the Lord, and from the glory of his power, when he shall come to be glorified in his saints, and be admired in all of them that believe (2 Thess. 1:7-10). By the power of their faith they have forsaken and overcome the world, who for the sake of the gospel now despise all perishable and temporal things and seek those things which are above (2 Cor. 4:18; Col. 3:1), where Christ sitteth at the right hand of the Father. For righteousness' sake they are now so unmercifully persecuted and put to death by tyrants and bloodthirsty men. For this is now the time when the heathen have come into the Lord's inheritance, defiling his holy temple, giving the dead bodies of his servants to be meat to the fowls of the heaven, and roasting the flesh of his saints on spits and offering it as prey and game to the wild beasts of the field. Their blood have they shed like water round about Jerusalem, and there was none to bury them (Ps. 79:1-3), and all because the great Babylonian harlot thirsts so greatly for the blood of the saints and witnesses of Jesus (Rev. 17:5; 18:24). She cannot be satisfied until she is fully drunken and the number of the servants of God (all of whom must be put to death for the sake of his Word) is fulfilled (Rev. 6:11). Then shall the almighty God judge and punish the Babylonian harlot, because she is the mother of all abominations on earth (Rev. 17:5), and the blood of all the saints is found in her (Rev. 18:24). She has deceived the world with her beautiful appearance (being arrayed in purple and scarlet color, and decked with gold and precious stones and pearls, having a golden cup in her hand full of all abominations and gives all her lovers and paramours to drink thereof); and the kings of the earth have committed fornication with her, and all nations have been made drunk with the wine of her fornication and sorcery. Therefore God shall punish her, and her plagues shall come unawares, and all who adhere to her and will not separate from her shall not go unpunished. O Lord! how will those then tremble and fear who now so haughtily revile the Lord and take truth captive (Is. 59:14, 15), who serve the Babylonian whore so faithfully, protecting her, and for her sake put the true Christians to death with fire, water, and the sword. On the other hand, how the servants of the Lord will rejoice, who have not received or accepted the mark of the beast, but who are sealed with the seal of the living God on their foreheads, of which it is written in the Revelation of John. John saw a great number of the servants of God who were sealed in their foreheads by the angel with the seal of the living God from among all the tribes of the children of Israel.

17.24 Menno Simons, "Encouragement to Christian Believers," 1556, *CWMS*, 1047-1048

Little children, fear not, but be comforted in the Lord. For he is such a faithful, pious King, to whom you have sworn and bowed your knees. Not the least of his promises shall fail you. He will be our shield and great reward. Therefore neither doubt nor waver, for it is but a small matter to endure the heat of the sun, tribulation, fear, oppression, temptation, plunder, persecution, prison, and death for a short time. The messenger is already at the door, who will say to us, Come ye blessed, enter into the glory of thy Lord. Then will our brief mourning be changed to laughter, our momentary pain into endless joy. These tyrants with their bloody mandates will have an end and all our persecutors, executioners, and torturers will cease. We will follow the Lamb, adorned in white garments with palms in our hands and crowns upon our head. Neither ill nor pain nor pangs of death will touch us longer, but we will forever exalt, praise, and thank in inexpressibly great joy and glory the Lamb who sits upon the throne.

Behold, my children, all the truly believing pious hearts comfort themselves with this approaching change. With it they possess their souls in patience, knowing well that their reward is great in heaven, and that on the other hand all the ungodly shall have their portion in the eternal, unquenchable fire, under the intolerable, dreadful sentence of God in the depth of hell, if they do not become converted and repent with all their hearts. Woe, woe, to these wretched people. To what an evil day were they born.

17.25   Menno Simons, "Teaching and Writing," 1539, *CWMS*, 303

Beloved reader, the Babylonian king, namely, the Antichrist, has through his servant, that is, through the false prophets and teachers, demolished the disobedient Jerusalem, the temple of the Lord, and so has imprisoned Israel these many years. Therefore I and my brethren in the Lord desire nothing, God is witness, than that we may to the honor of God so labor with his fallen city and temple and captive people according to the talent received of him, that we may rebuild that which is demolished, repair that which is damaged, and free those who are captives with the Word of God by the power of the Holy Spirit. And we would bring it back to its earlier estate, that is, in the freedom of the Spirit to the doctrine, sacraments, ceremonies, love and life of Christ Jesus and his holy apostles.

17.26   Menno Simons, "Reply to Gellius Faber," 1554, *CWMS*, 737, 742

On the other hand, the church of Antichrist is begotten of deceiving seduction through the spirit of error. Paul says, Now the Spirit speaketh expressly, that in the latter times some shall depart from the faith, giving heed to seducing spirits, and doctrines of devils; speaking lies in hypocrisy. Yes, reader, what else has the church of Christ laid low and the church of Antichrist raised up again, if not the vile, false doctrines of the learned ones, the many mutually contradictory councils, decretals, statutes, doctrines, and commandments of men? What is it that blinds the Germanic peoples today? What keeps them in their ungodliness, if not the frivolous doctrine of the preachers, the miserable infant baptism, the unscriptural, idolatrous Supper...?

. . . .

On the other hand, the ungodly, heathenish lying; the hating, envying, reviling, blaspheming; the unmerciful apprehending; the exiling, confiscating, and murdering, and the sentencing to water, fire, sword, and stake, seen in various localities, are plain signs of the church of Antichrist. For John saw that the Babylonian woman was drunken with the blood of the saints, and with the blood of the martyrs of Jesus. Rev. 17:6. He also saw that to the beast which arose from the sea, a mouth was given, speaking great things and blaspheming against God and his holy name, and his tabernacle or church, and them that dwell in heaven. And it was given unto him to make war with the saints, and to overcome them. Rev. 13:5, 6. Yes, my reader, this is the very way and work of the church of Antichrist, to hate, persecute, and put to the sword those whom she cannot enchant with the golden cup of her abominations.

O Lord! Dear Lord! Grant that the wrathful dragon may not entirely devour thy poor little flock, but that we, by thy grace, may in patience conquer by the sword of thy mouth; and may leave an abiding seed, which shall keep thy commandments, preserve thy testimony, and eternally praise thy great and glorious name. Amen, dear Lord. Amen.

17.27 Menno Simons, "Reply to Gellius Faber," 1554, CWMS, 775

But as to his assertion that the reign of Antichrist was as yet unknown, or weak, at the time of Augustine, it is not necessary to answer. Whoever will, let him read history, and he will find in great clarity that Antichrist was in full honour at the time of Augustine and that he ruled in the hearts of men with his doctrine.

17.28 Menno Simons, "Cross of the Saints," ca. 1554, *CWMS*, 613

Yes, dear brethren, the desirable day of your release is at hand; the day in which you shall stand with great constancy against those who have afflicted you, and have taken away your sweat and your toil, yes, your blood and your life. Then shall all those who pursue us be as ashes under the soles of our feet and they shall acknowledge too late that emperor, king, duke, prince, crown, scepter, majesty, power, sword, and mandate, were nothing but earth, dust, wind, and smoke.

With this day in view, all afflicted and oppressed Christians who now labor under the cross of Christ are comforted in the firm hope of the life to come; and they leave all tyrants with their heathenish mandates to God and his judgment. But they continue unmovable with Christ Jesus and his holy Word, and they construe all their doctrine, faith, sacraments, and life accordingly; and not in all eternity according to any other doctrine or mandate, even as the Father has commanded it from heaven and as Christ Jesus together with his holy apostles taught in all clarity and bequeathed it to all devout and pious children of God.

17.29 Menno Simons, "Instruction on Excommunication," 1558, *CWMS*, 961

In the second place, it is evident that also the bewitching spirit of Antichrist has made the whole world so drunk with the cup of abominations, has so rejected the doctrine of Christ and his holy prophets and his holy apostles, their sacraments, spirit, life, ordinances, usages, example, and true religion, that but little that is not of a salutary nature is left among men, so that it is difficult to restore that which has fallen into decay to its proper usage to which the Lord had ordained it.

For further reading:

Beachy, *Grace*, 56-61, 218-219.
Clasen, *Anabaptism*, 118-120.
Estep, *Anabaptist Story*, 198-200.
Friedmann, *Theology*, 101-114.
Keeney, *Dutch Anabaptist*, 175-190.
Krahn, *Dutch Anabaptism*, 93-164.
Littell, *Church*, 109-137.

Notes

1. From the Greek verb *dokein,* to appear. It means the view that Jesus only appeared to be human but was not so in reality.
2. The word denotes the view that Jesus had only one, namely a divine, nature.
3. Cf. Martin Luther, "Temporal Authority: to What Extent It Should Be Obeyed" in *Selected Writings of Martin Luther,* ed. T. G. Tappert, Philadelphia: Fortress Press, 1967, vol. 2, 294-308.
4. See article "Unitarianism" in *ME,* vol. 4, 773-774.
5. Original: *vermenscht.*
6. Original: *wesentlichen.*
7. Original: *leiblich mensch.*
8. Original: *tag.*
9. Original: *vorgift in plosseit.*
10. All true believers.
11. Synergism means that the process of justification was regarded as one in which God and man cooperated.
12. Col. 1:23. The Vulgate read: *"quod praedicatum est in universa creatura";* Erasmus: *"apud universam creaturam";* Martin Luther: *"unter aller kreatur."*
13. Rom. 1:20.
14. Original: *schaidwasser-nitric acid.*
15. Original: *unentpfindlich.*
16. This view of the sleep of the soul between physical death and the last judgment is called psychopannychism.
17. Original: *walbrediger,* i.e., those who preach about God's election and predestination.
18. Original: *vff alle Ziechen.*
19. The reference is presumably to Jesus although there is no antecedent.
20. Marpeck clearly means God's revealed Word, that Word about which we know. To go beyond that is to deal with things we know nothing about. This is presumption and rebellion, for it implies that we are not satisfied with what God has revealed.
21. See *The Mennonite Encyclopedia,* IV, 409-419 for details.
22. Breaking here means the initial plowing of virgin soil.
23. In other words, there is a church in Strassburg only as long as the faithful actually live in Strassburg. The presence of the cathedral does not say anything

about the presence of God, nor does the meticulous performance of preaching and the sacraments.

24. Paraphrase to be found in Yoder, *Legacy*, 141-145.

25. To save Jesus from any taint of sin Melchior Hoffman and Bernard Rothmann as well as Menno Simons and Dirk Philips argued that Jesus was born out of Mary but not of Mary. Being born of a human body would have tainted him with sin and made him incapable of being the Saviour.

26. Original: *ungeschmelts*.

27. The meaning of charismatic here is that in the earliest years of Swiss Anabaptism there was a consciousness of being guided by the Spirit. This was necessary since standard forms had not yet developed. This is characteristic of every movement and institution. See, for example, Emil Brunner, *The Misunderstanding of the Church*, chapters 3, 4, 5.

28. Proper church order meant first of all that those who were chosen to be minister had to be properly trained in the university. Second, they had to be appointed to their positions by public authority.

29. Enforcing its observance by law.

30. Many Sundays were also saints days.

31. See the recent reprint of the Froschauer Bible by Amos Hoover.

32. Quoted in 1539 by the Anabaptist Hans Umlauft, *Quellen: Bayern II*, 67-68. See also selection 15.6.

33. Cf. the statement by Pilgram Marpeck in 2.23. If the work is by Hans Hut as is proposed by Gottfried Seebass in his work *Müntzer's Erbe* (still unpublished), then we have here an example of possible dependence of Marpeck on Hut.

34. Original: *gelassenheit*. Here the word is evidently not a mystical term. It is rather the equivalent of Verlassenheit.

35. Cf. tripartite guide for the interpretation of Scripture suggested by Pilgram Marpeck in selection 7.12.

36. Theophylact (c. 1038-c. 1118), archbishop of Achreda, wrote commentaries on the New Testament widely esteemed. Cf. Cornelius, *Geschichte des Münsterischen Aufruhrs*, I, 226, 236, 238. Hubmaier, in contrast to Grebel, mistakenly thought Theophylact wrote AD 189 and cited him approvingly as a witness to apostolic usage. C. Sachsse, *Hubmaier*, p. 34.

37. The idea of the threefold baptism had a long history and is therefore not Hubmaier's invention. It was expressed by Augustine, Isidore of Seville, Peter Lombard, Thomas Aquinas, Gabriel Biel, and John Eck. See discussion in Christoph Windhorst, *Täuferisches Taufverständnis*, 1976, 162-166.

38. It is likely that Hut got the concept of a threefold baptism from Hubmaier.

39. Concerning infant baptism.

40. Presumably Eugenius II, 824-827.

41. Presumably Nicholas I, 858-867.

42. This is a reference to the document called *The Donation of Constantine*, which first appeared in the eighth century and which was shown to be a forgery by Lorenzo Valla in the fifteenth century. Apparently Keller did not know this.

43. *Didache*, 9. This work of the early church was rediscovered in 1873. However, it must have been known to people in the sixteenth century, or they found it in other writings of the early church which reproduced parts of it, such as Cyprian's Letter 62:13. Martin Luther also knew it and refers to it in his writing on the Lord's Supper of 1519.

44. The idea of the Supper as a symbol of unity had already been described by Erasmus. See Krahn, *Dutch Anabaptism*, 51.

45. The objection here appears to be against the perpetration of the priestly conception of administering the elements. To avoid any suggestion of a sacerdotal act, Müntzer, ordained to the old priesthood, should relinquish the distribution of the bread and wine to a server from out of the congregation.

46. The implication here seems to be to the shuffling of trained bears who do what they are trained to do correctly, but have no idea why they do it.

47. Original: *kanne*.

48. See footnote 43.

49. Luther.

50. Johann Eisermann, *Concerning the Common Good*, 1533.

51. In comparison to Christ.

52. Catholics and Protestants.

53. "The order of his Father" refers to the divine establishment of the governmental authority in the Old Testament with its external rules which were in force until the coming of Christ. See also selections 12.12 and 13.3.

54. Attributed to Jacob Hutter by Müller. Robert Friedmann disputed this attribution.

55. This is a direct use of article 6 of the Schleitheim Confession. See selection 13.3.

56. This is an emendation of the text on the basis of the German in *Muralt and Schmid: Quellen*, 219.

57. The Swiss Anabaptists.

58. A reference to the Peasant War of 1525. Hut here uses the argument of Thomas Müntzer to explain the defeat of the peasants.

59. Peasants War 1525.

60. It is possible that this work is not by Menno Simons. It bears no date and was first associated with the name of Menno in 1627. See Irvin B. Horst, *A Bibliography of Menno Simons*, 1962, 117-118.

61. This could be a reference to the Interim of Augsburg 1548, an interim religious settlement that was enforced militarily by the emperor, and which caused some Protestant leaders such as Martin Bucer to go into exile. If this surmise is correct, we have a date for the treatise from which this selection is taken.

62. On this point, which appears to express something less than thoroughgoing nonresistance see Stayer, *Anabaptists*, 323-324. The original Dutch is difficult to translate, but Stayer's translation of the last line "...unless it is a question of unweaponed service" seems to me to be closer to the original than Verduin's.

63. Jörg Maler was a leader among the Swiss Brethren but did not share their view on the oath.

64. This work is likely not by Denck alone, but who it was that participated in its composition is not apparent.

65. The reference is perhaps to the forcible Christianization of Germanic tribes by Charlemagne in the early ninth century.

66. A notable example of such a baptism of a pagan temple into a Christian church was the Pantheon in Rome, a temple to all the gods, consecrated as a Christian church in AD 609.

67. A reference to the practice of venerating the bread as the very body of Christ, i.e., of God.

68. A reference to the clergy who, in their ordination, were anointed with oil.

69. The idea of sealing was found originally in Ezekiel 9:4 where the mark was the Hebrew letter taw in the form of a T. This sealing is found also in the writings of Melchior Hoffman.

70. This was a construction of Hans Hut, a kind of summary of the whole Bible under seven headings, and the only correct way of understanding the Bible. The first three were: the covenant of God (gospel, faith, baptism), the body of Christ (the Lord's Supper), and the end of the world. See Packull, *Mysticism*, 77-87.

71. The original according to Schornbaum says "nie." It should be "hie"—hier—to make sense in this context.

72. Strassburg.

73. One of the two witnesses of Revelation 11:3.

74. Church writings.

75. Rothmann's knowledge here is very limited. Linus wrote nothing; Dionysius, Alexandrius, and Marcellus of Ancyra belong to the third and fourth centuries respectively.

76. Joel 3:10.

List of Anabaptist and Other Writers

Aurbacher, Kilian (dates unknown), was an early Anabaptist leader in Austerlitz, Moravia.

Bichter, Hans (dates unknown), a tailor's apprentice, was among the first converts to Anabaptism in Zürich, early 1525. He baptized a number of people in early March 1525. Soon after he recanted.

Bullinger, Heinrich (1504-1575). Reformer of Zürich after Zwingli's death (1531), who wrote extensively against Anabaptists.

Denck, Hans (ca. 1500-1527). A young humanist scholar who became an Anabaptist in 1525 and who wrote a number of theological works that were very influential in later Anabaptism. He died of the plague in Basel.

Grebel, Conrad (1498-1526). He was the first one to be baptized and was a leader of early Anabaptism in Zürich and its environs. He died of the plague.

Hoffman, Melchior (ca. 1495-1543). A leader of Anabaptism in Strassburg and the Netherlands who was convinced of the imminent coming of Christ and the judgment and who discussed these subjects in most of his many writings. He died in prison in Strassburg.

Hotz, Hans (dates unknown). An Anabaptist leader who was a very able spokesman at the colloquy between Anabaptists and the Reformed Church clergy in Bern in 1538.

Hubmaier, Balthasar (ca. 1480-1528). He was the Reformer of Waldshut and notable Anabaptist leader whose writings reflect his able scholarship. He was burned at the stake in Vienna.

Hübner, Hans (dates unknown), was a tailor from Zeegendorf, a small village southeast of Bamberg. He was baptized by Hans Hut.

Hut, Hans (?-1527). He was a follower of Thomas Müntzer and a very fruitful Anabaptist evangelist. He wrote much about suffering as the way to faith, and predicted the second advent for Pentecost, 1528. He died in prison in Augsburg.

Hutter, Jakob (?-1536). He was a Tyrolean who was a strong and effective Anabaptist leader in Tyrol and Moravia. Under his leadership

Anabaptists in Moravia adopted the community of goods in 1533. He died at the stake in Innsbruck.

Kautz, Jakob (1500-?), was a Lutheran preacher in Worms and became an Anabaptist in 1527. He was associated with Hans Denck.

Keller, Endres (dates unknown), was a member of a prominent family in Rothenburg on the Tauber, who spent many months in prison and suffered much torture for his faith. He later recanted.

Lemke (dates unknown) (Lemken Bruerren?), an Anabaptist elder in Jülich, and associate of Menno Simons.

Maler, Jörg (also Jörg Rothenfelder) (dates unknown). He was a Swiss Anabaptist, for a while associated with Pilgram Marpeck, and the copyist of the "Kunstbuch," in which a number of letters by Pilgram Marpeck were preserved.

Mändl, Hans (?-1560), was a very important leader of the Hutterites. He was frequently imprisoned on his missionary journeys and as frequently escaped. He died at the stake in Innsbruck.

Mantz, Felix (ca. 1498-1527). He was a member of the first Anabaptist church in Zürich, a co-worker of Grebel and Blaurock. He was executed by drowning in Zürich.

Marpeck, Pilgram (?-1556), was an important Anabaptist leader in Strassburg and Augsburg. He was an engineer by profession, but was also a very capable lay theologian, as his many writings reveal. He died a natural death in Augsburg.

Müller, Hans (dates unknown), was an Anabaptist from Medikon, southeast of Zürich. He wrote his plea for religious toleration from prison.

Nespitzer, Georg (dates unknown), was an active Anabaptist missionary, and leader of the congregation in Augsburg in 1528. He later left Anabaptism through the pressure of persecution.

Pfistermeyer, Hans (dates unknown). An outstanding Anabaptist leader in Aarau, Switzerland. He recanted his Anabaptist views in 1531 after having been convinced of his error by the Reformed clergy.

Philips, Dirk (1504-1568), an important Anabaptist leader in the Netherlands and North Germany. He was an associate of Menno Simons and wrote a number of treatises on matters of faith. He died a natural death near Emden.

Riedeman, Peter (1506-1556). One of the most important Hutterite leaders, and writer of the basic doctrinal statement of the Hutterites, the "Confession of Faith." He died a natural death in a Bruderhof at Protzko, Moravia.

Rothmann, Bernhard (c. 1495-c. 1535), was the Reformer of Münster, and Anabaptist theologian. His later writings eloquently defended the view that the Anabaptists were chosen by God to carry out his judgment on the godless. The circumstances of his death are unknown.

Sattler, Michael (ca. 1490-1527). Once the prior of a Benedictine

350

monastery, he became an Anabaptist sometime in 1526. He was the chief architect of the Schleitheim Confession of 1527, a document that confirmed the separation of Swiss Anabaptism from the Reformed church. He died by fire at Rottenburg.

Scharnschlager, Leupold (?-1563). He was an Anabaptist elder and longtime associate of Pilgram Marpeck. He was co-author with Marpeck of a long work against the views of Caspar Schwenckfeld. He died a natural death in Ilanz, Graubünden.

Schiemer, Leonhard (?-1528), a former Franciscan, became an Anabaptist in 1527. He had a very brief association with the church in Rattenberg, Tyrol, where he was imprisoned. He wrote a number of tracts of a moving spirituality. He died by the sword in Rattenberg.

Schlaffer, Hans (?-1528). A former priest, Schlaffer became an Anabaptist under the influence of Hans Hut. He wrote nine tracts in prison prior to his execution by the sword in Schwatz, Tyrol.

Schnabel, Georg (dates unknown), an Anabaptist leader from Hesse who wrote a long confession in prison and then escaped.

Simons, Menno (ca. 1496-1561), a former monk and priest, became an Anabaptist elder in 1536 and gave himself completely to the brotherhood until his death. He wrote much and died a natural death at Wüstenfelde in Holstein.

Spitelmaier, Ambrosius (ca. 1497-1528). He was an early Anabaptist leader first commissioned by Hans Hut. He wrote a long moving confession of faith. He died by the sword in Cadolzburg.

Stadler, Ulrich (?-1540), a Hutterite leader who wrote extensively on many subjects, but is especially known for his tracts on the inner and outer word and community of goods. He died a natural death at Bucovic, Moravia.

Umlauft, Hans (dates unknown). He was likely a former monk who had learned the trade of a cobbler, and who was a very effective evangelist. After recantation he seems to have joined the Hutterites.

Volk, Jörg (?-1528). He was a follower of Hans Hut and attended the Martyr Synod in Augsburg, 1527. He was executed in Bamberg.

Wagner, Jörg (?-1527). Although not an Anabaptist, Anabaptists shared the convictions expressed in his hymn. He was a martyr for his faith.

Weninger, Marti (dates unknown), was a weaver who was an Anabaptist spokesman in Switzerland, especially at the colloquy in Zofingen in 1532. He later recanted.

Zylis, Jacobs (dates unknown), was an Anabaptist elder, who, together with Lemke, criticized the harsh practice of banning among the Dutch Anabaptists.

Acknowledgments

I wish to acknowledge permission to use selections from the following:
Rollin Armour, *Anabaptist Baptism*, Scottdale, Pa.: Herald Press, 1966;
Heinold Fast, *Der Linke Flügel der Reformation*, Bremen: Carl
Schünemann Verlag, 1962; Heinold Fast, *Quellen zur Geschichte der
Täufer in der Schweiz. II. Band. Ostschweiz*, Zürich: Theologischer Verlag,
1973; Walter Fellmann, *Hans Denck. Schriften. 2. Teil. Religiöse Schriften*,
Gütersloh: C. Bertelsmann Verlag, 1956; Walter Fellmann, *Hans Denck.
Schriften. 3. Teil. Exegetische Schriften*, Gütersloh: C. Bertelsmann Verlag,
1960; Used by permission. *Jakob Huter: Leben, Frömmigkeit, Briefe*, copy-
right 1956 by Mennonite Publication Office, Newton, Kan.; Günther
Franz, *Urkundliche Quellen zur hessischen Reformationsgeschichte. IV.
Band. Wiedertäuferakten 1527-1626*, Marburg: N. G. Elwert'sche Verlags-
buchhandlung G. Braun, 1951; *Mennonite Quarterly Review*, XXV
(January 1951), XLV (January 1971), XXII (July 1948); Martin Haas,
*Quellen zur Geschichte der Täufer in der Schweiz. IV. Band. Drei
Täufergespräche*, Zürich: Theologischer Verlag, 1974; William Klassen and
Walter Klaassen, *The Writings of Pilgram Marpeck*, Kitchener, Ont., and
Scottdale, Pa.: Herald Press, 1978; Manfred Krebs, *Quellen zur Geschichte
der Täufer. IV. Band. Baden und Pfalz*, Gütersloh: C. Bertelsmann Verlag,
1951; Manfred Krebs and H. G. Rott, *Quellen zur Geschichte der Täufer.
VIII. Band. Elsass II. Teil.*, Gütersloh: Verlagshaus Gerd Mohn, 1960;
Clyde L. Manschreck, *A History of Christianity*,© 1964, pp. 86-87.
Adapted by permission of Prentice-Hall, Inc., Englewood Cliffs, N.J.; Lydia
Müller, *Glaubenszeugnisse oberdeutscher Taufgesinnter I*, Leipzig: M.
Heinsius Nachfolger, 1938; Leonhard von Muralt and Walter Schmid,
Quellen zur Geschichte der Täufer in der Schweiz, I. Band, Zürich: S.
Hirzel Verlag, 1952; *Account of Our Religion, Doctrine and Faith*, London:
Hodder and Stoughton in conjunction with the Plough Publishing House,
1950; Gordon Rupp, *Patterns of Reformation*, London: Epworth Press,
1969; Karl Schornbaum, *Quellen zur Geschichte der Täufer. II. Band.
Markgraftum Brandenburg*, Leipzig: M. Heinsius Nachfolger, 1934; Karl
Schornbaum, *Quellen zur Geschichte der Täufer. Band. Bayern, II.*

Abteilung, Gütersloh: C. Bertelsmann Verlag, 1951; taken from: *Die Schriftender Münsterischen Täufer und Ihrer Gegner I. Teil: Die Schriften Bernhard Rothmanns,* ed. by Robert Stupperich (Veröffentlichungen der Historischen Kommission Westfalens, XXXII), Münster: Aschendorffsche Verlagsbuchhandlung, Münster/Westfalen, 1970; John C. Wenger, *The Complete Writings of Menno Simons,* Scottdale, Pa.:Herald Press, 1956; Gunnar Westin and Torsten Bergsten, *Quellen zur Geschichte der Täufer. IX. Band. Balthasar Hubmaier: Schriften,* Gütersloh: Verlagshaus Gerd Mohn, 1962; John H. Yoder, *The Legacy of Michael Sattler,* Scottdale, Pa.: Herald Press, 1973; Lowell H. Zuck, *Christianity and Revolution,* Philadelphia: Temple University Press, 1975; *Spiritual and Anabaptist Writers,* edited by George Huntston Williams and Angel M. Mergal; Volume XXV: The Library of Christian Classics. Published in the U.S.A. by The Westminster Press, 1957. Used by permission.

354

Index of Persons

(Numbers in italics refer to pages in the introductions)